On Giants' S

Studies in Christian apologetics

Edgar C. Powell

"If I have seen further it is by standing on the shoulders of giants"
Isaac Newton (1642—1727)

DayOne

© Day One Publications 1999
First printed 1999

Scripture quotations are from The New King James Version.
© 1982 Thomas Nelson Inc.

British Library Cataloguing in Publication Data available
ISBN 0 902548 93 X

Published by Day One Publications
3 Epsom Business Park, Kiln Lane, Epsom, Surrey KT17 1JF.
☎ 01372 728 300 **FAX** 01372 722 400
email—sales@dayone.co.uk
www.dayone.co.uk

Designed by Steve Devane and printed by Clifford Frost Ltd, Wimbledon SW19 2SE

Dedication

This apologetic study is dedicated to the late
Dr D. Martyn Lloyd - Jones (my mentor in the
Faith) and to Sir Fred Catherwood and his
Bible class, both of which stimulated my
interest in the application of Christianity to
contemporary problems.

This book is indeed *'a challenge to the sceptic and comfort to the saint'*. This remarkable book affords a superb overview of the apologetic scene, adducing authors ancient and modern, from the ancient Greek philosophers to the evolutionist Richard Dawkins. At times racy and colloquial, with traces of humour, at other times more detached and academic, Mr Powell allows antagonists to speak for themselves before giving reasoned (and always courteous) counter-arguments. Unusually for an apologetic work, there is a positive and winsome presentation of the only saving Gospel. The whole is enhanced by impressively extensive bibliographies, stimulating 'Questions for Further study' and a Glossary of Technical Terms for good measure. Not to be missed.

The late **Dr Richard Alderson** (Editorial Linguist).

This classic treatment of his subject is carefully approached, cleverly thought out and clearly presented in such a manner that one's interest is caught from the outset, carefully maintained and deepened throughout. The author is not afraid to face up to critical attacks on the existence of God, and denunciations of faith, exploring them and applying Biblical and rational truths to expose the nonsensical theories propounded. The book is an academic approach intelligible and eminently readable for all concerned with this vital matter.

Dr Enid Parker (Bible Translator, Red Sea Mission).

We all know that Truth is coming increasingly under attack. Jesus, the Son of God (the Saviour of the world), the Gospel (Christian teaching) and the Word of God (the Bible) are now widely disregarded in the western nations. They are written off simply because it is thought that the authoritative teachings of distinguished scientists, philosophers, sociologists and educators, past and present, have fully discredited the historicity of Jesus Christ, the power of the Gospel and the veracity of the Bible.

On Giants' Shoulders: Studies in Christian Apologetics shows that this popular view rests upon a spread of misinformation, recognisable misinterpretation of the evidence and superficial thinking. For example, the underlying assumptions of the views of those who object to the Christian faith, when identified and evaluated are found to require for their acceptance as much, if not more faith than the Christian Gospel!

Here then is a book that provides a comprehensive and informed overview of the battle for the Truth, combined with valuable insights into the areas of truth and falsehood on which the contention for the faith is to be fought and won. All students who are concerned for Truth will find it helpful. *"Fight the good fight of faith"* (1 Tim. 6:12). *"This is the victory that overcometh the world, even our faith"* (1 John 5:4).

Dr Leonard Loose (Former Missionary to India & Biologist)

'An excellent teaching manual'—
Dr David Watts, Research Material Scientist, Manchester University.

Acknowledgments

My thanks are due to Timothy Mitchell, B. A. (Oxford) current Ph.D student—who debated and criticised some of the issues covered in this book, and to the late Dr. Richard Alderson who kindly commented on the proof; Margaret—my wife and family—who supported me in this venture. Any errors or opinions remain that of the author's alone, but thanks are due to those who also gave some specific advice, including Dr Leonard Loose, Dr Nick Needham and Paul Solly.

Contents

Our church is full of bright students and post-grads doing doctorates, theologians as well as scientists, so it is clear that neither higher criticism nor Darwinism can stand in the way of someone who has a living faith in Christ. And there are those who would leave it at that.

But we are called to be the salt of the earth and the light of the world and not to keep our religion for Sundays and not to opt out, keeping our faith and our secular profession in watertight compartments. We have to make a difference and that means bringing a Christian mind and Christian standards to our secular calling.

For the last thirty years, since the permissive Sixties, British thought and legislation has been ruled by secular humanism, which is governed by the belief that there is no Creator God, no external moral code to which we are all accountable and so we can make up our own moral rules as we go along. If the law disallows this, then the law must be changed. The result has been a disastrous destabilisation of our moral and social order. The rich have got richer and the poor, the sick and the old have been marginalised. Crime has soared, drugs are sold to school children, teachers who try to stop the pushers are murdered, corruption has begun to enter every walk of life. Dixon of Dock Green has been replaced by armed police and corruption has crept into public life.

At the root of this whole transformation is the belief that there is no God. That's nothing new. The Psalmist wrote three thousand years ago, *'The fool has said in his heart that there is no God.'* But today this foolish belief purports to be based on science and on new scholarly criticism of the Bible. So it is good that Edgar Powell has tackled these myths head on.

He is in good company. I find that the higher up you go in the academic ladder, the less certainty you find, certainly none of the certainty of the propagandists, a Huxley in Darwin's day and Dawkins today. I was having lunch once with Lord Blackett, who was then President of the Royal Society and I said that, when I thought of the human eye with its intricate design, I found it impossible to believe in evolution by chance. He said that I shouldn't worry, I was as much entitled, on the evidence, to believe in creation as he was in the theory of evolution and, in any case, for every current theory, there were a score of scientists dedicated to making their name by blowing it apart. So Edgar Powell is right to avoid the error of some creationists, who want to pin the Christian position to some unprovable alternative.

What he does is to point out that the theory of evolution and other theories of origins cannot be proved by the scientific method. It can be no more than metaphysical speculation, for it can neither be proved or falsified and, as the late Sir Karl Popper had said, '*What cannot be falsified is not science.*'

I was taught by the Regius Professor of History at Cambridge, Sir Herbert Butterfield, who wrote a seminal book on '*The origins of modern science.*' He found it firmly rooted in the Reformation, the ideas shuttling back and forwards between the French Huguenots, the Dutch and the English and emerging as a Puritan consensus. They believed that they should come to the Book of God's Works with the same reverence as they came to the Book of God's Word and remove the non-Christian medieval additions to both Christian doctrine and to natural science. In particular they excluded all enquiry into origins and concentrated on what God himself has revealed.

God was one, so the natural laws would be unified. God had made all things in order, so the natural laws would be orderly. Plants and animals could be classified. God reasons with us in both old and new Testaments. He shows moral cause and effect. So all God's creation will be rational and experimenting with cause and effect will give us the systems under which natural laws work. God had promised stability in the natural laws, from the time of the last great catastrophe to the end of time; so the natural laws can be stable. This is a "given" of the scientific method, which those who try to extrapolate backwards ignore.

Finally God the Creator is good, so the creation is for the benefit of mankind and we should learn all we can about the laws of nature and use this knowledge 'For the good of man's estate.'

What the Huxleys and the Dawkins have done is to destroy the basis of the scientific method by going back to metaphysics. So they have not made us a more scientific age, instead they have turned us back to every kind of heathen superstition. Today people no longer see any unity in nature, it looks to them, as to pagan tribes, disorderly, irrational, unstable and hostile. This is reflected in today's art, where we wear our inner beliefs on our sleeves. And when we see the art in the airport lounge we can be thankful that the plane we board is still built by the scientific method.

Not only in science and biblical criticism, but in all else that he has tackled, Edgar Powell has done today's Christian community a real service.

Sir Fred Catherwood
Balsham, Cambridge

The subject of Christian apologetics doesn't fire up everyone's imagination or enthusiasm. Indeed, even the highly intellectual Abraham Kuyper (pastor, theologian and later Prime Minister of the Netherlands) who was responsible for the founding of the Free University of Amsterdam doubted if such a subject has any real value. Thus, in the Stone Lectures of 1891 delivered at Princeton University under the title of *"Calvinism"* he stated *"There is no doubt that Christianity is imperilled by great and serious dangers. Two life systems are wrestling with one another, in mortal combat .... In this struggle Apologetics have advanced us not one single step"*. Today, many people, including Christians themselves, suspect the same. The author of this book thinks otherwise, and has sought to bring the subject of Apologetics within the grasp of non-academic persons using material from modern-day debates on a wide range of issues. Herein lies the value of the book, since it does not aim to tackle the issues at a deep level, but mostly to use the writings of well-known people to give confidence to the ordinary person that the Christian Faith is indeed a reasoned position to hold in today's materialistic society.

One of the main assets (and pleasures) of the book is the vast amount of quotation from thinkers ancient and modern. If you like good, pithy quotations (and I for one do!), this makes for an excellent read and a valuable source book. Particularly memorable is the saying of Galileo that the Bible is to *"teach us how one goes to heaven, not how heaven goes"*. Kepler's famous saying that science is *"thinking God's thoughts after Him"* is well used, particularly in the chapter on *"Science or scientism"*, which for me is the focal point in the book for our contemporary world. It is sometimes argued by Christians that "value-free knowledge" is impossible, and that presuppositions and interpretations colour everything, particularly in education.

This was strongly argued against by the brain scientist and Christian philosopher Donald MacKay in his book *The Open Mind*. He showed that in the natural sciences there is an objectivity which only declines into *"scientism"* when subjective world-views are allowed to intrude into the truly scientific method of observation and hypothesis generation based on data. Of course, such clarity inevitably becomes less evident in the *"social sciences"* where inter-human interaction provides biases which come from situations laden with pre-suppositions. However, it remains thankfully true, as Powell says in this chapter, that *"the scientific method is the same for either Christians or non-Christians"*. Thus, *"science cannot determine its own values"* (Gordon Clark). However, the last word in this chapter goes rightly to Einstein with his remark that *"science without religion is lame, religion without science is blind"*.

The book covers many of the *"chestnut"* debates which envelop the Bible-based believer in a society which has mutated the post-Reformation enthusiasm for the empirical sciences based on adoring wonder at God's work in nature, to a molecular reductionism which abstracts God out of His own Universe. The topics covered include the existence of God, the nature of man, the objectivity of truth, the problem of suffering, the possibility of miracles and the popular theories of evolution.

Apart from the many stimulating quotes, Powell has included several Tables which summarise the main thinking on specialist topics, together with many detailed end-notes to the chapters, and an overall Glossary of Terms (essential for the non-specialist reader). This multi-faceted explanation of the accepted jargon is an excellent attribute of the book. In addition, questions are included to draw out the reader into reflective and deeper thought. At this point, the book shows its use for teaching purposes.

Finally, the first chapter sets the scene as one of compassion for a suffering and confused world, rather than a battlefield for philosophical, intellectual debate. The book can be recommended, therefore, as stated in the introduction to *"challenge the sceptic and comfort the believer"*.

Professor Derek A Linkens
Research Professor (formerly Dean of Engineering)
Department of Automatic Control and Systems Engineering
The University of Sheffield.

"A man can no more diminish God's glory by refusing to worship Him than a lunatic can put out the sun by scribbling the word 'darkness' on the walls of his cell." C. S. Lewis.

Professor Richard Dawkins (Oxford Biologist) gives a scientist's case against belief in God. He says: *"Religious people split into three main groups when faced with science. I shall label them the "know-nothings", the "know-alls" and the "no-contests"…. The "no-contests" are rightly reconciled to the fact that religion cannot compete with science on its own ground…. The "know-nothings" or fundamentalists, are in one way more honest. They are true to history. They recognise one of religion's main functions was scientific: the explanation of existence, of the universe, or life. Historically, most religions have had or even been a cosmology and a biology. … the "know-alls" (I unkindly name them that because I find their position patronising), think religion is good for people, perhaps good for society".* [1]

Dawkins believes that the fact that belief in God still exists, is due to a lack of an adequate education system to promote evolution. This is an interesting comment. It is often believers who are said to be indoctrinated or brain-washed. Dawkins thinks insufficient evolutionary brain washing is going on! The problems and dilemma that Dawkins faces both scientifically and philosophically are not even mentioned in his speech. Some of those with whom he differs may similarly regard his comments as patronising. Dawkins does, however, manage to throw down a clear challenge to those who claim to hold religious beliefs: *"Faith is the great cop-out, the great excuse to evade the need to think and evaluate evidence. Faith is belief in spite of, even perhaps because of, the lack of evidence."* Such comments fail to realise that man himself is placing *"faith"* in the power of autonomous (independent) reason, and the validity of such logic in a chance universe. It also dismisses the wealth of evidence that does not fit into Dawkins' world view, and fails to account for man's persistence in believing in God.

In this life we would be considered foolish to attempt a long journey without consulting a map, but people think nothing of drifting through life, without asking themselves whether this material universe is all. They rest secure in the notion that evolution, it is claimed, is no longer a theory, but fact. We are told everything in the cosmos, from heavenly bodies to human beings, has developed, and continues to develop through evolutionary processes. The theory of organic evolution, originally a scientific model propounded to account for the diversity of animal and plant life, together with the principle of *"uniformitarianism"* (the present is the key to the past) based on Lyell's selective field evidences, have, through the idea of progressive historical change permeated the whole of Western culture. Indeed scientific dogma such as these are being absorbed by large numbers of people, consciously or otherwise, as an ideology of existence—*"a basis of faith"*.

The need for On Giants' Shoulders: Studies in Christian Apologetics

The approach of this book is to evaluate and contrast the alternatives to such a secular viewpoint. We have quoted opponents of Christianity, believing their admissions or praise carries greater weight in making our alternative case more persuasive or viable. The text in general is a challenge to open minded thinkers to examine answers to some of the more significant criticisms of Christianity; and an apologetic tool for Ministers and Christian workers. Sir Isaac Newton said: *"If I have seen further it is by standing on the shoulders of giants."* We have the benefit of the divine wisdom of Apostles and Prophets, and researches of seers and scientists to give us understanding of today's world. In this sense we can see further, and have guiding principles for life in the new millenium, D.V.

Firstly, we see the need for Christians to be equipped to engage in the battle for the minds of men. Like the fisherman—who's **"Gone Fishing!"** we must be prepared to know how best to cast out the gospel net. We take some time, however, to explain the need for a reasoned defence of the faith, along with noting some of its limitations. Next, we examine in **"A fading cosmic smile?"** whether operationally the notion of God is irrelevant in the modern universe. The question of God's existence is raised, and if there is a grand Architect behind any design in nature. The major "proofs" for God are reviewed, namely the need for a great First cause, the design argument, and the moral argument that claims man as a moral being reflects his creator. In addition—the congruity argument is used to summarise the different viewpoints. Basically, this says: if you have the right key to the door, it opens the door! If your system of thought fits the facts, it must be the correct one.

"You are what you eat?" looks at the ramifications of people being a *"mere collection of atoms."* What is the self? Is there a ghost in the machine? If we have a soul, is this detectable by scientific means? What are the consequences of seeing man as only genetic material? "Is there a God?" looks at a rationale for God's existence, and the fact that we all have *"belief systems."* Consideration is also given as to whether God is proved to be non-existent by logical traps and the problem of evil. The impact of atheism on ethics is also briefly examined—having looked at obstacles to faith and the possibility of God's existence, how has God (if he exists) chosen to reveal himself? In "Truth unchanged, unchanging", we review the validity of the claim that God has revealed himself not only in the natural world—the so-called *"book of nature"*- but also in a special revelation—the *"book of Scripture."* Has the Bible got any credibility? As the most criticised book in the world, can we still trust the Bible?

"Science or scientism" examines the nature and limitations of true science, and whether there is a point when science becomes scientism. "Only one way?" follows this issue of truth, to see if it is correct to synthesise knowledge to come to valid religious truths, or whether there is only one way? Is the answer of Christianity unique in any way? Is there only one way to be rescued? "Vanity of vanities?" reviews the Christian doctrine of ultimate punishment, and its implications both for justice in man-made systems and for God. If there is a God of love, how can he send people to Hell? What is the significance of ultimate justice for man-made systems of justice? Another common objection to belief in God is that of suffering and disaster: "Tragedies—why?" seeks to illustrate the answer the Bible gives to the problem of suffering. Another stumbling block, for some, is the possibility of believing in miracles in our scientific age. Many imply that belief in miracles is for the gullible. "It ain't necessarily so ..."

seeks to look at this both philosophically and theologically to demonstrate that this is unjustified.

"**Evolution—on the rocks?**" reviews the area that is claimed to be one of the strongest supports for a belief in Evolution: fossil series. The nature of the evidence and credibility of the "proofs" is carefully scrutinised. Next "**On Giants' Shoulders**" looks at a mix of reasons that indicate Christianity is both credible and believable, as an alternative to the secular world-system. It also summarises the main arguments of the book, including the effect of the view that there is no God has on ethics. To be able to see further than those who have gone before, is possible for the modern Christian apologist, as they can stand not only on the shoulders of prophets and apostles, but great scientists and seers who have studied the book of nature.

Two appendices deal with how this all works out in practice: "**Nice one, Cyril**" presents a case study of a real life encounter between these two opposing viewpoints, and indicates lines of reasoning that challenge the sceptic and comfort the saint, particularly outlining the significance and evidence for the resurrection. It is to the literary giant C. S. Lewis that we go in "**The Man, the Myth, the Legend.**" This appendix reflects on the influence of the best known British apologist in the twentieth century. He applied his Christian principles in a different sphere: linguistics. As someone who was a Professor of English, Lewis had the ability to relay the Christian message in the layman's vernacular. Despite limitations in his theological understanding, he had a zeal to see people give up atheism, and come to trust in the God of the Bible and His Son, Jesus Christ.

One of the most profound and problematic questions we face is whether or not to believe in God. The level of complexity in answering this question and its implications, in this book, is usually kept to that of the intelligent layman. Occasionally, more technical phrases or concepts are used in the particular discipline under scrutiny. This is true, for instance, of the chapter dealing with "**Evolution—on the rocks?**"—which reviews the evidence for micro-evolution in a fossil series, but clearly, in such a debate, specific geological terms need to be mentioned. If the reader perseveres with any such more technical areas, they will still gain the vital principles that question the accepted interpretation. We will mention some of the reasons for the general antagonism of the modern mind-set to belief in Christianity and suggest various solutions and evidence which shows that Christianity is both believable, vital, and truthful in its claims.

In *On Giants' Shoulders: Studies in Christian Apologetics* it would be easy to get lost in technicalities, semantics and dealing with red herrings. Each problem could merit a book on its own! As one problem is solved, it may give rise to another! Rather like the climber who thinks he has reached the mountain peak, only to find there is yet another to be tackled first! To answer all permutations and implications of any question would clearly be impossible. This approach would be too long and complex for our present purposes. Instead the main principles are reviewed—alternatives and solutions are offered to genuine intellectual enquiries. The text seeks to illustrate the credibility and relevance of the gospel, as it is the most up-to-date message for today. It is trusting in God's word that enables us to live life to the full, life with a capital 'L'. If we are to have faith that can remove mountains (such as any obstacles to faith), then we must have a willingness to review our philosophy of life. Is it true, for instance, that the materialist is postulating certain properties of matter which supposedly govern the evolution of life, that cannot be observed, and therefore must be accepted or rejected by faith, not on the grounds of evidence or logic?

The text is arranged by topic so that its usefulness to seekers and searchers after truth is enhanced. Ultimately it may stimulate enquiring minds to find out more about the purpose and meaning of life, and that *"Thou (God) hast made us for yourself, and our hearts are restless till they find their rest in Thee."* Sometimes we approach a subject in which we are interested with the zeal of a gold rush prospector: hopefully readers will find nuggets of truth that stimulate them to find out more about the Bible, the Book of Books. This author seeks to give reasonably short answers to the "blockbuster" questions raised, in the hope it will stimulate the reader to take up some of the fuller explanations; further reading is indicated at the end of each chapter, and a glossary of terms is provided at the end of the book. The series of **Questions for Further study** are designed to emphasise the line of argument, and to stretch the reader to apply apologetic principles for themselves. It is partly because Christians have tended to have apologetics low on their agenda, that their 'credit-rating' in the world's eyes has declined. With a heightened awareness of this battle for the truth—we will be able to fulfill Bunyan's words: *"Then fancies flee away! I'll fear not what men say, I'll labour night and day to be a pilgrim".*

E. C. P.
Dulwich, London.
February, 1999.

1:   **R. Dawkins** (1992) *A scientist's case against God,* (a speech by Professor R.Dawkins at the Edinburgh International Science Festival on 15th April, 1992), The Independent, 20 April, 1992, p. 17.

Gone Fishing!—the do's and don'ts of witness

"Fishermen like to cast their nets where there are plenty of fish; and fishers of men delight to be where there are many who are enclosed in the gospel net." C. H. Spurgeon [1]

This chapter examines the need for effective Christian testimony, based on a knowledge of contemporary events and world-viewpoints. It spells out the characteristics of a good "fisherman" and explains the biblical need for apologetics. It argues for a proper defence of the faith against those who imply this is unnecessary or even unbiblical.

Casting out the Gospel net

A fisherman and an evangelist have many points in common. A fisherman selects those pieces of equipment (be it net; fish hooks; bait—maggots, worms or flies) that are most appropriate to his fishing conditions and the type of fish he hopes to catch. So must Christians when they *"cast out the gospel net"*, use the most appropriate arguments to attract and capture the different types of unbeliever. Paul showed an appreciation of this need to vary his approach. He was willing to be *"All things to all men, that I may by all means save some"* (1 Cor. 9:22) as long as no biblical principle was contravened and sincerity or truth were not compromised. To be a good fisherman for the Lord Jesus, we need to be: adaptable (able to speak to all types of people); humble (able to get things across in a sympathetic or winsome way); able to witness by life and lip; relevant (able to use contemporary events to highlight the need for the gospel) and prepared (in our knowledge and by prayer).

◆ 1 Adaptability

Spurgeon comments on the soul winners' need to be flexible—like a man who can come alongside the sceptic and also show the flexibility of a rider who needs to mount and control a wild horse: *"The power of adaptation to high and low, learned and ignorant, sad and frivolous, is no mean gift. If, like Nelson, we can lay our vessel side by side with the enemy, and come to close quarters without delay, we shall do considerable execution. Show me the man who can make use of any conversation and any topic, to drive home saving truth upon the conscience and heart. He who can ride a well-trained horse, properly saddled, does well; but the fellow who can leap upon the wild horse of the prairie, and ride him bare-backed, is a genius indeed. "All things to all men", rightly interpreted, is a motto worthy of the great apostle of the Gentiles, and of all who, like him, would win souls for Jesus ."* 2

◆ 2 Humility

Our approach, when giving a reason for the hope within us, must always be one of humility. It is often said that you can *"win the argument, but lose the soul."* No one is attracted to the bigot or fanatic who thinks exclusively of making his own opinion heard. Dr Mark Guy Pearse says: *"I watched an old man trout-fishing the other day, pulling them out one after another briskly. 'You manage it very cleverly, old friend,' I said, 'I have passed a good many below who don't seem to be doing anything.' The old man replied, 'Well, you see, sir, there be three rules for trout-fishing, and it is no good trying if you don't mind them. The first is, keep yourself out of sight; and the second is, keep yourself further out of sight; and the third is keep yourself further out of sight still. Then you'll do it."* Dr Pearse comments: *"Good for catching men, too, I thought, as I went on my way ."* 3

◆ 3 Witness

Clearly, effective witnessing involves sensitivity and humility and more than simply being unobtrusive! Paul makes it clear in Romans chapter 10: 9 *"That if you confess with your mouth the Lord Jesus, and believe in your heart that God raised him from the dead, you will be saved."* Confession is the external evidence and fruit of faith. The psalmist puts this succinctly, *"Let the redeemed of the Lord say so!"* (Psalm 107:2). Paul in contrast, paints another picture in Romans 1: 14, where he says, *"I am a debtor ...*

both to wise and unwise." If we see someone suffering some illness from which we have just found a cure for ourselves, we cannot but desire to help them. We feel indebted to help them—we must tell them about the cure and where to get it. Paul had found the One who could help cure men and women's spiritual diseases. He could not stop himself telling others about the great Physician of souls. You might say, *"Surely the important thing in witness is holiness of life."* Of course this is right. But a silent witness can never replace the need to tell others of the Saviour's love. How can they hear without a preacher, or testimony?

◆ 4 Relevant

As Christians one of the most exciting things that we can be is *"fishers of men"*. To be a soul winner as C. H. Spurgeon would say, is a vital part of our witness by word and deed. Often when faced by the objections of the unbeliever we can flounder, unable to *"give a reason for the hope that is in us"* in an effective manner. To comment on everyday life, we must be aware of what's happening in the world, so we can be up-to-date in our application of the truth. We need—to some degree—to be able to take a diagnostic approach—'problem and cure'. We are called upon to show the relevance of our faith in our *"no blame, no shame"* culture.

Modern teenagers are cynical about ancient beliefs, but credulous of modern ones. Some Welsh teenagers on the radio recently were clear that going to church had no relevance, but all accepted the existence of extra-terrestrials and their landing in New Mexico in 1947! They believe, *"New is true, old is mould"*. Logic informs us, however, that time has no necessary connection with truth. Indeed, Francis Schaeffer reminds us that Christianity is based on a God who has revealed to us eternal truth: *"What is the first hypothesis for evangelism? That God is there, and is the kind of God that the Bible says he is, and that he is not silent but has given us propositional truth."* To apply this truth, involves us in an awareness of the culture around us.

The apostle Paul on Mars Hill, Athens, did not hesitate to make a point of contact with the thinkers there, by quoting an inscription to the *"Unknown God"* and also their Grecian poets (e.g. Cleanthes) and Cilician poets (e.g. Aratus). Before he spoke, he familiarised and prepared himself with a knowledge of the culture and beliefs of the Athenians. Matthew Henry graphically comments on Paul's Mars Hill testimony: *"By this it appears not only that Paul was himself a scholar, but that human learning is ... serviceable to a gospel minister, especially for convincing of those that are without; for it enables him to beat them at their own weapons, and to cut off Goliath's head with his own sword."*

◆ 5 Preparation

One thing I learned about fishing on my honeymoon in Norfolk was that it seemed initially an easy business. You just had to lay out the net in the water, in the evening, then come back in the morning when the tide had gone out and pick up the fish! How wrong can you be? First, the poacher gets up far earlier and picks out the best fish. Then, when you have taken out the few mackerel left, the hard work begins. The net has to be hauled in and repaired (if necessary) but by far the most arduous task is the hours spent removing all the seaweed caught in the net! Gospel work is like that! It needs preparation (not least prayer). A lot of hard work, patience and effort goes in, but those caught in the gospel net may be few, or stolen away by false teachers or cults. There will, however, be blessing as it is Jesus the Son of God who says, " *I will make you fishers of men"* . Evangelism is truth demanding a verdict. God's word, we are promised, will not return to Him without significant impact.

What is apologetics?

At its simplest level it is positively defending the truth of God's word. It is not giving an apology! It is seeking to cut the ground from under the unbelievers feet, so (s)he must face the reality of the Living God. The Christian should always be ready to give a reason for the hope that is in them (I Peter 3:15-16). There are important elements to include in such apologetics: **Proof**—giving a rational basis for faith; **defence**—dealing with the actual objections to belief; and **offence**—uncovering the foolishness of unbelieving thought. The Psalmist says *"the fool has said in his heart there is no God"*(Psalm 14:1). There is nothing especially modern about rejecting God. Solomon in all his wisdom advises: *"The fear of the Lord is the beginning of knowledge"* (Proverbs 1:7).

Apologetics examines Christianity's most basic presuppositions or assumptions—why we should start with Christian presuppositions rather than others. As philosophers can legitimately defend various positions so apologists can legitimately defend Christianity. Apologetics may not create belief, but it creates the atmosphere in which belief can come to life. Gresham Machen, the well known defender of the faith, said: *"Certainly a Christianity that avoids argument is not the Christianity of the New Testament."* 4 Benjamin B. Warfield (another theologian) noted, *"The action of the Holy Spirit in giving faith is not apart from evidence, but along with evidence; and in the first instance consists in preparing the soul for the reception of evidence."* 5 Pastor Tim Keller (New York City) says perceptively in his notes on *The Gospel and the Secular Mind (1997):* *"It is becoming increasingly difficult for Christians to just share the gospel without doing apologetics. The old canned quickie training programmes cannot prepare a Christian for dealing with the range of intellectual and personal difficulties people have with the Christian faith. They need to hear the preacher week in and week out dealing winsomely and intelligently with the problems of non-believers."*

Wise as serpents, gentle as doves

There are, and have been those, who caution against involvement in philosophy. John Wesley reminds a fellow Pastor in one of his letters: *"You would have a philosophical religion; but there can be no such thing. Religion is the most plain simple thing in the world. It is only, 'We love him, because he first loved us.' So far as you add philosophy to religion, just so far you spoil it."*6 Certainly a philosophy which excludes the light of Scripture is unprofitable. Thomas Aquinas (1225-74)—an Italian theologian—pointed out, *"Everything that is, is treated of in philosophical science—even God Himself; so that there is a part of philosophy called theology, or divine science, as Aristotle has proved ... Therefore, besides philosophical science, there is no need of any further knowledge."*7 Some of the greatest Christians have been great philosophers, like St. Augustine of Hippo, or more recently the Dutch thinker—Herman Dooyeweerd. Clearly we need to be careful to maintain a balanced position, and to include the light of Scripture to enable us to be, *"Wise as serpents and* *harmless as doves"* (Matthew 10: 16). Rev. W. B. Godbey notes—*"… we are still to carry with us the good, common sense with which we are born, and to utilise all the intelligence God gives us, 'watching' lest we enter into temptation."*[8] **See Endnote 1:** on Thomas Aquinas.

Strangely enough, C. H. Spurgeon is sometimes quoted as being against apologetics. He is reported as saying: *"Defend the Bible? I would as soon defend a lion. All you need to do is let it out … it needs no defence."* This is a comment from one of the greatest defenders of the truth! Clearly Spurgeon as a preacher felt God's word needed to be proclaimed authoritatively. In his life and witness, he indulged in biblical apologetics. So this comment is clearly one of emphasis. No-one can be argued into the kingdom of God: *"Man proposes, but God disposes."* Doubtless Spurgeon was against the development of an arid intellectualism, that made its roots exclusively in worldly wisdom, or that played excessively to man's pride. In this sense I agree with Spurgeon—if you take apologetics as a high flown philosophical debate (for a few initiated folk) that does not touch down in reality! True apologetics is about applying Christian truth to everyday life.

Elsewhere, Spurgeon exhorts us in words that could have been written yesterday, *"We must defend the Faith; for what would have become of us if our fathers had not maintained it? … Must we not play the man as they did? If not we do not, are we not censuring our Fathers? It is very pretty, is it not, to read of Luther and his brave deeds. Of course, everybody admires Luther! Yes, yes, but you do not want anyone else to do the same today … Yet imagine that in those ages past, Luther, Zwingli, Calvin, and their co-peers had said, 'The world is out of order; but if we try to set it right we shall only make a great row, and get ourselves into disgrace. Let us go to our chambers, put on our night-caps and sleep over bad times, and perhaps when we wake up, things would have grown better.' Such conduct upon their part would have entailed upon us a heritage of error. These men loved the Faith and the name of Jesus too well to see them trampled on. Note that we owe them, and let us pay to our sons the debt we owe to our fathers."*

Another argument against apologetics is that it's fighting the Lord's battles in Saul's armour. That is using worldly or inappropriate means to bring gospel success. You may remember the account of David and Goliath recorded in I Samuel 17:31-39. David being unused to Saul's heavy suit of armour, declined to use it and fought with a catapult and stones. This made it plain that David fought and conquered in faith, using the feeblest and despised instruments of a shepherd. The idea is that the armour is like the heavy arguments of apologetics rather than a simple word of testimony. Clearly—if the story of David and Goliath is applied to defending the faith—it teaches us to use the most appropriate type of equipment (or arguments) or practised skills that fit our *"opponent."* You don't need to use long terms to argue with someone about God's existence (like the ontological or cosmological arguments for the existence of God). All you need to say in such a case is, *"In the beginning—God"* and *"He is the great First cause of all things"* -which makes these two points. Who could oppose the work of brilliant apologists like Billy Bray the Cornish miner, or others who have testified simply but profoundly in their different fields of work?

Apologetics' roots

The basic movement in historic Christian apologetics takes its roots from the apostles of the New Testament, was developed by Augustine, and comes to fruition in later Christians like Aquinas. It is in essence the approach used by the old Princetonian theologians like Warfield and Hodge in the tradition of Calvin. It has been popularly represented in more modern times by apologists like Clive S. Lewis, Cornelius Van Til, Francis Schaeffer, and Josh Mc Dowell. What is the basic starting point of the present study? We propose that **Christian theism** is a rationally necessary position. We claim that Christianity alone is reasonable for people to hold. It is wholly irrational to hold any other position than that of Christianity. Christianity alone does not slay reason on the altar of "Chance". The only "proof" of Christianity is that unless its truth is presupposed there is no possibility of "proving" anything at all. We don't need to peer down a telescope to try to find God, because the very fact we exist (fearfully and wonderfully made) should convince us there is a God.

The Christian apologist is interested in proclaiming and defending the truths that Christ is the Son of God and the Bible is the Word of God. Prior to establishing these main pillars on which the uniqueness of Christianity is built, is the pivotal truth of the existence of God. Our failure to get involved in pre-evangelism, is to leave our young people (or friends) at the mercy of those who will soon expose them to thoughts and ideas that seek to completely undermine the Christian position. Such neglect tends also to confirm the media presentation of Christians as gullible and in need of some psychological props.

The Scriptural justification for apologetics springs from key verses like I Peter 3:15. Sanctify in your hearts Christ as Lord, being ready always to give answers (apologia) to every man that asks you a reason concerning the hope that is in you, yet with meekness and fear. The word apologia, translated answer, apology or defence occurs in several other Scriptures. For instance 2 Timothy 4:16 where Paul says, *"At my first defence no one stood with me ..."* At my first apology; this word signifies a defence or vindication, in the manner lawyers prepare a reasoned marshalling of arguments to vindicate their clients. Paul thought a good answer an absolute necessity. He was anxious that each of his readers would know how to give an answer which in each case will meet this necessity. He proclaims elsewhere, " ... *knowing that I am set for the defence of the gospel"* (Philippians 1:17). This is the meaning of what we call the 'apologies of the primitive fathers'; they were vindications or defences of Christianity. Scripture elsewhere exhorts believers to: *"earnestly contend for the faith which was once delivered unto the saints"* (Jude 3). The apostle Paul used such powerful and persuasive reasoning, that King Agrippa said, *"Paul, you are beside yourself! Much learning is driving you mad! But he* [Paul] *said, "I am not mad, most noble Festus, but speak the words of truth and reason"* (Acts 26: 24-25).

Broadly speaking, there are two major approaches one can take to apologetics: to argue from the truth of God's Word, or to take the stance of *"neutral ground"* and try to build on commonly accepted truths. The latter *"block house"* methodology or approach assumes that people given sufficient evidence will succumb to the superior weight of evidence in favour of the Christian position and turn to seek God. Unfortunately, we find that however much evidence is presented people always tend to find another objection. To argue from this common ground does not give us any absolute certainties, one person's opinion is as good (or as bad) as another's.

There are five main issues that systems of apologetics vary on:

1. **The starting point,** e.g. reason—presenting the facts alone, as if reason is autonomous (an independent entity); or a presuppositional approach (which starts with God and his special revelation rather than man's unaided reason). Arthur Pink states, *"In the beginning God." This is not only the first word of Holy Scripture but it must be the firm axiom of all true philosophy—the philosophy of human history, for example. It is failure to do this which leaves unsolved the 'riddle of the universe.'* [9] This is basically the approach followed in this defence of the faith.

2. **The common ground** or **point of contact** with non-Christians, e.g. observable facts, the laws of logic; or an appeal to everyone's suppressed knowledge of God. It is the latter that is emphasised in our reasoning with people. Calvin says for instance: *"That there exists in the human mind and indeed by natural instinct, some sense of Deity, we hold to be beyond dispute, since God himself, to prevent any man pretending ignorance, has endued all men with some idea of his Godhead ."* [10]

3. **The test for truth:** or standard by which we accept what is true, e.g. truth must agree or cohere with the evidence and rational categories, so all true beliefs must be consistent with one another. It is difficult, however, to prove a negative proposition. An evolutionist may claim that once upon a time there was a creature that had a pigment spot and during a period of many millions of years this pigment spot developed into a human eye. Could you prove it did not happen? It is easy to make fantastic assertions, but it is difficult (if not impossible!) to prove they are not true. For instance, could humans become frogs or flies?!

4. **The role of reasoning:** in practice we judge between conflicting world views on the grounds of defined or specified criteria and evidence. Professor C. Van Til (Apologist) has noted, *"Logical laws must operate in*

a vacuum unless they are based on the presupposition of Christian truth. They operate as laws of thinking implanted in man's constitution as image bearer of God."[11] The limitation of reason is well expressed by Samuel Coleridge, *"Water cannot rise higher than its source, neither can human reason."* Finally:

5. The basis of faith in God, Christ and Scripture: For example, a Christian apologist argues:
(i) logic is dependent on God and not God on logic (speaking in the realm of being—metaphysics);
(ii) all things depend on God for their existence (i.e. that the existence of God is ontologically necessary) otherwise nothing could be either known or proven to be true; **See Endnote 2;**
(iii) that the basis for Christian truth is neither reason nor experience but the authority of God as expressed in Scripture so as Vance Havner commented, *"God's Word is its own best argument"*;
(iv) that there is a revelation of God in nature that humankind is wilfully repressing or holding down as Thomas Brooks queried, *"What are the heavens, the earth, the sea, but a sheet of royal paper, written all over with the wisdom and power of God?"*; and
(v) that God has revealed himself in His Word, the Bible, acting as *"a window in this prison world through which we may look into eternity."*

This defence of the faith in *On Giants' Shoulders* presents Christian apologetics—facts and arguments usable as a tool for Christian witness. Each section deals with a range of vital issues, including those that are often skated over in some apologetic manuals (like the exclusiveness of the gospel, the problem of evil, suffering, existence of ultimate justice). Contrasts are drawn between the atheistic and Christian alternatives on each topic, to show that believers need not feel cornered by attacks on their position. Our methodology uses "evidences" so long as the presuppositions of those used in such evidence are known and made clear.

The antagonistic views which are answered—in defence of the Faith—are those that students will meet head-on in University, and from that angle this 'apologia' will provide a source of encouragement to Christians to maintain their testimony, knowing there is an answer. For that reason I have quoted opponents (especially Professor Dawkins) as their outspoken challenge to the Christian gospel must be answered. Despite this, it is not possible to present any antagonists views in entirity—each topic would then involve a book on its own! The criticism of selectivity, can always be levelled against those who seek to pinpoint weaknesses in their opponents armour! Apologetics challenges the sceptic and comforts the believer. To be forewarned is to be forearmed, and it is right to learn even from a foe.

Apologetics in practice

Francis Schaeffer once said if he were on an aeroplane flight for an hour—with a fellow traveller—he would spend most of the time talking about Genesis chapters 1-3—creation and evolution (i.e. indulging in apologetics) and the last few minutes explaining the gospel. There is a clear need to overcome the *"credibility gap"* in part created by the media's portrayal of people of faith as 'blinkered', or unable to face the "fact"that man is in a mechanistic universe. Dr Schaeffer wrote extensively on topics like *The God who is there* and *Escape from Reason*, which dealt with the emptiness of life and culture without the God of Scripture.

When we have found the pearl of great price (Jesus), we want others to know Him too. Mark 1:17 says: *"And Jesus said unto them, Come you after me, and I will make you to become fishers of men."* Spurgeon commenting on this says: *"Only by coming after Jesus can we obtain our heart's desire, and be really useful to our fellow men. Oh, how we long to be successful fishers for Jesus! ... We must keep to our preaching [and witness] as our Master did, for by this means souls are saved. We must preach our Lord's doctrine, and proclaim a full and free gospel; for this is the net in which souls are taken. ... We must work under divine anointing, depending upon the sacred Spirit. Thus, coming after Jesus, and not running before Him, nor aside from Him, we shall be fishers of men."*[12]

"I will make you fishers of men, if you follow me". Think of the profundity of this illustration used by the Lord Jesus Christ—the master teacher, when he told the fishermen that he would make them fishers of men rather than fishers of fish! John Calvin commenting on this passage points out the reason for casting out the gospel net—to provide a lifeline to

rescue us from a troubled world: *"As to the meaning of the metaphor, 'fishers of men', there is no necessity for a minute investigation. Yet, as it is drawn from the present occurrence [Luke 5:10], the allusion which Christ made to fishing, when he spoke of preaching the Gospel, was appropriate: for men stray and wander in the world, as in a great and troubled sea, till they are gathered in by the Gospel."* [13]

References

1. **C. H. Spurgeon** (1997) *C. H. Spurgeon's Sermon Collection* , vol. 4., Christian Library, Ages Software, Albany, OR, USA, p. 388.
2. **J. B. Mc Clure** (ed.) (1997) *Pearls From Many Seas,*, C.H. Spurgeon: Affability in conversation, Christian Library, Ages Software, Albany, OR, USA, p. 62 . p.23.
3. **J. Wilbur Chapman** (1996) Present Day Parables, M. Guy Pearse, *Fishers of men*, Christian Library, Ages Software, Albany, OR, USA, p. 62 .
4. **J. Gresham Machen** (1951) *What is Christianity?* Eerdmans, Grand Rapids, pp.126-30.
5. **B. B. Warfield** (1932) *Studies in Theology*, Oxford University, N.Y., p.15.
6. **J. Wesley,** *The Complete Works of John Wesley: Letters, Essays* , Vol. 9, Christian Library, Ages Software, Albany, OR, USA, p. 536.
7. **T. Aquinas** (1997) *Summa Theologica*, Christian Library, Ages Software, Albany, OR, USA, p. 5.
8. **W. B. Godfrey** (1997) Commentary on the New Testament, volume 6, Gospel Harmony, Part 1, Christian Library, Ages Software, Albany, OR, USA, p. 271.
9. **A. Pink** (1997) *The Godhead*, Christian Library, Ages Software, Albany, OR, USA, p. 4.
10. **J. Calvin** (1997) *The Institutes of Christian Religion*, Christian Library, Ages Software, Albany, OR, USA, p. 63 .
11. **C. Van Til** (1972) *Toward a Reformed Apologetics*, Van Til summary, p. 5. The works of Cornelius Van Til (1895-1997) on CD Rom can be obtained from: http://www.gospelcom.net/wts/bookstore/vantil/ It is also possible to listen to "Christ and the Scripture, the Christian view of education and culture; history and nature of apologetics" broadcast over the net in .ra format (i.e. in real audio format.)
12. **C. H. Spurgeon** (1997) *Faith's Checkbook, May 29 Fishers Follow Him*, Christian ` Library, Ages Software, Albany, OR, USA, p. 167 .

13. **J. Calvin** (1997) *Harmony of the Gospels*, Christian Library, Ages Software, Albany, OR, USA, p. 211.

Resources:

See **Appendix 1 Nice One Cyril**, for a case study of apologetics. For an example of an apologist who used a block house methodology see **Appendix 2 on C. S. Lewis** who concentrated on the 'facts.' In practice, Christian apologists are not always entirely consistent in their approaches to presenting the truth, but nevertheless do a valuable job in exposing erroneous views. For instance, ultimately even a Van Tillian appeals to reason to establish their case (see **J. M. Frame** (1994) *Apologetics to the Glory of God*, chapter 3 Apologetics as Proof: Some Methodological Considerations, pp. 57-88.)

Recommended books:

At a **popular level** is : Josh Mc Dowell (1988) *Answers to tough questions*, Scripture Press, ISBN O-946515-51-4.
General level: William Edgar (1996) *Reasons of the Heart,* Baker Book House Co., ISBN 0-8010-51138-X.

More scholarly works are:

Gordon R. Lewis (1997) *Testing Christianity's Truth Claims*, The Moody Bible Institute, Chicago, ISBN 0-8024-8595-2.
J. M. Frame (1994)*Apologetics to the Glory of God*, Presbyterian & Reformed Publishing, New Jersey, ISBN 0-87552-243-2.
Francis A. Schaeffer (1996) *Complete Works*, 5 volumes, Crossway Books, Wheaton, Illinois, 60187, USA, ISBN 0-89107-331-0.

Key Texts:

Matthew 4: 17-23; Isaiah 41:21 (Challenge to unbelievers)

Endnote: 1 Thomas Aquinas

There is a vigorous defence of Aquinas by Reformed theologian Norman Geisler in his book *Thomas Aquinas: An Evangelical Appraisal*, Grand Rapids: Baker Book House Company, 1991, pp. 1-43, in which he reviews the criticisms often made against Aquinas' writings. It is worth checking both Geisler's comments and *Summa Theologica* for oneself to see that many points of criticism are not founded on fact. Geisler says in the above appraisal, *"The time is overdue for all secret believers to join in a positive word of gratitude for the masterful expression and defence of the historic Christian faith bequeathed to us by this humble giant of the faith. As for myself, I gladly confess that the highest compliment that could be paid to me as a Christian philosopher, apologist, and theologian is to call me 'Thomistic.' This, of course. does not mean I accept everything Aquinas wrote naively and uncritically. It does mean that I believe he was one of the greatest systematic minds the Christian church has ever had, and that I see a lot farther standing on his shoulders than by attacking him in the back. No, I do not agree with everything he ever wrote. On the other hand, neither do I agree with everything I ever wrote. But seven hundred years from now no one will even recognise my name, while Aquinas' works will still be used with great profit"* p.9.

Endnote: 2 Ontological argument:

An a priori argument for the existence of God from the idea of God. God is defined as a self-existing or necessarily existing Being. Therefore God cannot not exist. His ontological Being is argued from what we mean by God. No evidence is necessary.

Questions for Further study

1   What was Calvin's comment on the phrase "fishers of men"?
2   What are the qualities required to make us effective witnesses?
3   What are the three essential elements of good apologetics?
4   What are the dangers of apologetics, that made Spurgeon cautious about them?
5   Is apologetics a new phenomenon in the Christian church?
6   What are the main things a Christian apologist is anxious to defend?
7   Is the word apologetics (apologia) used in Scripture, if so give instances?
8   What Scriptures would you use to prove the need for Christians to use apologetics?
9   How would you dispel the notion, "New is true, old is mould"?
10   In an age that is sceptical about Christianity, was Schaeffer right to spend so long on apologetic groundwork?

Food for Thought

*   "What I live by, I impart." St. Augustine of Hippo
*   "For My sake and the gospel's, go
     And tell redemption's story:
     His heralds answer, 'Be it so,
     And Thine, Lord, all the glory!'"   E. H. Bickersteth

A fading Cosmic smile: is the need for God disappearing?

" When men cease to believe in God, they do not believe in nothing; they believe in anything." G. K. Chesterton.

T he question of God's existence is reviewed: certainly the "God of the gaps", sometimes invoked to explain mysteries or inadequate scientific theories, is dead. Julian Huxley, Karl Marx and Friedrich Nietzsche all hoped this was the end of the notion of "God". The only God they dispose of is a "God" who is the projection of man's mind. Are contemporary believers gullible obscurantists? Humanity is a mix of believers and unbelievers, so it must surely include some gullible people in both categories. Isn't the atheist, however, as "foolish"to trust in broken systems and the tinsel of this world which lets them down? Unbelief is not modern, and we can surmount every intellectual difficulty, if we are prepared to face the facts. The "proofs" of God are introduced and examined. The ontological, cosmological, teleological, anthropological (or moral) and congruity arguments are explained in layman's terms. These arguments show that far from believers being "irrational" in their beliefs, there is a whole system of cogent thought, flowing from the acceptance of the reality of God.

Introduction

"The time has come," the Walrus said, "To talk of many things: Of shoes—and ships—and sealing-wax- Of cabbages- and kings- And why the sea is boiling hot- And whether pigs have wings." This may be a strange introduction to a discussion about beliefs, but we are going to *"talk of many things"*! The philosophical significance of Lewis Carroll's *Alice's Adventures in Wonderland* and *Through the Looking Glass*—has not escaped profound thinkers! Gilbert K. Chesterton noted the fact that Alice's story had already fallen under the heavy hands of scholars who

were making Carroll's writings, *"cold and monumental like a classic tomb."*[1]

"Poor, poor, little Alice!" bemoaned G. K. Chesterton. *"She has not only been caught and made to do lessons; she has been forced to inflict lessons on others. Alice is not only a schoolgirl but a schoolmistress."*[2] **See Endnote 1.** The powerful "nonsense" that Lewis Carroll wrote, clearly captured the mind of a famous British philosopher who adapted one of Carroll's illustrations as a prediction of the future of the notion of God. The biologist, Julian Huxley, wrote: *"Operationally, God is beginning to resemble not a ruler but the last fading smile of a cosmic Cheshire cat."* What did he mean? Cleverly, Huxley alludes to a scene in *Alice's Adventures in Wonderland*, a fantasy world where a little girl named Alice falls down a rabbit hole into a fantastic, illogical world. Alice is portrayed as a shrewd character able to see through the pretence and hypocrisy of the adult world. In her adventures Alice consults a Cheshire Cat, a character that would often fade from sight until nothing but his grin remained visible.

Huxley uses this idea to say that as knowledge advances and man comes of age, the need for God as a ruler of the universe or in people's thinking will fade away. This reflects Julian Huxley's view of God. Operationally, he thinks the need for God is doomed. Certainly, the type of *"god"* that Huxley imagines is dead. He is an operational principle, a *"god"* of the unknown, who is invoked to fill in the gaps in our scientific or philosophical knowledge. Otherwise he is the result of some form of psychological conditioning, perhaps in childhood: invoked to give some measure of security in an insecure world. These notions are far removed from the living Triune God of the Bible: they do, however, underline the view of the Bible itself that unaided reason cannot find the true God: *"Can man by searching find out God?"* He can find only the type of *"god"* (a product of man's mind) that Huxley disposes of! Other thinkers have claimed there is no God to dispose of, so that effectively *"God is dead"*.

Julian Huxley wrote a book called *Religion without Revelation* (1927, revised 1957) in which he suggested that humans could find an outlet for their religious zeal in thinking of their destiny rather than about theistic creeds. Like his grandfather, Thomas Huxley, Julian was particularly interested in concepts of evolution and growth, and processing these in the light of both philosophical and scientific developments. Other thinkers, too, have advocated the abandonment of the idea of God.

Karl Marx and Nietzsche

Karl Marx (1818-1883) the famous political philosopher and definer of communism, claimed that religion is the opium of the people. Liberation comes from *"coming of age"*, and being enlightened to the view that there is no need of a first cause. Others (like Friedrich Nietzsche, 1844-1900) have sought to *"think God out of existence, then we have a future!"* Nietzsche founded his morality on what he saw as the most basic human drive, the will to have power. He criticised Christianity and other philosophers' moral systems as *"slave moralities"* because, in his view, they chained all members of society with universal rules of ethics. As Don A. Carson (theologian) has written: *"Nietzsche could argue that abandonment of any notion of God was immensely liberating. "Once you said 'God' when you gazed upon distant seas; but now I have taught you to say 'superman'." But human history has rightly destroyed much of this form of arrogance. Since Nietzsche's day a succession of brutal tyrants and wars they have spawned, ongoing struggles with racism, grinding poverty, urban violence, and the evils of massive bureaucracies have done much to temper enthusiasm for the notion that the death of God is a triumph of the human spirit."*[3]

Credibility gap

There is a big credibility gap in many people's minds—created in part by the popular portrayal of believers as gullible obscurantists, like ostriches with their heads in the sand, *"unable to face the facts."* Perhaps this is most graphically stated by James Harvey Johnson of the Thinkers Club: *"Religious beliefs are against common sense. There are no angels, devils, heavens, hells, ghosts, witches, nor miracles. These superstitious beliefs are promoted for the purpose of making the gullible believe that by paying money to the priest class they will be favoured by one of the gods. There is nothing supernatural—nothing contrary to natural law."*

Others attack the discernment and intellectual credibility of people who believe in God. Oxford Professor of Philosophy—Richard Swinburne writing in his book on *Is there a God* says: *"My own view … is that none of the great religions can make any serious claim on the basis of particular historical evidence for the truth of their purported revelations, apart from the Christian religion."* David Hall, a critical reviewer, says: *"If a man is naive enough to believe that, he is obviously naive enough to believe anything."* He continues: *"This book is further evidence that intelligence and academic ability are no guarantee of sound judgement in religion, as the number of fundamentalists with degrees in the sciences well illustrates ."* 4

Why create?
Hall is also incredulous at the purpose of a God creating such a Universe. He says: *"If God is indeed the creator and sustainer of the universe one is prompted to enquire what it is for. Since God is, by Swinburne's definition, a person with desires and purposes, he must have some aim in mind in embarking on and sustaining the enterprise. All that we are offered by way of explanation is that the universe gives rise to freely-acting human beings. Why an omnipotent God needs such infinitely vast means in terms of time and space in order to produce such a short-lived and puny result is hard to understand. Why, indeed, would a freely-acting human being be worth the creation of any universe at all, especially when it entails the possibility of the instantiation of the evils we all know, evils that would not have existed at all had the infinitely good God remained just that and refrained from creation?"* 5 Replies to these queries are dealt with in greater detail in chapter 4, but the logic of a sceptic like Hall here, could also have been written by a modern day Augustine: *"Why, indeed, has man been created with any significance in this vast Universe?"* The Psalmist spells out the answer in Psalm 8: 3-8, which wonders—in view of the vast starry heavens—*"What is man that you are mindful of him?"*

Christianity is not an irrational leap of faith
In reality it is just the opposite to Johnson's or Hall's views—as Christian truth is addressed to thinkers, not the gullible: *"Come let us reason together"* said Isaiah. Paul the Apostle says: *"Test all things; hold fast what is good"* (I Thessalonians 5:21). Christianity is not a blind *" leap of faith"*

in the dark, neither does it ask believers to commit intellectual suicide; its claim is to be grounded in historic fact. Are Christians any more or any less gullible than non-believers? Does the world and its pleasures provide the lasting happiness it boasts? Does the experimentation in morality bring happy families, peace, joy, and health to those with loose sexual habits? Such views and life-styles may be thought *"liberating"*- but are they? Aren't such folk *"captives"* to their own passions or drives?

Some have thought that only the present counts: Henry Ford, the car maker, claimed: *"History is more or less bunk. It's tradition. We want to live in the present and the only history that is worth a tinker's damn is the history we make today."* Was he right? Only if you are so limited in your outlook as not to realise that the present depends on the past. Long ago, Cicero, the Roman orator and statesman wisely said, *"to know nothing of what happened before you were born is to remain a child."* A knowledge of history confirms that the phenomenon of *unbelief* is not modern. There have always been genuine intellectual problems that can trip us up. In all aspects of life—cultural, ethical, psychological, scientific, socio-logical—we no longer express ourselves or understand our world as our forbears did even a hundred years ago. This work argues that the seeker or Christian can surmount every modern obstacle to faith, and so remove any mountains of unbelief or doubt. What have been the arguments given by philosophers and theologians as proof of the being of God?

Proofs of God's existence

Those who argue from the viewpoint of **natural theism**, believe it is possible to learn about God through studying the natural realm and using man's reasoning powers. Typically knowledge of a Supreme Being (obtained in this fashion) comes from three sources in the natural realm: (i) intuition, (ii) tradition and (iii) reason. We shall examine this evidence, to see how far it can provide valid justification for the notion of God. The French writer Voltaire (1694-1778) commented, *"If God did not exist, it would be necessary to invent him."*

◆ i: Intuition

The fact man knows intuitively about God is evidenced by every civilisation having some belief in an afterlife and in a higher power or god. This knowledge does not need to be taught, and manifests itself also in every society having a concept of right and wrong. This latter notion implies that good actions will be rewarded by God, and wrong actions will invoke the displeasure of God. The apostle Paul, in fact talks in Romans 1:19 of, *"what may be known of God is manifest in them, for God has shown it to them."*

◆ ii: Tradition

To a certain point much of what we know about God today came from past generations who have committed their findings on this matter to paper. Certainly the data we have recorded in the Old Testament may have been tradition before it was set down by Moses (called *"a man learned in the Egyptians"*).

◆ iii: Reason

Reason is typically thought of as a faculty of humans and not the lower animals. The intellect has the capacity to abstract, comprehend, relate, reflect, notice similarities and differences; it also implies the ability to infer. Three categories of reason are generally recognised: (1) evidencing; (2) motivating; and (3) causally necessitating, although discussion of these is beyond our present purposes. We will consider, however, the two main types of reasoning—deductive and inductive.

◆ 1: Cause to Effect: Deductive reasoning

A priori means proceeding from causes to effects. The **a priori** argument is the testimony given by reason. It is that which can be known to be true without reference to experience, except in so far as experience is necessary to understand the terms. It proceeds from causes to effects. In our context, a priori reasoning includes proofs drawn from the necessity that such a being as God is, must exist: arguments of this type do not produce any thing in evidence which is derived from his works. The **ontological argument** (see Figure 2.1 **"Proofs for the existence of God"**) is an a priori argument and says basically that man could not have the idea of a perfect infinite being unless something exists that corresponds to it. We must

Figure 2.1: Proofs for the existence of God.

POPULAR NAME	TECHNICAL NAME	TYPE	METHOD	SUPPORTER(S)	STATUS / COMMENT	TYPICAL SECULAR ALTERNATIVE
1. Idea of a Perfect Being	Ontological Argument	Cause to Effect	Deductive: A priori	C. Van Til with his "Ontological Trinity" J. Frame GL Bahnsen	Accepted as an assumed starting point.	Atheism
2. First Cause of all things	Cosmological Argument	Effect to Cause	Inductive: A posteriori	Thomas Aquinas.	Every effect must have a cause.	S. Hawking's Cosmology
3. Intelligent Designer to Universe:	Teleological Argument	Effect to Cause	Inductive: A posteriori	William Paley Michael J. Behe	As biological mechanisms would be useless until complete, there must be an intelligent designer.	R. Dawkin's Blind Watch-Maker; or Selfish Gene. S. Gould: God a poor engineer.
4. Man a microcosm	Anthropological or Moral Argument	Effect to Cause	Inductive: A posteriori	John Calvin Francis Schaeffer	Man made in God's image; also acts as point of contact.	Man product of Evolution. Freudianism.
5. Force of cumulative arguments	Congruity Argument	Both sorts: Cause to Effect, Effect to Cause.	Synthesis	Josh Mc Dowell Clive S. Lewis	Weight of evidence can show reasonableness of belief in God. "If a key fits the lock, it is the correct key"	Logical Positivism: Man a mere collocation of atoms.

assume that the infinite being made us aware of Himself. Ontological comes from the Greek word "ontos" or being. Aristotle refers to it as "First philosophy." In part, this seeks to describe the nature of the ultimate being (the one, the absolute, the perfect eternal form) and to show that all things depend upon it for their existence. Descartes, the father of modern philosophy stated that we have the idea of an infinite and perfect Being, this idea cannot have derived from the imperfect and finite things. There must, therefore, be an infinite and perfect Being who is the cause. The human mind does seem capable, however, of imagining entities that do not exist like, *"the force be with you"* or fairies and unicorns. Hume dismisses the whole argument by saying, *"But Caesar, or the angel Gabriel, or any being that never existed may be a false proposition, but still is perfectly conceivable and implies no contradiction."*[6] Whilst the **ontological argument** has this weakness, it is possible to make an ontological assumption, which may be the starting point or presupposition of your discourse. Thus it is an a priori argument for the existence of God from the idea of God. God is defined as a self-existing or necessarily existing Being. Therefore God cannot not exist. His ontological Being is argued from what we mean by God. No evidence as such is necessary. Several apologists take this stance, including the late Cornelius Van Til.

◆ 2: Effect to Cause: Inductive reasoning

There are several arguments based on inductive reasoning for belief in God. The inductive method is to proceed from facts to a conclusion, i.e. reasoning from particular facts to general principles. For instance, if you touch two electric wires in a socket, you feel something. From the fact of this pain, you draw the conclusion it is unwise to touch electric wires in a socket—unless you have first checked the power is switched off! The **a posteriori** argument is a process by which we proceed logically from the facts of experience to causes. The argument from effect to cause is technically known as **"argumentum a posteriori"** so that if you see an effect you know it must have a cause. For instance, if you find a well designed aeroplane, you conclude it is made by a designer and his team—and is not the result of a tornado blowing through a metal scrapyard!

This line of argumentation moves from the end product that we exist and the world in which we live (creation), then argues backwards to what was in the past. The **a posteriori** arguments are:

◆ **A:** the **cosmological argument**, by which it is proved that there must be a first Cause of all things, as every effect must have a cause;
◆ **B:** The **teleological**, or argument from design. We see everywhere the operations of an intelligent Cause in nature; and
◆ **C:** The **anthropological argument**, based on the moral consciousness and the history of mankind, which exhibits a moral order and purpose, which can only be explained by the supposition of the existence of God. Now let us review these arguments in greater detail.

◆ A: Cosmological argument

The so-called **Cosmological argument** comes from the term "cosmos" meaning orderly. In essence this says that we can observe the great and vast universe and we must assume, therefore, there was a great and vast power that was able to create this. Either something must be eternal or something comes from nothing. Something does not come from nothing. Therefore something is eternal. Relating to these points, there have been four main arguments (or positions) in the past.

Firstly, it is claimed nature is eternal—so there is no need of a cause. Secondly, it can be argued matter is eternal and is self-developing. Thirdly, matter is eternal but its present arrangement is due to the influence of God. Aristotle, Plato and other philosophers thought man must have some purpose or else why would God influence matter. Fourthly, that matter was created for the express purpose of, and by, Almighty God—as is confirmed by His Revelation.

The **cosmological argument** thus reasons: Everything—whether substance or phenomenon—owes its existence to some producing cause. The universe, at least as its present form is concerned, is a thing begun and owes its existence to a cause equal to its production. This cause must be indefinitely great. This position assumes:

(1) If there is an effect there was a cause.
(2) The effect depends on the cause for its being.
(3) Nature cannot in and of itself produce itself. Hence there had to have

been a cause for the effect of nature. So there is a power somewhere because there are effects everywhere.

◆ B: Teleological argument

Another argument for a great designer is that of teleology, frequently associated with the work of biologist William Paley. Simply put this says: we can see design in nature thus we must conclude that creation was designed and created by a being that has both design and order. The term *"telos"* (Greek) means designer or end. The teleological argument thus:

◆ **1:** gives the explanation of phenomena by the purpose that they serve rather than by postulated causes.

◆ **2:** In theology it means the teaching that the world (inorganic as well as organic) is an ordered design. Therefore the cause of the world is an intelligent Designer. Order and useful bringing together pervading a system imply intelligence and purpose as the cause of that order and arrangement together. As order and collocation (things arranged together or side by side) are found in varying degrees throughout the Universe, there must be an intelligence adequate to the production of this order, and a will to direct this collocation to useful ends. The universe is full of examples of design (e.g. plants and animals). Even Darwin shuddered when he contemplated the complexity and design of the human eye. Some philosophers claim that the order and design come from the natural working of the laws of nature. Although, if this is true, where did the orderly laws of nature originate—if not from an orderly God?

Biologist Dr Leonard Loose's *"What, are we blind too?"* discusses whether natural selection can be an intelligent and directing force. He says: *"It is, therefore, flagrantly inconsistent to adopt the principles and results of Artificial Selection as the model of Natural Selection, and yet ignore the means by which those principles were discovered and the results obtained. The means were wholly personal and threefold: purposeful evaluation of the living organism; the exercise of a rare degree of human intelligence; human expertise acquired by years of experience. Without these qualities, selection must "assuredly fail", "nothing can be effected" as Darwin so emphatically believed. Thus Natural Selection, if it is to succeed, must possess powers comparable to these powers of the successful plant and animal breeder! Even Paley, it must be noted in passing, never claimed such skills for living things, other than for God and Man. Yet Dawkins approves of Darwin and dismisses Paley! "Paley's argument … is wrong, gloriously and utterly wrong. The analogy between telescope and eye, between watch and living organism is false" (Blind Watchmaker p. 5). Darwin on the other hand is acknowledged to be "one of the most revolutionary thinkers of all time" (Ibid. p. 4). It seems rather odd, to say the least, that Natural Selection, the great idea of this great thinker, should be described by Dawkins in these terms: "It has no mind and no mind's eye. It does not plan for the future. It has no vision, no foresight, no sight at all" (Ibid. p. 5). … The fact is, that in passing from the sphere of selection by man, to selection by nature, Darwin stepped from scientific fact to scientific fiction."* [7]

Argument from Un-design

The most forceful argument against a created universe involves what we might call the 'Argument from Un-design'. This reasoning basically reverses the argument from design and implies God (if He exists) is a bodger. Professor Stephen Gould is associated with this argument and he suggests that the Panda's thumb is not actually a thumb but a bone protrusion which can be interpreted as a bit of sloppy engineering. Therefore, if God is the creator, He is a lousy engineer. As the God of the Bible cannot be a poor designer, He does not exist. Evolution tends to talk exclusively in terms of engineering and design features and says that creatures and plant forms and their diversity show a 'least cost engineering solution.' A bird's wing, for instance, is assessed in terms of its flexibility, light weight, surface area, strength, warmth and repairability needed for flight. Dr Gould tends to think of God exclusively in terms of the Great Designer/Architect working like a Divine Engineer. His view fails to recognise that God is also a Great Artist. The Panda's thumb, is in fact, God delighting in his creation, creating new wonders. God may use common patterns—but He is not restricted to them. He is not limited, say, to ten species of monochrome bacteria! The Panda's thumb works perfectly; it is an example of God's creativity and artistic skill.

◆ C: Anthropological argument

Man has a spiritual side that did not occur by chance. We must assume a spiritual being created him. This so-called, **"Anthropological argument"** states that:

◆ **1:** Man's intellectual and moral nature requires as its originator an intellectual and moral Being. The mind cannot evolve from matter, neither can spirit evolve from flesh. Consequently, a Being having both mind and spirit must have created man.

◆ **2:** Man's moral nature proves the existence of a holy Lawgiver and Judge. Otherwise, conscience cannot be satisfactorily explained.

◆ **3:** Man's emotional and volitional nature requires for its author a Being, who can furnish in Himself a satisfying object of human affection and an end which will call forth man's highest activities and ensure his highest progress. Calvin has commented along these lines: *"Hence certain of the philosophers have not improperly called man a microcosm [miniature world] as being a rare specimen of divine power, wisdom, goodness, and containing within himself wonders sufficient to occupy our minds, if we are willing so to employ them."*[8]

◆ D: Moral argument

Inasmuch as man has these unusual qualities not found in any other animal (including the power of speech) it is possible for man, on the basis of what he is, to have some concept of what the makeup of that creator would be. Man is composed of both material and immaterial elements. We can assume that due to our makeup, a creator would probably have some of those same characteristics which he gave to us: life, intellect, sensibility, will and conscience. Some submit people's moral nature as indicative of a moral God as well. Indeed, this whole thought is known as the Moral argument.

In summarising the three main a posteriori arguments it can be stated:

◆ **1:** In the **cosmological argument**, the existence of the cosmos, originating in time, constitutes proof of a First Cause who is self-existent and eternal and who possesses intelligence power and will. As Thomas

Watson commented, *"To create requires infinite power. All the world cannot make a fly."*

◆ **2:** In the **teleological argument** the evidence of design extends the proof of the intelligence of the First Cause into details of telescopic grandeur and microscopic perfection far beyond the minuscule ability of man to discover or comprehend. It was the philosopher John Stuart Mill (1706-73) who said, *"The argument from design is irresistible. Nature does testify to its Creator"*. Perhaps the most surprising comment on this argument comes from the great sceptic philosopher David Hume. He said, *"The whole frame of nature bespeaks an intelligent author, and no rational enquirer can, after serious reflection, suspend his belief a moment with regard to the primary principles of genuine Theism and Religion."*[9] This admission shows that even Hume felt the force of this argument, whether he believed it or not!

◆ **3:** In the **anthropological argument**, though confirming the proofs advanced in the two preceding arguments, an added indication is secured which suggests the elements in the First Cause of intellect, sensibility and will, which are the essentials of personality. Man has a conscience. The moral feature of conscience in man indicates that his Creator is the One who actuates holiness, justice, goodness and truth.

Historically speaking, there have been numerous attempts to prove the reality of God. St. Anselm (medieval scholar) argued the very idea of God—a being than whom no more perfect can be conceived entails his existence, for existence is itself an aspect of perfection. Philosophers have renounced the logical validity of such a transition from idea to factual existence, but this ontological argument is still discussed. Whilst Thomas Aquinas (the 13th century theologian) rejected the ontological argument he nevertheless proposed five other proofs for God's existence:
(i) the fact of change requires an agent of change;
(ii) the chain of causation needs to be grounded in a first cause that is itself uncaused; (iii) the contingent facts of the world (facts that might not have been as they are) assume or presuppose a necessary being;
iv) one can observe a gradation of things as higher and lower, and this

points to a perfect reality at the top of the hierarchy; and (v) the order and design of nature demand as their source a being possessing the highest wisdom.[10] Whilst Immanuel Kant (18th century philosopher) rejected these arguments for God's existence, he argued there was a need for God to support and be guarantor of the moral life. See Endnote 2.

The correct key

Referring back to the arguments or *"proofs for God's existence"* we note that in the Cosmological thought God possessed a self-determining will. In the teleological thinking we found God had a mind to produce design and power to enact that design. In the anthropological or moral argument we saw God has sensibility. These are all properties of God's creation, as well. There is another line of argument: known as **congruity**. This simply states that if you have a system of thought that fits the facts of the effect then you must assume the system of thought contains facts that are correct about the cause, because they are harmoniously related. In other words, if the key fits the lock then it is the correct key to the door. If an infinite God fits the facts that we know, then He is the answer we seek.

These proposed arguments show belief in God is reasonable and determined by the presuppositions or frame of reference adopted by the enquirer. Clearly Christianity is not a leap in the dark or into irrational thought. Nor is it as a little boy once said, *"believing things we know to be untrue"*! The arguments for the reality of God have been submitted to extensive criticism, and they are still being reformulated to meet these criticisms. It is true that no one argument makes an infallible *"proof"* for God's existence, but the arguments do have a cumulative force. They amount to a strong probability, especially alongside supporting religious experience. Doubtless there are valid aspects to all these arguments, but logic itself runs out eventually, when one is dealing with a God who is greater than our Universe.

Far from God becoming like *"a fading cosmic smile"*, Calvin says: *"Still, none who have the use of their eyes can be ignorant of the divine skill manifested so copiously in the endless variety, yet distinct and well ordered array, of the heavenly host; and, therefore it is plain that the Lord has furnished every man with abundant proofs of his wisdom. The same is true in regard to the structure of the human frame. To determine the connection of its parts, its symmetry and beauty .... requires singular acuteness; and yet all men acknowledge that the human body bears on its face such proofs of ingenious contrivance as are sufficient to proclaim the admirable wisdom of its Maker.*"[11] It is this aspect of the composition of humans that we now examine in the next chapter.

References:

1   **L. Carroll** (1982) *The Annotated Alice*, Introduction by M. Gardner, Penguin Books, ISBN 0 1400 1387 3, p. 7.
2   **Ibid,** p. 7.
3   **D. A. Carson** (1996) *The Gagging of God*, Apollos, Leicester, ISBN 0-85111-7678, pp. 206-7.
4   **D. Hall** (1996) reviews *Is there a God?* by Richard Swinburne, Philosophy Now, Issue 15, Spring/Summer, Ipswich, ISBN 0961-5970, p. 44.
5   **Ibid,** p. 44.
6   **D. Hume** *Inquiry concerning Human Understanding* XII (iii).
7   **L. Loose** (1988) *What, are we blind too?* pp. 11-12. Unpublished pamphlet.
8   **J. Calvin** (1559) *Institutes of the Christian Religion*, Christian Digital Library version 5, Ages Software, Albany, OR97321, p. 74.
9   **D. Hume** (1980) *Dialogues Concerning Natural Religion*, from Introduction by Editor Richard H. Popkin, Hackett Publishers, Indianaplois, Cambridge, ISBN 0-915144-45-X, p. xiii.
10   **T. Aquinas** (1997) *Summa Theologica: An Evangelical Appraisal by Norman Geisler*, Books for the Ages, Ages Software, Albany, OR., USA, pp. 2-39.
11   **J. Calvin** (1559) Ibid.

Further Reading:
   J. Blanchard (1985) *Right with God*, Banner of Truth, Edinburgh, ISBN 0 85151 045 0
   R. Creswell (1990) *Why Believe?* STL Books, Bromley, Kent, ISBN 1 85078 079 X.
   B. Palmer (1996) *Cure for Life*, Summit Publishing Ltd, Milton Keynes, ISBN 1-9010-7407-2.

Chapter 2

Key Text:

Acts: 17: 23 *"For as I was passing through and considering the objects of your worship, I even found an altar with this inscription: To the unknown God. Therefore, the one whom you worship without knowing, him I proclaim to you."*

Endnote 1:

Some argue that Carroll pokes fun at evolution in reality. For instance M. Bowden (1998) writes: *"Alice's neck grows in length (Lamark's explanation of the giraffe's neck) and she is chased by a big puppy (a 'Beagle' puppy—referring to Darwin's ship. Darwin was hurt by this caricature.) Carroll almost certainly went to the famous Oxford debate between Wilberforce and Huxley (which, incidentally, is grossly misreported and was not won by Huxley ... Carroll represents this event and much of the ensuing controversy in the kitchen scene ... where the cook (Sir Richard Owen) is stirring a pot with too much pepper (producing a lot of 'hot air') and everybody sneezes except the cook and the Cheshire cat (Dean Stanley who came from Cheshire and had much influence with Queen Victoria and others—he could afford to smile!)"*. From: *True Science Agrees With the Bible*, Sovereign Publications, Bromley, Kent, pp. 252-3.

Endnote 2:

What is the present status of these concepts in University departments? There are philosophers like Alvin Plantinga (Notre Dame University) a Reformed analytical philosopher, who has rebutted arguments against belief in God. He seeks to show belief in theism is justifiable in books like *God and Other Minds* (1967) and in *God, Freedom and Evil* (1974). He is now writing a three volume trilogy on warrant ('that which turns belief into knowledge'). Plantinga's modal version, however, claims that God is a logically necessary being and then moves from the alleged possibility of God's necessary existence to God's actual necessary existence. Graham Oppy (1995) has written a whole book on the ontological argument: *Ontological Arguments and Belief in God*. The cosmological argument—in one form—states that if there exists a contingent being, there must be a necessary being to, as it were, explain its existence. Peter van Inwagen, puts forward an *a priori* version of the argument in his book *Metaphysics* (1993). The teleological argument has been supported recently by Richard Swinburne (1979) in his book *The Existence of God*. He uses probability theory in his book. Arguments about the problem of evil and suffering continue to abound; since 1960, over 3600 articles and books have been written on this issue. Alvin

Plantinga has shown it is impossibly difficult to establish any sound proof of God's non-existence using this argument.

Questions for Further Study

1   To what extent is Julian Huxley's view of God correct? Is this the Christian view of God?
2   How do you account for the credibility gap, between Christian believers and non-believers?
3   What conditions the modern mind-set to be dubious about the Christian Faith?
4   In what ways would you illustrate the failure of humanism to bring the liberation and freedom, that are claimed for it?
5   Is Christianity an "irrational leap of faith"?
6   How would you answer someone who saw no value in History?
7   On what aspect of God's character does the Christian base his/her conviction that there is an answer to every problem?
8   Is the ontological argument dead?
9   What is the cosmological argument for God's existence?
10 "The announcement of Watson and Crick on the DNA code is for me the real proof of the existence of God." Salvador Dali (1904-1989) Spanish surrealist artist. For the Spanish artist Salvador Dali, the discovery of DNA was real proof of the existence of God. What is he implying about the genetic code?
11 What is the teleological argument for God's existence?
12 What is the anthropological argument for God's existence?
13 List the main arguments for the existence of a Supreme being. Which do you find most convincing (or not) and why?
14 As it is not possible to prove God's existence in any infallible way to a sceptic, is there any value in arguments that can indicate God's existence?

Food for Thought

* "Let us not lose the Bible, but with diligence, in fear and invocation of God, read and preach it. While that remains and flourishes, all prospers with the state; 'tis head and empress of all arts and faculties. Let but divinity fall, and I would not give a straw for the rest." Martin Luther.
*"The whole case of the Bible is that the trouble with man is not intellectual (in the mind) but moral (in the heart)." Dr. D. Martyn Lloyd-Jones.

You are what you eat ... are we just flesh and blood?

"I can explain my body and my brain, but there's something more: I can't explain my own existence. What makes me a unique being?" Sir John Eccles—Nobel Prize Winner in brain physiology. [1]

From a materialistic viewpoint, we can be reduced to a biochemical system. Is it true or scientifically proven, that we are solely materialistic beings with no soul or eternal components? The views of Russell (philosopher), Huxley (biologist), Dennett (neuro-scientist) and Dawkins (biologist) are reviewed. Dennett's idea that the brain is an evolutionary "botch-up," a piece of bricolage, that resulted from fishes to man evolution—is scrutinised. Is the idea of "self"or "mind" valid, or as sceptics put it, "Is there a ghost in the machine?"There is evidence from the incurable "religiosity" of man, that people are "hard-wired" to believe in God. Also examined is the nature of the human race, "Are we basically 'good' or 'bad'?" The Bible has a noble and uplifting view of man, as "made in the image of God" with an eternal soul—rather than humans as "a mere accidental collocation of atoms".

From dust to dust?

"*Know yourself* ", the wise Greek thinkers advised, but it is hard to look at ourselves realistically. We are told by secular scientists that we are made of dust. In fact, they claim "*star dust* ". We are a mere collection of atoms: on average a 70-kilogram person is made up of: enough **carbon** to make **9,000 pencils**, enough **phosphorus** to make **2,200 match heads**, enough **fat** to make **7 bars of soap**, enough **water** to fill a **45 litre barrel** , enough **iron** to make a **2-inch nail**, and small amounts of other raw materials!

Leaving aside the question of our composition and origins, we wonder at our existence in this universe of time and space: *"Why are we here?"* Are we moral beings created by God? Can all human experiences be adequately explained in terms of the brain firing neurons? What makes us unique? Is there a non-physical part to our make-up? How do all these issues impinge on peoples' free-will? These are some of the main items addressed in this section.

Mere collocations of atoms?

Is there no purpose to our lives in this vast Universe? What have famous secular thinkers such as Bertrand Russell—philosopher, Aldous Huxley—novelist and critic, Daniel Dennett—contemporary cognitive-scientist and Richard Dawkins—Oxford biologist 'said about mankind's existence? (See **Figure 3.1**, **"Four Viewpoints".**) Bertrand Russell's response as a radical but consistent humanistic thinker was: *"Man is the product of causes which had no prevision [foresight] of the end they were achieving; that his origin, his growth, his hopes and fears, his loves and his beliefs, are but the outcome of accidental collocations of atoms; that no fire, no heroism, no intensity of thought and feeling, can preserve an individual life beyond the grave; .... all the noonday brightness of human genius, is destined to extinction in the vast death of the solar system, and the whole temple of man's achievement must inevitably be buried beneath the debris of a Universe in ruins—all these things, if not quite beyond dispute, are yet so nearly certain that no philosophy which rejects them can hope to stand."* [2]

As a British philosopher and mathematician, Russell's emphasis on logical analysis influenced the course of 20th-century philosophy. In 1950 he received the Nobel Prize for Literature and was recognised as *"the champion of humanity and freedom of thought."* He was a strong logical positivist (with its emphasis on empiricism), who attempted to explain all factual knowledge as constructed out of immediate experiences. Bertrand Russell, however, expressed disappointment at his life's work at fifty-nine. He came to realise the failure of logical positivism to provide illumination in his life, and wrote in his autobiography: *"When I survey my life, it seems to be a useless one, devoted to impossible ideals ... And what of philosophy? The best years of my life were given to the Principles of Mathematics, in the hope of finding somewhere some certain knowledge. The whole of this effort, in spite of three big volumes, ended inwardly in doubt and bewilderment. As regards metaphysics, when, under the influence of Moore, I first threw off the belief in German idealism, I experienced the delight of believing that the sensible world is real. Bit by bit under the influence of physics, this delight has faded ... I do not believe that the constructive efforts of present day philosophers and men of science have anything approaching the validity that attaches to their destructive criticism ...*" 3

Figure 3 .1 Four Viewpoints.

YOU ARE WHAT YOU EAT?

TOPIC	Philosopher	Novelist & Critic	Philosopher & Scientist	Biologist Cognitive
	Bertrand Russell (1872—1970)	Aldous Huxley (1894—1963)	Daniel C. Dennett (1942—Present)	Richard Dawkins (1941—Present)
Belief	Logical Positivist (Empiricist)	Humanist—Mystic (Nihilist in 1920's)	Behaviourist (Biological determinist)	Logical Positivist (Evolutionist)
View of Humanity	Man is an accidental collocation of atoms.	Man is a product of evolution.	Man is a conscious robot; brain—a mass of largely superfluous circuitry or "amateur gadgetry."	Man determined by genes, but also has freewill. "We are gene survival machines."
Destiny/ Purpose?	To find true love. No afterlife; ultimate pessimism.	Wrote nihilistic novels; sceptical about any after-life: "ignore death until the last moment."	Self is a delusion; man is simply a biological organism.	Death is the end; integration into the void.

Toward the end of his life, Bertrand Russell became aware of *"being given to himself in his ability to love"*: He wrote, *"I have sought love, first because it brings ecstasy—ecstasy so great that I would often have sacrificed all the rest of my life for a few hours of this joy. I have sought it, next, because it relieves loneliness—that terrible loneliness in which one shivering consciousness looks over the rim of the world into the cold unfathomable lifeless abyss. I have sought it, finally, because in the union of love I have seen, in mystic miniature, the prefiguring vision of a heaven that saints and poets have imagined. This is what I sought, and though it might seem too good for human life, this is what—at last—I have found."*[4] Is a transient love the best we can hope for? Does human life count for so little?

When it's over, it's over?

For Aldous Huxley too, there was no hope beyond the grave, death simply meant, *'when it's over, it's over.'* As a writer his novels *Antic Hay* (1923) and *Point Counter Point* (1928) illustrate the nihilistic mood of the 1920's. Nihilism is basically the rejection of all moral and religious principles. In an extreme form it is a scepticism that maintains that nothing has a real existence. Huxley's best known work was *Brave New World* (1932)—an ironic vision of a future utopia. Later, he became very interested in mysticism and parapsychology, and *The Doors of Perception* (1954) and its sequel, *Heaven and Hell* (1956), deal with Huxley's experiences with hallucinogenic drugs (e.g. LSD). It seems that Huxley's viewpoint is that when all is said and done, life has no ultimate purpose. He wrote, *"Ignore death till the last moment; then when it cannot be ignored any longer have yourself squirted full of morphia and shuffle off in a corner"* from *Time Must Have A Stop (1944)*. In sympathy with this novelist's viewpoint—the issue of our true worth, is considered by some contemporary scientists as little more than biochemical systems—which are advanced robots. Are we then just *"conditioned robots"*?

Cognitive scientist's viewpoint

For Daniel C. Dennett—Director of the Centre for Cognitive Studies at Tuft's University, Massachusetts—*homo sapiens* is a race of conscious robots. He claims we are robots in an unusual sense, because not only do we respond to signals but we initiate actions in their absence. We may fail to respond to signals because our attention is elsewhere. We may not be programmed, but we invent our program as we go. As we have our agendas, we create our environments as well as responding to them. By so doing, he believes, we continuously create ourselves. [5]

Puppets on a DNA string?

Modern materialist scientists like Oxford biologist Professor Richard Dawkins also believe we are controlled by a mix of our genetic make-up and freewill. Steven Rose (Professor of Biology at the Open University) thinks we are more than mere DNA puppets, conditioned by our genes. By focusing exclusively on molecules, Professor Rose says, biologists lose the bigger picture. He believes that life is shaped by an *"elaborate web of interactions that occurs within cells, organisms and ecosystems, in which DNA plays one part among many."* [6] Further Professor Rose insists that far from being puppets of our DNA , we create our own futures. He concedes that these so-called *"lifelines"* are shaped by circumstances that we are sometimes powerless to change.

Reporting on Rose's latest book *Lifelines*, a science reporter—Anjana Ahuja—says: *"In Professor Rose's eyes, we are either slaves to our genes or we are not. If we are enslaved, then we cannot have free will because our genes have already pre-programmed us to behave in a particular way. Professor Dawkins, an ultra-Darwinist (someone who believes that organisms are primed by their genes to reproduce and thus continue the genetic line), resolves this by saying that as well as being in thrall [or captive] to our genes, we are also blessed with free will, allowing some control over our destinies."*

A screaming gap

Our science reporter continues, *"Somewhat mischievously, Professor Rose says that if Professor Dawkins really was enslaved by his genes, he would be 'breeding like crazy'. He adds: 'Because Dawkins realises life is more complex, he adds that we have the power to overthrow our genes, we now have this power that comes from nowhere to overrule our genes. It is a screaming gap. Quite rightly, Dawkins doesn't like the corner he has*

painted himself into, and therefore says 'hang on, we've got free will'.
Do we not possess the ability to control our biology—the urge to
procreate, for example—if it is socially appropriate to do so? Yes says
Professor Rose, but 'our freedom is inherent in the living processes that
constitute us'. The ability to construct our own 'lifelines' is actually built
into our genes. 'In that way, I am even more of a materialist than
Dawkins,' he shrugs."[7]

Dawkin's Unweaving the Rainbow

As a result of recognising that modern science has appeared to have a
joyless message—lessening life's specialness—Richard Dawkins has
written his latest book, *Unweaving the Rainbow*. This title is based on
Keats' criticism of Newton. Keats believed Newton's scientific analysis of
white light had destroyed the poetry of the rainbow, reducing it to an
array of prismatic colours. Dawkins is keen that we should appreciate the
wonder of the universe. Dawkins quotes a colleague—Peter Atkins (1984)
from his book on *The Second Law*—where Atkins purges 'cosmic senti-
mentality': "*We are the children of chaos, and the deep structure of*
change is decay. At root, there is only corruption, and the unstemmable
tide of chaos. Gone is purpose; all that is left is direction. This is the
bleakness we have to accept as we peer deeply and dispassionately into
the heart of the Universe."[8]

Professor Dawkins seeks to put a nice spin on this by saying that there is,
however, personal hope: "*Presumably there is indeed no purpose in the*
ultimate fate of the cosmos, but do any of us really tie our life's hopes to
the ultimate fate of the cosmos anyway? Of course we don't; not if we are
sane. Our lives are ruled by all sorts of closer, warmer, human ambitions
and perceptions. To accuse science of robbing life of the warmth that
makes it worth living is so preposterously mistaken, so diametrically
opposite to my own feelings and those of most working scientists ..."[9]
Scientists, do seek to assess the impact of our genes on our behaviour, if
not our ultimate destiny.

Controlling factors: Nature versus nurture

Is it our genes or the environment that is most important in determining our social behaviour? This long established so-called *"nature versus nurture"* debate, is resolved by seeing any living creatures' behaviour as an interaction between these two factors. It's likely today (considering the nurture aspect) that we are controlled in our behaviour by life's circumstances, our education and the accepted *"world-view"* or fashions. A healthy body and mind are encouraged by our *"package-orientated"* society—with its emphasis on the *"feel-good factor"* and looking fit. Perfect bodies are promoted by TV programmes like *Gladiators* and glamour soaps such as *Baywatch*. Some (young or old) feel it necessary to undergo plastic surgery to create the body shape or image that they want.

Only flesh and blood?

Today, we have much advertising and effort spent on keeping fit (eating healthy food, regular exercise, and personal hygiene). We may be physically what we eat, but this completely ignores our spiritual make-up. Sadly, people only seem to face up to their spiritual side or their mortality on the death of someone they know or admire. Such has been the case in the passing of Diana, Princess of Wales, which set off a wave of national mourning. As journalist Judith Williamson writes: *"So for most of us, if we are honest, the greatest shock of Diana's death was the sudden pulling of a central thread from the dense weave of cultural life, leaving raw edges and unravelling holes. The holes expose some of our underlying feelings, usually well-wrapped: a sense of the world's sadness, remorse, perhaps, at Britain's past sorry decades; sadness of loss in our own lives, and simply, of ourselves. But these real and painful feelings are knitted back almost at once into the great web of stories, meanings and explanations: as quickly as possible we make sense of it all again. If death tells us anything, it is how little, really, we know about what it all means—and how low our tolerance is for facing that unknowing."*[10]

An immortal soul

Some scientists have proclaimed that death is the end, our biochemical system ceases to function. Sir Arthur Keith, an eminent surgeon, once claimed that he had never found a *"soul"* when he had cut open a human body. This naturalistic view fails to realise that the **soul,** which is the inner self (mind), is immaterial and immortal. The philosopher David Hume, of course, admitted no such thing. He proposed that, *"The physical arguments from the analogy of nature are strong for the mortality of the soul; and are really the only philosophical arguments which ought to be admitted with regard to this question, or indeed any question of fact."*[11]

The Bible, however, teaches that we do have an eternal soul. Jesus said, *"And do not fear those who kill the body but cannot kill the soul. But rather fear Him [God] who is able to destroy both soul and body in hell"* (Matthew: 10:28). The worst our enemies can do is to destroy our physical life, but this does not prevent a blessed resurrection to life everlasting of our eternal souls. To God, however, belongs the power of 'the second death', which is eternal destruction. Calvin clearly recognised the thrust of the passage: *"In God's hand alone is the power of life and death. ... Does this not make evident, that this shadowy life of the body has become more worth to us than the eternal state of the soul; indeed, that the heavenly Kingdom of God is of no value with us, compared with the fleeting, vanishing shade of this present life? ... Recognise that you have been given immortal souls, which being under the judgment of God alone, do not come under the authority of men."*[12] Some see evidences of our spiritual side in Near Death Experiences, but it is difficult to draw any conclusive evidence from this new area of research. **See Endnote 1** on **Out of the Body Experiences.**

Theologians have defended the soul's immortality on several grounds: Firstly, being immaterial and indivisible by nature, the soul is independent of the body and indestructible, i.e. does not depend for its existence on time and space; Secondly, the instinctive, universal and persistent belief of humankind that there is life after death argues for its reality, as *"eternity is written in his heart"*. The soul co-exists with the body and inherits the body. The whole person, soul as much as body, is a wonderful divine creation (see, for example, Job 10: 8-12; Psalm 139: 13-16). The issue of whether soul and spirit refer to the same thing is clarified by the late Professor William Hendriksen (theologian): *"What, then, is the soul, and what is the spirit of man? Both terms refer to that part of the human personality which is immaterial and invisible. There is only one such element, even though at least two names are given to it"* [soul and spirit].[13] **See Endnote: 2.**

A God-shaped blank

Humans have a unique religious capacity, a faculty definitely not found, even in embryonic form, in any other animal. The committed non-theist Thomas H. Huxley (biologist) confessed that *"There is a blank in the human heart and it is a God-shaped blank."* When a computer starts up, it has certain information built into it, to enable it to know what to do, when it is turned on. Such vital instructions are stored in a chip. This is known as firmware, as the instructions are "hard-wired" to the silicon chip. These instructions are not lost therefore, when the computer is switched off. So, to use this analogy, we are *"hard-wired to believe in God."* Paul, the apostle, says in Romans 1 : 18 that we seek to suppress or hold down such truth in unrighteousness. For a naturalist (like Huxley), however, the puzzle was why the purposeless mechanical process of a *"struggle for existence"* and *"survival of the fittest"* produced an animal with a God-shaped blank. We are conscious beings! We have a spiritual dimension. Contrast this with Daniel Dennett's behaviourist view that our brains are a mass of largely superfluous circuitry. This he believes is mainly due to an evolutionary mechanism, which uses the ready-made as the basis for *"new technology."*

Brain's incredible complexity

The human nervous system is a vast communications network. Over 12 billion nerve cells or neurons in the brain communicate with millions more in the body. The basic logic device inside the human brain can be considered to be the neuron. The inputs into this basic logic element are via the dendrites, i.e. it is the dendrites that carry the input logic signals to the main cell body. A typical neuron inside the human brain might have an average of 1,000 dendrites feeding in signals. **See Endnote 3.** There are two types of neural connections, known as excitatory and inhibitory connections. An excitatory connection is one which tells a neuron to fire a signal if the threshold level is exceeded. Inside the human brain, these neurons are interconnected by "synapses". The brain is capable of many parallel connections, and has **many millions of neurons** such as those mentioned here!

Professor Dennett, however, believes the human brain is a piece of bricolage, a sort of "do it yourself" creation: it is composed of a reptilian brain over which is imposed a mammalian brain, and over both of which is superimposed a neomammalian brain. Though much of our brain is made of *"amateur gadgetry"*which has no useful function, it amazingly works— though *"its links lead nowhere."* This view of our amazingly complex brain is so minimalist as to be unbelievable! Stated more positively, *"There is probably nothing to be found in the universe that is more complicated than the human brain. In fact, all our hopes of understanding it or ourselves may rest on this question: "Can my brain possibly understand my brain?"*[14]

No real self—no 'ghost in the machine'

Dennett thinks that in all this superabundant, often pointless, wiring it is impossible to locate a controller—traditionally thought of as our self-consciousness or mind—who is in charge of the whole. It was Oxford philosopher Gilbert Ryle (1900-76) who first used the expression *"the dogma of the ghost in the machine"* to mean the concept of mind. Dan Dennett thinks there is less of a ghost in the machine, but more of a vast haunted house, populated by numerous ghosts. The idea being conveyed here is that if we feel like a boat that drifts along on the *"stream of consciousness"* in neurological terms (the flow of neurons in the brain) there is no boat, or anybody to steer it—there is only the stream. Dennett implies we do not have thoughts, but that we are thoughts! The neuroscientist argues that if for every "mind" event there is a corresponding "brain" event, what need is there to postulate a duality? In biological terms our sense of self is thus no more than a useful fiction, the "I" is mainly a grammatical construction. Self, he thinks, is an illusion.

A sceptical question

The sceptic may be tempted to ask Dennett, *"If this sense of self is an illusion, how can we deceive ourselves?"* If we are ourselves fictions, then no one story we tell about ourselves has any more truth than any other. Dennett would argue that the sense of self (however poorly defined) which we all possess is a superimposition on our biology resulting from our mutual or social interactions. Dennett wrote a book entitled *Consciousness Explained*, by which he really meant consciousness explained away!

However, the *"ghost in the machine"* will not go away by virtue of being pluralised into *"multiple ghosts"*. Even Popper admitted: *"I said in Oxford in 1950 that I believe in the ghost in the machine. That is to say, I think that the self in a sense plays on the brain, as a pianist plays on a piano or as a driver plays on the controls of a car."* [15] Despite this, Popper's *"self"* is still nothing more than physical. Our self consciousness will not disappear, however much it is explained away by imaginary experiences. Dennett shows how far one can go within the limits of an atheistic scientific world picture. The story he tells of how we became conscious robots is clearly not the whole story, even if one accepts his evolutionary presuppositions.

Roger Caldwell tries to deal with the implications of Dennett's position from his naturalistic viewpoint. He says: *"However elusive the sense of self may be, however lacking in a biological base, we nonetheless are judged as individuals before a court of law, whether legal proper, or that of family and friends, or that of our own consciences. If we are the products of our genes, we nonetheless are forced to take some responsibility for the products of those products [e.g. our actions]. There is little doubt too that, on the Darwinian scheme, our systems of ethics developed to ensure our survival as a social species. But what happens when we become consciously aware of that truth? Is the result that we then cease to be bound by that code of ethics—that it becomes merely one option amongst many? To ask such questions is to cease to think of ourselves merely as biological organisms, which is the level at which Dennett primarily moves, but rather as creatures who move in the artificial world which they have constructed for themselves."* [16]

Another viewpoint

At this point it is worth noting that strict materialistic views of man that ignore the mind come into conflict with studies by researchers like neuro-physiologist Wilder Penfield, which indicate a simultaneous double consciousness in human beings. Dr. Wilder Penfield was gradually convinced that the monistic view did not adequately account for the facts. He wrote, *"Something else finds its dwelling place between the sensory complex and the motor mechanism ... There is a switchboard operator as well as a switchboard".* [16] If one of these consciousnesses is the brain state, where does the other state come from that is conscious of the first? The visual system, for instance, shows the need for the mind or self at the end of the information processing system in the brain to give rise to our awareness of reality. This view of Penfield is not far from the Hebrew-Christian model, which regards the human being as an immaterial soul and physical body co-existing and working together as one functioning unit.

A key question

Here is another pertinent question about the human condition: *"Are people basically 'good' or 'bad'?"* Some people like to think that we are basically good. The Bible says every part of our nature is polluted in some way. If we are basically decent and respect one another, why do we need keys? If we are all honest, then it should be possible to leave everything unlocked. Crazy?! One commercial area that has seen tremendous growth is security and surveillance systems: house alarms, car alarms, video cameras, etc. So the test for those who think the Bible is wrong to call us sinners because we are basically good is: *"Have you thrown away your keys yet?"* Nevertheless, some parody the teaching of our tendency to do wrong by saying they cannot believe *"cradles are corrupt places"*! Also, that the *"born-bad model is defunct."* This, despite the incessant reports in our daily newspapers to confirm our fallen nature.

Original sin

In contrast, Mary Kenny (Daily Express columnist) says, *"I believe in the doctrine of original sin, not just because that is what I have been taught but because my experience of life has shown it to be true. Human beings are born with an amazing capacity for evil deeds. From the gulags and death camps to the massacres of Rwanda and Burundi, we see the evidence paraded all around us. And I think we can see this capacity for evil within ourselves."*[17] The fact is that the Bible says we all have feet of clay. We are prone to sin. *"For all have sinned, and fall short of the glory of God"* (Romans 3: 23). The Psalmist confesses, *"I was brought forth in iniquity, and in sin my mother conceived me"* (Psalm 51: 5). This does not mean we are 100% bad in all we do, but rather that everything we do (however 'good') is polluted in some way by the effects of sin. I once asked the late John Murray (Professor of Theology, Westminster Seminary) *"What is a good work?"* He replied, *"One that is directed by God's word, motivated by His Holy Spirit, and done to the glory of God."* How such considerations underline our fallen nature! We do things for our own self esteem, to please others ... but God looks on the heart.

Total depravity does imply then that the inherent corruption extends to every part of our nature—including our faculties and powers of both soul and body; it also indicates that there is no spiritual good (i.e. in relation to God) in the sinner at all, but only a tendency to wrong doing. On the other hand, it does not imply every person is as thoroughly depraved as they can become, that man has lost his innate knowledge of God—or ability to discern right and wrong. Again, the Bible's teaching does not mean sinful humanity cannot admire virtuous acts in relations with others, or necessarily indulges in every possible sin.

Born noble versus genetic predisposition

There are now mainly two alternatives to the biblical view of human nature. Firstly, the philosopher Rousseau's idea—that man is born noble but corrupted by society, or secondly the frightening new triumphalism of genetics—that we are born with certain genes and these predispose humans to conditions and behaviour that little, short of genetic engineering or powerful drugs, can alter. Rousseau's viewpoint soon leads to disillusionment, generally through the experience of parenthood or teaching children. As Kenny comments, *"Children are undoubtedly born with certain innate characteristics and show these long before society has a chance to corrupt them."*[18]

The genetic option is very deterministic if, as some biologists claim, there is a *"criminal"* gene and people can be genetically constituted to be villains, so what is the point of human responsibility or morality? If accepted, could this lead to a *Brave New World* where those with such a *"criminal"* gene would be genetically modified or aborted? Would such *"treatment"* alleviate the need for prison, justified on the basis it is more cost effective or efficient? There clearly are some individuals born with serious personality problems. In a morally chaotic world these may never learn anything but the rules and values of the concrete jungle.

Are you what you eat, just a collection of atoms? If so, where does your sense of identity come from? Steven Rose answers, *"We have a coherent sense of identity despite the turnover of molecules. How is it that memory persists even though our biology changes through lifetime? It lies in the interactions, not in the molecules. Free will and determinism are misleading ways of understanding the human condition. It is precisely our biology that makes us free."*[19] A somewhat confusing response! This recognition, however, that there is more to life and our identity than any mechanistic description or viewpoint can determine, is significant from a Christian viewpoint. It seems that scientists having got rid of the concept of mind and soul are wanting to retain concepts like consciousness and freewill. Roger Penrose (Mathematician) has suggested that as there is a higher emergent level of activity in the brain—basically a result of neural activity—it doesn't follow the laws of physics that we know of. Penrose thinks the physical world of atoms and quantum physics hasn't resolved all the problems that Einstein left unsolved. When this is resolved, this new physics will, Penrose believes, explain freewill and consciousness.

Conclusion

We should not hesitate to admit that man is more than science can measure. Yes, we are made of about 100 million million cells, as Dawkins would say, *"Each one of us is a city of cells, and each cell a town of bacteria. You are a gigantic megalopolis of bacteria."* [20] Why should we expect or try to reach high moral qualities, if humans are nothing more than animal material and destined to evaporate with our body chemicals? C. S. Lewis noted perceptively, *"The real objection is that if man chooses to treat himself as raw material, raw material he will be: not raw material to be manipulated as he fondly imagined, by himself, but by mere appetite, that is, mere nature ..."*[21]

It is biologist Thomas Huxley's suggestion, however, that we have hearts with a *"God-shaped blank"* that holds a key to our further investigations: in a modern idiom, *" we are hard-wired to believe in God."* The Bible says that we are *"fearfully and wonderfully made; marvellous are your works, and that my soul knows very well"* (Psalm 139:14). We are living souls. Solomon reminds us that : *"He* [God] *has also set eternity in the hearts of men"* (Ecclesiastes 3:11). This faculty for awareness of our spiritual side is part of our being made in the *"image of God"*. If man is an incurably religious creature with self awareness and God consciousness—a capacity to worship, it raises the question of whether there is a true God and religion. It is this vital issue we shall examine in the next chapter.

References:

1 **Newsweek,** 21 June, 1971, p. 66.
2 **B. Russell** (1957) Why I am not a Christian, George Allen & Unwin, New York, p. 107.
3 **B. Russell** (1968) Autobiography of Bertrand Russell Vol. II , George Allen & Unwin.
4 **Ibid.**
5 **R. Caldwell** (1997) Dan Dennett and the Conscious Robot, Philosophy Now, Issue No. 18, Summer 1997, Ipswich, ISBN 0961 5970, pp. 16-18.
6 **Anjana Ahuja** (1997) Life beyond genes, The Times, October 6, 1997.
7 **Ibid.** Professor S. Rose's book is: Lifelines: Biology, Freedom, Determinism, Penguin.
8 **R. Dawkins** (1998) Unweaving the Rainbow, Penguin Press, London, ISBN 0- 713-99214-X, p.ix.
9 **Ibid.,** pp. ix-x.
10 **J. Williamson** (1997) A glimpse of the void, The Weekend Guardian, September 13, 1997, p. 8.
11 **D. Hume** (1963) Essays Moral Political and Literary, Oxford University Press, London, W.1, p. 602.
12 **J. Calvin** (1972) A Harmony of the Gospels, Volume 1, Torrence edition, The St. Andrews Press , Edinburgh, ISBN 0 7152 0160 3, pp. 305-6.
13 **W. Hendriksen** (1980) The Bible on the Life Hereafter, Baker Book House, Grand Rapids, Michigan, ISBN: 0 8010 4189 9, pp. 38-9.
14 **M. P. Cosgrove** (1987) The Amazing Body Human, Baker Book House Co., Grand Rapids, ISBN 0 810 2517 6, p. 145.
14 **K. R. Popper & J. C. Eccles** (1977) The Self and its Brain, New York: Springer- Verlag, pp. 495-6.
15 **R. Caldwell** (1997) Ibid, p. 18.

16 **W. Penfield** (1975) *The Mystery of the Mind*, Princeton University Press, Princeton, p. xiii.

17 **M. Kenny** (1997) *The sins of society*, Report, Association of Teachers & Lecturers, p. 11.

18 **M. Kenny** (1997) Ibid, p. 10.

19 **A. Ahuja** (1997) op. cit.

20 **R. Dawkins** (1998) Ibid., p. 9.

21 **C. S. Lewis** (1947) *The Abolition of Man*, Macmillan Co., p. 84.

Endnote: 1

Out of the body experiences / Near Death Experiences (NDEs)
Some on the brink of death report a sensation of overwhelming bliss, and resent being brought back to normal life again. Others, however, have shown that **Near Death Experiences (NDEs)** have been horrific. One woman reported: *"It was an awful feeling—like I was going down a big hole and I couldn't get up. I was going into this big pit. I was going further and further down, and trying to claw my way back up and kept slipping"* . In a fascinating book on *"Before Death Comes ... "* Dr. Maurice Rawlings describes how he himself was resuscitating a man having a frightening *"out of the body experience"* who insisted that he pray for him. As a result Dr. Rawlings went home and began to read the Bible to find out what it said about hell. He says, *"My former belief that death was merely oblivion was being shattered. I was now convinced that there is life after death after all, and that not all of it is good."*
Dr. Maurice Rawlings became a committed Christian, and expert on near death *"out of the body"* experiences. Scientists admit they do not fully comprehend **Near Death Experiences.** Rational explanations such as hallucination, lack of oxygen to the brain, or the effects of drugs in the last few seconds of consciousness, do not seem adequate. Some claim these NDEs have involved patients who were registering no measurable brain activity. Certainly scientists are to investigate this area in greater detail. The University of Coventry, for instance, have appointed a psychologist Dr. Tony Lawrence, to undertake such studies. He thinks some negative NDEs are remembered as the absence of experience and that there is nothing after life. More research is needed to throw further light on this area, and any possible significance for the existence of man's spiritual side.

Chapter 3

Endnote: 2

T. C. Hammond (1954) *In Understanding Be Men*, I. V. F., pp. 72-6, gives a useful summary of a long and complex subject, entitled 'Body, Soul and Spirit'. He mentions the majority view that there are two components of man's being. This bipartite view (body and soul with the spirit as the essence, or another aspect, of the soul) refers to the whole life of a person, e.g., *"Let every soul be subject to the higher power"* (Romans 13:1) as well as the immaterial part of humankind which survives death.

Endnote: 3

Students of electronics know that a logic gate is an electronic device to control the flow of signals, and the commonest of these are AND, OR and NOT gates: Such may think a 12-input AND gate has a lot of inputs!

Further Reading:

D.A. Carson (1996) *The Gagging of God*, Apollos, Leicester, ISBN 0-85111-7678, pp. 206-7.

M. P. Cosgrove (1977) *The Essence of Human Nature*, Zondervan Publishing House, ISBN 0-310-35711-X.

A. C. Custance (1980) *The Mysterious Matter of Mind*, Probe Ministries International, ISBN 0-310-38011-1.

J. Frame (1995) *Cornelius Van Til*, Presbyterian & Reformed Publishing Co, Nutley, New Jersey, ISBN 0-87552-245-9. Distributed in U.K. by Evangelical Press.

Key text:

Psalm 8: 4, 5 *"What is man that You are mindful of him. And the son of man that You visit him? For You have made him a little lower than the angels, And You have crowned him with glory and honour."*

Questions for further study

1   *"The whole is more than the sum of the parts."* Can this concept be applied to the human body?
2   Bertrand Russell's view of life saw no hope or purpose in it all. How did he eventually console himself?
3   What conclusion did Bertrand Russell come to over his own philosophical reasonings?

4 What is logical positivism, and what is it based on?

5 What does it mean when we say Aldous Huxley's writings reflect the nihilistic mood of the 1920's?

6 Huxley's best known work was *Brave New World* (1932) which explores the idea of eugenics. Does it reflect the thinking and reality of the state of science in the new millennium?

7 Dan Dennett (cognitive-scientist) thinks humans are "conscious robots"—but how far do we differ from the animals who are also driven by physiological drives (such as the need for food)?

8 What is the problem for Richard Dawkins who believes in genetic determinism? How does he try to escape from this position?

9 How can the "nature versus nurture" debate be resolved?

10 Are soul and spirit the same element?

11 "We are hard-wired to believe in God." Explain what is meant by this, and any biblical support for such a concept?

12 How does Dan Dennett's view of the brain fail to give credit to its amazing complexity?

13 Dennett believes our sense of self is an illusion. Does Popper agree with him?

14 What is "the ghost in the machine"?

15 How does Roger Caldwell respond to Dennett's neurological viewpoint?

16 What does Wilder Penfield's research indicate about the notion of mind?

17 Is the born-bad model defunct?

18 C. S. Lewis spells out the result of believing we are just raw material. What would be that effect according to Lewis? Do you agree?

Food for thought:

* *"Because we are the handiwork of God it follows that all our problems and solutions are theological."* A. W. Tozer

* *"The very existence of the fear of death, which is the root of practically all human fears, is a clear indication that death is unnatural even though its incidence is universal."* Akbar Abdul- Haqq.

* *"Man is born with a fractured will. He wants to go his own way."* John E. Marshall.

* *"If a philosophy of life cannot help me to die, then in a sense it cannot help me to live."* Dr David Martyn Lloyd-Jones.

Is there a God?

"There is a great difference between those who say, "We wish to be gods," and those who say, "We wish to be God's." Bolton Davidheiser (Writer & Biologist)

Whilst it is not possible to "prove the existence of God" in an experiment, it can be argued that unless God is assumed, we are left with profound moral and philosophical problems (both epistemological and metaphysical)—if God is not a reality. This was recognised by Hume, who defines the "is-ought" problem—also designated the naturalistic fallacy. Ultimately, nothing can be certain if God's truth is not valid. Reasoning is either based on a materialistic belief system or a system that admits God is behind all of reality (as the Christian philosopher Dooyeweerd has pointed out). The conclusions we come to are not the result of the inevitability and persuasiveness of the evidence, but our original inclinations or presuppositions.

Introduction

The term *"God"* is used in many ways, but is often applied to that which is thought to be a (or the) fundamental source of one's existence and/or values. To be consistent, if God is the first cause and creator of all things, thinking beings could not even ask these questions—as they would not exist! Wherever you begin your view of life, it makes unprovable assumptions. How? If there is no God, then we are saying that matter is eternal—nobody created it. It always existed. But how can we be sure? Are humans all-knowing? Is this position any different from that of those who say God is eternal, He always was and is, the beginning and the end? The believer claims God was the first uncaused being, who made *"all things by the word of his power"*.

There are many who mock the believability of the Bible's claims and who prefer to rely on man's unaided reason. Typical of such an attitude is the late Bertrand Russell who said: *"There's a Bible on that shelf there. But I keep it next to Voltaire—poison and antidote [cure]."*[1] Another thinker who had similar views was Julian Huxley. In his opinion: *"Operationally, God is beginning to resemble not a ruler but the last fading smile of a cosmic Cheshire cat"*[2], which implies that God (if he exists) is irrelevant, and shows that atheists would be glad to see the back of the notion of God. At a more basic level, many have asked *"Who made God?"* Again, other thinkers present logical problems: *"If God is all powerful (Almighty), can he create an immovable object?"* or *"How can you explain the origin of evil?"* These are some of the issues raised by people who think they've trapped the Christian believer into a logical hole they cannot get out of! The issues we must face, on whichever side of the divide we fall (God, no God), leave us with the alternative not only God or no God, but of man alone in the universe as an independent being with no ultimate purpose. We are then condemned to chaos and old Night. See Figure 4.1, "Logical Traps Examined".

God no explanation?

David Hall, a reviewer of a book entitled, *Is there a God?* by Professor Richard Swinburne (Nolloth Professor of the Philosophy of the Christian Religion at Oxford) comments, *"Swinburne believes in the existence of this God because he finds it the best explanation for everything that exists: 'We find that the view there is a God explains everything we observe, not just some narrow range of data' (p. 2). This means he is unperturbed by the thought that an explanation that explains everything is practically equivalent to no explanation at all. A God that 'has the whole world in his hands', is simply an emotionally reassuring way of admitting that things are the way they are; if an explanation quite literally explains everything nothing can ever count as evidence against it ."*[3] However, this intellectual conundrum set up by Hall—taken at face value—also destroys his own naturalistic base: for if *"evolution"* is substituted for the word *"God"* (as the only viable alternative) in the first part of his equation, we see that the same sort of criticism applies to it as well. See Figure 4.1, "Logical Traps Examined."

Figure 4.1 Logical Traps Examined

Problem	Solution	Comment
God no explanation: as the notion of God "explains everything" it is no explanation at all.	The alternative, Evolution could also be dismissed in this fashion. The choice between the two positions (God, no God) is still a matter of faith, or a priori assumptions - not scientific evidence.	Failure to distinguish between ultimate (originating) causes and proximate (near) causes. E.g. first man and woman may have been a special creation, (Supernatural first cause) but in contrast, our existence is a result of our parents' procreation (proximate causes.)
No need for a creator God. Universe has its own self organising principle within it—an objective value. Idea known as axiarchism.	This is a remarkable idea. It attributes to matter "god-like" properties, as a master-mind that gives direction to the universe. It shows the length to which man will go to avoid the notion of a personal God. over against a Creator God—which believers openly admit is a result of faith: (Hebrews 11: 3).	It is an untestable hypothesis. It is axiomatic, that what is, is; and whilst the universes present state can be explained by postulating an "organising principle", it requires faith or prior belief to accept this view,
The problem of moral evil. Epicurus: "Either God can prevent evil and chooses not to, and so is not good, or desires to prevent it and cannot, and so is not all-powerful."	Augustine said evil is the absence of good, like dark-ness is the absence of light. Evil crept in when man - given free will, chose less complete goods; or in Adam's case fundamental "evils". "God decreed it in order to demonstrate his nature." Even if evolutionists reject this answer, they are still left with the reality of evil. Philosophers find it hard to define.	This is the "privation argument." Augustine's view is the principle of "evil" is finite, and "good" is infinite. He shows how sin can come from perfection and thus absolves God, from any guilt. Evolutionists admit the existence of good, altruism, philanthropy, etc. is a problem for their scheme of origins, because it does not make evolutionary sense.
If God is all powerful - Almighty—can He create an immovable object? If He cannot, how can He claim to be all powerful?	This is an argument that depends on the definition of Almighty. Clearly there are things God cannot do, like create a being equal to himself. Nor can He lie, or deny Himself.	It is possible to create a series of logical traps, but this often proves the limitations of words rather than making a statement about God's existence.

Swinburne's comment that God explains everything—'*not just a narrow range of data*'—is parenthesis. He clearly believes in the distinction between ultimate and proximate causes. Whilst God is conceived as the ultimate cause of all things, it does not exclude more localised explanations of how, for instance, a mechanism works or biological system develops (proximate causes). To a Christian, science is discovering God's laws and so is (to use Kepler's famous phrase) *"thinking God's thoughts after Him."* Hall seems oblivious to all this and appears to fall into the trap that reflects the idea, *"Science is fact, faith is fiction."*

David Hall continues his analysis by claiming Swinburne sets up a *"spurious opposition between a personal God who brings about the universe by deliberate design, and an atheist materialism whose only available explanation is atoms in a void coming together by 'coincidence'. As if it is impossible to be an atheist without being a materialist, and as if there are no plausible alternative metaphysical explanations of the universe other than that of the Western religions."*[4]

Reductive materialism

Hall is anxious to suggest Strabo of Lampsacus' explanation of a naturalism that refuses any explanation of things in the universe by anything outside the universe. He insists that **reductive materialism** does not entail that the universe consists of nothing but mindless matter. Mind (however this be defined) is just as much in the universe as anything else. If reductive materialism does explain everything there is, then having a creator God outside the universe is unwarranted. In fact, *"It is difficult to see what advantage there is in positing a God outside the universe who creates and sustains it, rather than regarding the universe as the terminus of explanation. The whole idea that the world needs something to sustain it in existence through time is simply a hangover from Aristotelian physics. If God can exist through time without anything further to sustain it, why not the universe?"*[5]

The alternative to a creator God is the idea of everything coming about by chance from (for example) the so-called Big Bang, and then eventually humanity emerging from a primordial soup. Jean-Paul Sartre (1905-1980), a French existentialist thinker, reflecting this said, *"All is ooze, that is chaos"*. As a result of secular views, people become no more than a little ooze, wallowing about in ooze—making universal logical negations in ooze (for instance, denying the existence of God). Typically this *"universal negation"* is expressed by the Zoology Professor who said, *"Evolution is a theory universally accepted, not because it can be proved true, but because the alternative, 'special creation', is clearly impossible."*[6]

Axiarchism

Hall suggests that a possible purpose of the universe can be justified by using the concept of **axiarchism**: *"This is the idea that it is objective value, rather than a personal God, which has a creative capacity and thus brings the universe into existence. The universe would then exist because it is objective value, rather than a personal God, which has a creative capacity and thus brings the universe into existence. The universe would then exist because it is on the whole better, more valuable, that it does than that it does not, despite the evil it contains (See J. Leslie, Value & Existence, 1979)."*[7] This notion seems quite remarkable: to talk of an *"objective value"* being able to have a creative capacity, is an example of projecting man's thoughts to create another impossible *"material god"* which clearly means it is purely a fanciful figment of human imagination. It could be argued that it is easier to believe in an all powerful Creator God, than have faith in the capacity of any impersonal *"objective value"* as the justification for the Universe's existence.

Moral Evil

The reason why an all-powerful God allowed evil in the Universe has occupied the minds of thinking people throughout the centuries. It was Epicurus (a Greek thinker) who posed this logical teaser: either God can prevent evil and chooses not to (and so, he postulated, is not good) or chooses to prevent it and cannot (and so is not all-powerful). It is vital to distinguish between sin and the evil consequences of sin (such as disease and death). In essence, sin is more specific than *"evil"*. Sin denotes a definite kind of evil, namely a moral evil for which man is responsible and which brings him under a sentence of condemnation. Louis Berkhof explains the point clearly: *"The modern tendency to regard sin merely as a wrong done to one's fellow being misses the point entirely, for such a wrong can be called sin only as far as it is contrary to the will of God. Sin is correctly defined in Scripture as 'lawlessness' (I John 3:4)."* [8]

Augustine of Hippo (354-430)—theologian, offered the following explanation: Evil is the absence of good, in the same way as darkness is the absence of light. It is possible for something created good to diminish in goodness, to become corrupted. Evil crept in when creatures endowed with free will—the angels, lesser spirits (which became demons) and human beings—turned away from higher, or more complete goods, and chose lesser ones. It is arguable that Adam (and Satan) did not just choose merely *"lesser goods"* but fundamental evils.

A painting that had only light in it would not be very interesting: it would have no contrast. The artist must use darker shades to emphasise the different features present. So, it is suggested that God allowed evil to come, so that in the end a greater good may prevail. Augustine also realised the principle that evil was finite (limited and ultimately to be overcome) and that of good was infinite (as God is to reign in heaven—the eternal city of God). Augustine shows how sin can come from perfection and thus absolves God from the guilt of creating sin. Our painting analogy suggests that, sin having been committed, the greatest good may come by allowing sin to prevail in the short term. Thus to answer Epicurus: God is not the author of sin, but when sin came into the cosmos, he chose to allow the sinful cosmos to continue (in sin and with the evil consequences of sin), in order that greater good might come (so it is still possible to say that God is good).

According to Augustine, what at first appears to be evil may be understood to be good in the context of eternity. The Bible teaches that God is able to bring good out of evil. The supreme example here is the cruel death of His eternal Son (Jesus) on a cross, which has made possible the ultimate salvation of people. Dr. Jay E. Adams (practical theologian) puts the problem as: How can there be evil in a good God's world? The answer is, *"God decreed it in order to demonstrate his nature.... in this way according to his own good reasons for his glory."*[9]

Dr Francis Schaeffer (apologist) said that Christianity's answer to the problem of evil, *"rests in the historic, space-time, real and complete Fall. ...... there was an unprogrammed man who made a choice, and actually rebelled against God."* Schaeffer argued that if you rejected this historic Christian answer , *"you have to face Baudelaire's profound statement, 'If there is a God, He is the devil', or Archibald MacLeish's statement in his play J. B., "If he is a God he cannot be good, if he is good he cannot be God ...Without Christianity's answer that God made a significant man in a significant history with evil being the result of Satan's and then man's historic space-time revolt, there is no answer but to accept Baudelaire's statement with tears."*[10] **See Endnote 1.**

The issue of the origin of evil is clearly an emotive one. David Hall reviews Swinburne's latest book: *Is there a God?*[11]. His chapter giving an understanding of *"Why God Allows Evil"*, Hall calls a *"nauseating spectacle of specious reasoning."* He states, *"In explanation of moral evil his [Swinburne's] basic argument is that: 'Being allowed to suffer to make possible a great good is a privilege, even if the privilege is forced upon you.' (p. 102). And the 'great good' that this suffering makes possible is that it is the means whereby the one who inflicts the suffering has: 'the opportunity to make a significant choice between good and evil which otherwise he would not have had.' (p. 106). So the greatest privilege that God bestows upon his chosen people is that it gives the rest of us the choice of whether or not to be Nazis. How purblind of the six million not to realise how favoured they were. For anyone unconvinced by this reasoning there is the old stand-by that the good God provides a compensatory blissful afterlife for those who suffer most; unfortunately this boon was not revealed to the chosen people but to their persecutors."*[12]

An answer to Hall's criticisms is as follows: Swinburne's argument that man now has a choice between "good" and "evil" actions is clearly not intended to be a justification of evil. It is a consequence of the existence of evil, and whether humanity chooses or degenerates into following a Nazi philosophy (attributable to a belief in the survival of the fittest) is clearly a result of man's sinful actions. Hitler's evil persecution of the Jewish nation is an example of how depraved people become when they neglect God's laws. The prospect of Heaven is held out to anyone who believes in God's Son (John 3:16) and so Hall's quip, *"unfortunately this boon was not revealed to the chosen people but to their persecutors"* is inaccurate. See also **Endnote 2.**

Hall continues his sarcastic critique: *"A final evidence of God's compassion and generosity is that no matter how terrible anyone's suffering might be it is apparent that 'one human can hurt another for no more than eighty years or so.' (p. 106). As for the suffering of the animal creation we can comfort ourselves with the thought that 'it is most unlikely that they suffer nearly as much as humans do' (p. 110)."*[13] Swinburne's comment that there is a limit to our suffering from human persecutors is axiomatic, as death itself is a consequence of mankind's original Fall. Doubtless all the many thousands of Christians who were made into human torches, or dressed in animal skins and ravaged by wild dogs (or lions) in Roman times, were victims (like the Jews) of man's inhumanity to man.[14]

The Fall also affected the rest of creation, which *"groans and labours ... until now"* (Romans 8: 22) and nature became *"Red in tooth and claw."* God's plan of redemption, both for humans and nature, plus the prospect of *"a new Heavens and a new earth"*, are evidence of God's concern for this fallen world. The need to see us as responsible moral beings (with consciences) is what differentiates Christianity from any form of fatalism. There are points about God's nature (e.g. his omnipotence), where Hall correctly identifies and argues that Swinburne has not presented the traditional teaching of Western religion. See End note: 3

Origin of good and evil?

To say you don't believe in God because of the problem of evil is still to remain in a dilemma. How do you explain evil's existence in the world— conditioning? Natural selection or some form of competitive mechanism? Surely, no-one needs convincing of the reality of "evil" including "man's inhumanity to man"? Just read your daily newspaper! Whatever your naturalistic explanation, you will still be left with the reality of evil, and the fact that its existence does not disprove God's existence. Clearly as an agnostic or atheist you must have a natural explanation for it! The problem for secularists is: *"How did good arise? Why is there love, altruism (the opposite of selfishness) and philanthropy?"* Professor Richard Dawkins queries: *"Much as we may wish to believe otherwise, universal love and the welfare of the species as a whole are concepts which simply do not make evolutionary sense.*"[15] Another, different set of problems that critics make, may be classified as "logical traps".

Traps examined

I well remember the student who set this logical trap for me. *"If God is all powerful (Almighty), can he create an immovable object?"* The idea that God—if he should be Almighty—could create an immovable object is to display a misunderstanding of the term *"Almighty"* by implying that such a being could create something equal to itself. Such a semantic argument turns on the idea that nothing should be impossible to an Almighty One. This is clearly not true of the God revealed in the Bible, for it is said of him, that he cannot lie, nor can he deny himself. The person who creates this *'snare'* is rather like a drowning person in the ocean, trying to make a ladder of water to escape! The venture is doomed to failure! To use claimed autonomous human logic, which is based on a meaningless flow of neurons in the brain, can prove nothing for certain. In this sense no logical trap can ever work! It is impossible to use such "logic" to prove God does or does not exist. In fact, humans have to play at being a "god" themselves to have sufficient knowledge to make such an absolute statement.

Evidences for God?

Julian Huxley (philosopher) graphically stated *"Operationally, God is beginning to resemble not a ruler but the last fading smile of a cosmic Cheshire cat."* What did he mean? Huxley is saying that as science advances and explains more and more, the need to invoke the concept of *"God"* decreases. He doubtless believed God is a projection of the human mind. Like the Lewis Carroll's scene in *Alice in Wonderland*, where Carroll imagines the fading smile of a cosmic Cheshire cat, Huxley is suggesting that God is fading from man's consciousness and thought-patterns, till soon there will be no sign of Him at all. This comment shows a complete misunderstanding and finite view of the nature of God. Huxley (like Freud) understood God to be a mere human construct and unreal, whereas the Bible teaches that God is a living Trinity. Huxley's notion of God is only a *"god of the gaps"* in scientific knowledge, but not the biblical God who made all things *ex nihilo* (out of nothing). His views of God are not only deficient in scope but also in nature!

Mind behind the Universe?

There are important *"classical arguments"* for God's existence, all of which would take a considerable time to review, e.g. the so-called *"onto-logical"* argument for God, and so on, which have been mentioned in chapter 2 and which are ably discussed by Frame elsewhere.[16] We shall discuss *"teleology"* which is the proposition (in theology) that the universe has design and purpose. Teleology is concerned with the teaching that seeks to explain the Universe in terms of final causes or ends. In philosophy, *"teleology" sometimes* refers to something else—the explanation of phenomena by the purpose they serve, rather than postulated causes. In this philosophical context, the activity does not presuppose a designer, as various philosophical approaches to the environment have shown. For example, Gaian philosophers and scientist's see the earth as an organic whole, hence have a particular set of human ethics towards the environment, other humans, etc. **See Endnote: 4.** It should be noted that holding to teleological beliefs does not necessarily conflict with scientific research. The latter, seeks the explanation of phenomena by postulated causes.

Design in the dock

Many scientists try studiously to avoid saying anything in nature has a purpose or design. This results from the fact that the average scientist does not feel qualified to speak of design and thus make a teleological statement, which they prefer to leave to the philosophers. If the world's design is intelligent, an ultimate Designer must exist. This idea of a supreme architect or mind behind it all is alien to some atheistic naturalists. Most scientists are persons of integrity, and they hold to a vast range of teleological beliefs, which they genuinely seek to separate from the experiments they perform (see comment from Behe). The idea of a designer is no more alien to the atheistic scientist or lay person. To many scientists life is certainly more than a mere matter of biochemistry. Even David Attenborough in *Life on Earth* and *Wildlife on One*, occasionally slipped into talking about design when showing various incredible features of wildlife specimens! The film commentator on *Taking to the Air* on the evolutionary development of the world of animal flight said, *"Every aspect of a bird's body is specifically designed for flight."*[17]

Although secular scientists recognise the desire of people to see (or impose) order on complexity, they think it is explicable. Psychologists speak of the *"Aha! phenomena"* or having a *"gestalt"* when we see a pattern in what at first glance seems to be a random pattern of dots. The question concerns whether we are imposing the order onto reality, or whether there are 'laws' or statistical norms to be discovered. This debate is largely within the evolutionist world. Creationists agree with most evolutionist scientists that there is real order that may be discovered. The question of real concern between creationists and most evolutionist scientists, is over the origin of those laws—given by God, absolute in themselves, attributes of fundamental matter, or beyond human reasoning? Scientific progress depends on building up better models of reality, which increase our understanding of nature and the Universe.

A complex item—by chance?

If you think of the so-called "created order" as a mechanical watch, with all the complex mechanism inside, is it realistic to say there was no watchmaker? That the watch just came together by fortuitous circumstances? There is an interesting story told of a parent, who carefully planted seeds in the garden, in the pattern of their child's name. When the flowers appeared in the garden, and the young child noticed their name standing out in the flower bed, imagine his surprise to be told this happened by chance! The child was not convinced!

The Darwinian model (according to one of the elder statesman of biology, Ernst Mayr) is firmly established. Dawkins' essential thesis is that Darwinian selection is blind: *"Natural selection, the blind unconscious, automatic process which Darwin discovered, and which we now know is the explanation for the existence and apparently purposeful form of all life, has no purpose in mind. It has no mind, and no mind's eye. It does not plan for the future. It has no vision, no foresight, no sight at all. If it can be said to play the role of watchmaker in nature, it is the blind watchmaker.*"[18] The divine designer is dethroned by the *"blind watchmaker"*. There is no innate drive to complex life, intelligence and consciousness. Dawkins thinks we are simply *"gene survival machines"*.

Intelligent Universe

Other scientists are not so convinced of the power of *"chance caught on the wing"* as this evolutionary process has been called—as each evolutionary step is pure accident. One such was Sir Fred Hoyle (an astronomer), who voiced his doubts in his book, *The Intelligent Universe*. Chief among the facts that would not agree with Dawkins' views are revealed in his answer to the following questions:

◆ 1 Did life start by random processes?

Sir Fred Hoyle answers *"No"* because he says: *"Imagine a blindfolded person trying to solve the Rubik cubes. The chance against achieving perfect colour matching is about 50,000,000,000,000,000,000 to 1. These odds are roughly the same as those against just one of our body's 200,000 proteins having evolved randomly, by chance."*

◆ 2 Could chance operate on such a large scale?

Hoyle answers *"No"* because he says: *"The Universe, as observed by astronomers, would not be large enough to hold all the monkeys needed to write even one scene from Shakespeare, or hold all their typewriters, and certainly not the wastepaper baskets for the rubbish they would type."*

◆ 3 Is Darwin's theory of evolution still plausible?

Hoyle answers *"No"* because he says: *"The rich assembly of plants found on the Earth cannot have been produced by a truism of this minor order."*

◆ 4 Did life originate on Earth?

Hoyle answers *"No"* because he says: *"There is not a shred of objective evidence to support the hypothesis that life began in an organic soup here on Earth."* [19] Hoyle also admitted that believing order will come out of the chaos, was like saying given enough time a jumbo jet would develop out of a whirlwind blowing through a scrapyard of aeroplane parts! Fred Hoyle solves the problem of origins by suggesting we have descended from life seeded from the depths of space, and that these seeds of life can still be found today. He believes that the complexity of life on earth cannot have been caused by a sequence of random processes, but must have come from a cosmic intelligence.

With Dawkins it seems that we are asked to believe that all the amazing creatures we see around us with unusual *"adaptations"* are not the result of a creative mind, but of the impersonal forces of nature—his *"blind watchmaker"*. Think, for example, of the angler fish which can catch its prey with its own on-board fishing rod. It has an appendage which it lets out, waggles, and then hooks in any creature silly enough to try and swallow it! We could examine numerous examples: for instance the bat with its sonar. If the sonar system of echo-location in the bat evolved, then this amazing system would have to evolve at the same time as the wing membrane, as without its sonar no bat could survive. Bats fly in the dark and their sonar helps them to see. They send out signals -high pitched squeaks—at 50,000 and 200,000 vibrations per second. Bats are provided with special equipment to both send and receive signals. The point we are making here could be illustrated by millions of other creatures with unique features (like spider's spinettes for building their webs) which would have absolutely no reason to develop over time, because they are of no use until fully functional.

On the back burner

In the United States an attack on Charles Darwin's theory has come from an unexpected quarter. Professor of Biochemistry at Lehigh University— Michael Behe—(with no religious axe to grind) has written a best-seller 'Darwin's *Black Box*' where he comments: *"The scientific community contains many excellent scientists who think that there is something beyond nature, and many excellent scientists who do not. How then will science 'officially' treat the question of the identity of the designer? Will biochemistry textbooks have to be written with explicit statements that 'God did it'? No. The question of the identity of the designer will simply be ignored by science. The history of science is replete with examples of basic-but-difficult questions being put on the back burner. For example, Newton declined to explain what caused gravity, Darwin offered no explanation for the origin of vision or life, Maxwell refused to specify a medium for light waves once the ether was debunked, and cosmologists in general have ignored the question of what caused the Big Bang."* He concludes: *"The reluctance of science to embrace the conclusion of intelligent design that its long, hard labours made manifest has no justifiable foundation. Scientific chauvinism is an understandable emotion, but it should not be allowed to affect serious intellectual issues."* [20]

Behe's Darwinian Mousetrap!

One debate that has as much fire in it as when it first began is the question of whether life evolved or was created. The debate is always heightened by Oxford zoologist Richard Dawkins' outspoken comments against those who believe the Bible. Basically, this author of *'The Selfish Gene'* thinks we are self-replicating robots who live in a purposeless Universe—where all is Chaos and Old Night.

Behe asserts that complex molecular systems are the result of intelligent design and cannot have evolved by chance. This has been interpreted by Darwinists to mean God and they vehemently oppose the book. Professor Peter Van Inwagen (philosopher) says: *"If Darwinians respond to this important book by ignoring it, misrepresenting it, or ridiculing it, that will be evidence in favour of the widespread suspicion that Darwinism today functions more as an ideology than as a scientific theory. If they can successfully answer Behe's arguments, that will be important evidence in favour of Darwinism."* [21]

Step-by-step?

Professor Behe explains that modern biochemistry has revealed a stunning miniature world, that does not support Darwinism. This world is made of *'molecular machines'* which act as the nuts and bolts of biological systems. At this microscopic level, there are unbridgeable gaps, which do not support Darwin's ideas of a step-by-step evolution (what the zoologist Dewer once called the *"transformist illusion"*). Darwin claimed his theory would *'absolutely break down'* if it could be shown that any complex organ could not have been formed by many successive, slight modifications. Recent research has also shown the recapitulation theory to be impossible and incorrect. [22] See **Endnote 5.**

Behe's Darwinian Mousetrap

Behe argues that molecular systems are irreducibly complex. He uses the very simple example of a mousetrap made of a spring, hammer, catch, base and holding bar. Individually, none of these parts has any trapping ability. All are essential for the trap to work. Behe says that molecular systems could never have evolved by randomly acquiring separate bits of the system, as there would be no function to select—until all the pieces were properly organised to work together. Behe demonstrates using the examples of vision, blood-clotting, cellular transport, and others, that the biochemical world is made up of an arsenal of chemical machines, each comprised of finely calibrated, interdependent parts. Behe has reportedly challenged Dawkins (via American TV) to a debate, but Dawkins has declined, pleading inadequate knowledge of biochemistry. Another critique of evolution appeared in *The Facts of Life* by Richard Milton (1993) [23] who is an agnostic science journalist. The fact that most stunned Milton was that Richard Dawkins never answered his arguments, but just made a personal attack on him. A case of *"don't confuse me with facts, my mind's made up!"*?

There are many *"evidences"* for the existence of God, beginning with man's need for God, reflecting mans own spiritual makeup: his conscience, and awareness of *"right and wrong"*. Other evidences for a spiritual realm are studied in parapsychology and illustrated later by an account of a man (Victor Ernest) who got involved in spiritualism.

Proofs for man's spiritual makeup

It was the committed atheist Thomas H. Huxley, who confessed that there is a blank in the human heart and that it is a God-shaped blank. Human beings are incurably religious. Edmund Burke (politician) said: *"Man is by his constitution a religious animal."* Go to the remotest tribe, in the furthermost part of the earth, and you will find they have notion of *"gods"* whom they revere and worship. People have a conscience which alerts them to *"rights"* and *"wrongs"*. These will show some fairly comprehensive convictions—like murder is wrong—but clearly not entirely true for cannibals! Why are there such belief systems? Some suggest it is to keep moral order and preserve a system of respect. Many societies have an awareness of an *"after-life"* and a spirit world. The Scriptures teach that people seek to hold down or suppress the knowledge that God exists in their conscience" .... *who hold [down] the truth in unrighteousness"* Romans 1:18), and that we are made in the *"image of God"*. These surviving created *"remnants"*, including the conscience, along with the teaching of Romans 1: 20-21 account for our religious capacity. This states *"For since the creation of the world his invisible attributes are clearly seen being understood by the things that are made, even his eternal power and Godhead, so they are without excuse, because, although they knew God, they did not glorify him as God"* This accounts for man's religious capacity, and the diversity of beliefs that came from the loss of humans' intimate fellowship with God.

There are those who talk of a sixth sense or having a spiritual *"spark"*, to account for humans' capacity to worship. This shows itself in the continuance of the major world religions—and this is a topic we shall return to later. The contemporary world has different manifestations of people's sense of the divine or search for spiritual meaning: the tendency to idolise 'film stars' has religious roots. In the U.S.A. and Canada, there are over 1,200 newspapers that have astrology sections. In the U.K. in 1985, a Gallup survey revealed that over 50% of British teenagers thought astrology worked in some form. President Reagan regularly consulted an astrologer to see what his day would bring forth. Even the national lottery has the 'finger of fate' pointing from the stars. At a more popular level this is seen in the 'X' Files series with the belief that *"the truth is out there somewhere"*, where aliens and extra-terrestrial life, UFOs and clones become the order of the day. Here, however, it could be argued that when people cease to believe in the true God, they don't believe in nothing, they believe in anything.

More things in Heaven and Earth

Even in the so-called *"civilised world"* there is an incredible interest in the paranormal. There is Parapsychology—which investigates alleged phenomena and abilities that apparently cannot be explained by conventional scientific theories. This is not recommended territory for Christians (see the prohibition on such activities in Deut. 18: 10-12) but does indicate that strange things happen, which may be due to a hostile spiritual realm. There are indeed weird and wonderful phenomena in the world, which often defy human explanation. The evidence for another spiritual realm comes from what is termed the *"paranormal"*. Shakespeare's character talks of *"More things in Heaven and earth ... than are dreamt of in your philosophy ..."* (Hamlet 1:5). Clearly there is a whole realm that is still an anathema to science: ghosts, spiritualism, demon possession, black magic, and so on. These issues have been dealt with extensively elsewhere [24]. One example, of interest, is that of one-time spiritualist Victor Ernest.

I talked with spirits

Victor Ernest became a Christian Pastor, but he was once a spirit medium. He acknowledged that much of the occult demonstrations of power are clever hoaxes, but he shows that evil spirits do invade the natural world, when humans surrender themselves to them. Invisible spirits do sometimes lift tables, knock on walls and speak through mediums at seances. His book is written to deter people from dabbling in the mysterious spirit world, as it exposes them to the influence or even control of evil spirits.

Ernest explains: *"I now saw spiritualism in a very different light. The Bible taught me the truth about spirits and spirit phenomena, and I became deeply alarmed by the spreading invasion of evil spirits into human life. Many people think that spirit phenomena are accomplished by trickery, sleight of hand, or black magic. I agree that many mysterious happenings associated with prominent psychics and small-town fortune-tellers are hoaxes—perhaps 85 per cent of them, but I believe the rest are actual deeds of evil spirits counterfeiting the power of the Holy Spirit. At one trumpet seance, to prove there was no hocus-pocus involved, the control spirit sent the trumpet sailing between the chair on which I was sitting. Since I was in my home, I knew no props had been arranged and that no strings were attached."*[25] Despite this sort of evidence, some scientists are not impressed, because it does not fit into their *"frame of reference"*. This issue is now examined further, as we look at the impact of a person's *"belief system."*

It's not fish if my net won't catch it

A key principle in any belief system is that *"no philosophy can exceed its initial assumptions."* For instance, if no God is accepted, then anything which suggests he might exist or have acted will be excluded! It does not fit into that person's initial atheistic *"frame of reference"*. Nature will consequently be treated as if it is an autonomous (self governing) system. Atheistic scientists in practice are saying: *"It's not fish if my net won't catch it"*. Note, however, it is the scientists themselves who are setting up what they will accept as valid truth or evidence. They set the size of the mesh that catch the fish!

Sir Arthur Eddington used this illustration: You send a young scientist out fishing, and ask for a report on the size of fish caught. He makes a startling discovery: there are no fish less than four inches! An old fisherman wisely tells him to check the size of the net mesh before he releases his amazing discovery on the world that *"there are no fish less than four inches long"*! The nets have four-inch holes, so it is not surprising that it is the way you have set up your examination (your frame of reference) that has determined the outcome. Sometimes, philosophers and scientists are unaware of their initial presuppositions, and how these can influence the outcome of their theories.

One geologist claimed that creationism can be dismissed, as *"What creationist method has ever accurately located oil traps, gas, minerals, etc.?"* This comment shows some fundamental misunderstandings! In fact it was the early Catastrophists—the creationists—who were the *"hard-nosed empiricists"* of their day. In so far as geological research methods are based on empiricism, it is clear they will work, used by either a creationist or an evolutionary geologist: A geomagnetic survey will reveal magnetic anomalies and help locate oil and gas traps. The presence of mineral lodes can be detected by geochemical methods, also by geological and aerial surveys. The use of micro-fossils as indicative of the presence of oil does not prove or disprove the evolutionary interpretation that may be placed on the data. Neither is belief in the theory of evolution on the part of the mudlogger essential to successfully locate the oil! In so far as your geological methods are based on sound scientific methodology, their success depends on this, and does not necessarily "prove" the overriding philosophy of the day. The now widely recognised rapidly formed turbidites were correctly described in terms of their lithology (rock and particle content) long before they were interpreted as deposits resulting from rapid density currents at sea.

Behind the moon

Another classic illustration of one's mind-set determining one's perception of reality occurred when the atheistic Russian astronaut reported he hadn't seen God, when he went round the other side of the moon. Any Bible believer could have told him that God is invisible, because God is Spirit! For those who think that nature must have a supernature over and above it, there will be a completely different viewpoint. The reality people study around themselves will be the same for both groups. The believing scientist can also discover what exists and the way it works, but as one *"thinking God's thoughts after him."* The dilemma of modern knowledge has been jovially portrayed by saying: researchers learn more and more about less and less, until they end up knowing everything about nothing! Clearly a funny conundrum, but correct in implying that to know anything thoroughly a student must know it comprehensively.

Give me the facts, man, the facts!

For the agnostic or atheist, the ultimate reference point in determining truth is man himself (or herself) whereas the theist (believer) has a higher source of authority. The differences in starting points will affect interpretation of phenomena. The idea that we are like neutral detectives who say: *"Give me the facts, man, the facts"* is unrealistic. We select which data we think are significant, and our pre-suppositions influence the significance (or interpretation) we put on them. The evolutionary biologist will see common structures between creatures as common descent, whereas the believer interprets this as down to a common designer. Historians like Dr. H. A. L. Fisher will see *"no generalisations, only one safe rule for the historian ... the play of the contingent and unforeseen"* [26] , or as Henry

Ford put it crudely, *"history is bunk"*. In contrast the believer (like Augustine of Hippo, or Calvin—who saw history as the theatre of God's glory) will see the forces of good and evil at play, and God's directive will at work in the world's history. *"I read the newspaper,"* said John Newton (famous hymnwriter and preacher) *"that I may see how my Heavenly Father governs the world"*. This discussion underlines an important point: facts and the interpretation of facts, cannot be separated: see **Endnote 6**.

To err is human: impact on ethics

The impact on morality of this different starting point is monumental. David Hume, the Scottish philosopher argued that it is impossible in principle to reach conclusions about what ought to be done from assumptions stating only what is the case. In his *Treatise on Human Nature* (1740) Hume stated what has become known as the naturalistic fallacy or *"is-ought"* problem. He said: *"In every system of morality which I have hitherto met with, I have always remark'd, that the author proceeds for some time in the ordinary way of reasoning ... when of a sudden I am surpris'd to find, that instead of the usual copulations of propositions, 'is' and 'is not', I meet with no proposition that is not connected with an 'ought' or an 'ought not'. This change is imperceptible but is, however, of the last consequence."*[27]

David Hume was making a logical point, that in any argument, its conclusion cannot contain anything not in its original assumptions. If we say, for instance, *"Oranges are round and buses are red; therefore bananas are mauve"* you can tell immediately my argument is false, even if you have never seen a banana, as my assumptions did not mention bananas and so there is no way that my conclusions can mention them. The impact of this simple piece of logic on moral philosophy is tremendous!

In the 1960's there were still arguments over the validity of Hume's Law, which had been ticking away like a time bomb under moral philosophy. The main protagonists were Max Black, Peter Geach and John Searle who tried to find logical justification for moving from "is" to "ought". This fundamental point remains unsolved. Any ethical system which derives its rules about how we should behave solely from information about the world must be flawed, even if the error or weakness is not immediately detected.

This issue of whether ethics must therefore depend on God is still very much a live debate: in a recent book, *Does God exist?* J. P. Moreland (theist) discusses such issues with Kai Nielsen (atheist). Moreland says that without an Ultimate Good—that is, God, *"there is no reason to choose one course of action rather than another, and that this defeats the atheist's claim to be able—or necessarily willing—to lead a moral life. For Moreland, moral absolutes exist, while Nielsen thinks they do not, but Nielsen as a Marxist, believes that people will make choices which are ultimately beneficial rather than otherwise."*[28] Atheists must accept a relativistic morality—able to change over time—and *"everyone doing that which is right in their own eyes."* Ultimately their final reference point is man and his interpretation of what is noble and good. Theists, on the other hand, have a clear-cut *"right and wrong"* which is unchanging—for instance the ten commandments, which provide guiding principles on acceptable behaviour. Undoubtedly, some sceptics would be right in their incredulity at recent moral pronouncements from the *"establishment"* but Jesus (in contrast to liberal clerics) put it simply, *"If you love me, keep my commandments"* (John 14: 15).

Malcolm Muggeridge, the well known journalist, said: *"When mortal men try to live without God, they infallibly succumb to megalomania or erotomania, or both. The raised fist or the raised phallus: Nietzsche or D. H. Lawrence. Pascal said this, and the contemporary world bears it out."* [29] In other words if we ignore God, our attention eventually turns to self or sex, and ultimately death will only be integration into the void, which unbelievers think is their final fate. As humans are the guardians of the life and resources of this planet, the picture may not be that much better. Incidents with 'Swampy' the eco-warrior—who burrows under proposed sites for roads or runways—show that economics generally comes before ecology!

The *"Gaia hypothesis"* describes how the ecosystem of a planet can be viewed as a single system. Its creator, James Lovelock, wrote: *"I would sooner expect a goat to succeed as a gardener than expect humans to become stewards of the Earth."*[30] In contrast, Christopher Merchant, an environmental physicist who believes in absolutes, has said: *"Love your neighbour as yourself" (Matthew 22:39) is a culturally invariant principle. As you can see from the reference, it isn't a new idea—others have formulated similar laws, and even Jesus was quoting a much older source. As a principle, it is easy to learn and the practice of it lasts a lifetime."* [31]

Starting point

The issue of God and objections to his existence have been reviewed (like the problem of evil), and the need for an ultimate starting point has been recommended: without God, man has no other hope than to trust in himself and his own autonomous knowledge. Despite the claim that absolutes are for fanatics and holymen, we see that without absolute standards or an ultimate reference point man is left in a morass or quagmire that he cannot escape from. The next issue we examine, *"Truth unchanged, unchanging"* deals with whether we are left with only man's changing opinion to guide us, or whether there are credible reasons to accept that God has *'revealed'* himself. Unless the latter were true, Christians would believe we are on the shifting sands and tumultuous seas of human opinion, and like the Titanic—the so-called unsinkable ship—doomed to founder on the hidden iceberg of comprehensive knowledge. To be absolutely sure of anything, an atheist must know everything, but even a genius can make mistakes. Einstein, by introducing a cosmological constant into his equations, failed to predict an expanding universe, he called this *"the biggest mistake of my life."* We are still finite and fallible! When asked whether he would die for his beliefs, Bertrand Russell, the British philosopher, said: *"Of course not. After all, I may be wrong."* [32] Not only may great men make mistakes, but logic itself has limitations.

But on what grounds can atheists be sure any logic is valid? *"Basic to all non-Christian philosophies are certain far-reaching pre-theoretical commitments or presuppositions which are basically religious. Man assumes the self-sufficiency and autonomy of his philosophical thought. He makes God relative, and his thought, or some aspect of creation, absolute. As a result of this attitude, man, in his pretended autonomy, immediately finds that, not only is the world of everyday experience a problem, but that he is a problem to himself. Wherever man has, in terms of this presupposition, tried to think philosophically, he has found it all too easy ..... to end up in scepticism even concerning his own existence, or at least of his thinking processes ."* [33]

Conclusion

It is true that Christians may have problems in believing, and those who hold to other systems may apparently have fewer problems in believing what they believe! The difference is not in our subjective problems of belief, but in the fact that the objective redemption and revelation of God are both true and sufficient (so that there are no problems in the objective reality, even though our weak minds find problems) and that other systems are neither. *Matthew Henry's Commentary* on Psalm 19:1 says, *"The heavens so declare the glory of God, and proclaim his wisdom, power and goodness, that all ungodly men are left without excuse. They speak themselves to be works of God's hands; for they must have a Creator who is eternal, infinitely wise, powerful and good."*

References:

1   Reported by **Kenneth Harris,** talking to **Bertrand Russell** in **D. Chapman,** editor (1993*) Who said what?* Chancellor Press, London, p. 337 (ref 13: 924).
2   **J. Huxley** (1957) *Religion without Revelation.*
3   **D. Hall** (1996) reviews *Is there a God?* by Richard Swinburne, Philosophy Now, Issue 15, Spring/Summer, Ipswich, ISBN 0961-5970, p. 43.
4   **Ibid,** pp. 43-44.
5   **Ibid,** p. 44.
6   **D. M. S. Watson** (1929), Professor of Zoology, University of London, *The Times*, London, 3/08/29
7   **D. Hall** (1996) Ibid, p. 44.
8   **L. Berkhof** (1962) *A summary of Christian doctrine*, Banner of Truth, London, pp. 68-
9   Quoted in J. M. Frame (1994) *Apologetics to the Glory of God*, Presbyterian & Reformed Publishing, New Jersey, ISBN 0-87552-243-2, pp. 246-7.
10 **F. A. Schaeffer** (1968) *Escape from Reason*, I. V. F., London, ISBN 85110 340 5, p. 81.
11 **R. Swinburne** (1996) *Is there a God?* Oxford University Press, ISBN: 0-19- 823545-3.
12 **D. Hall** (1996) Ibid, p. 44.
13 **Ibid.**
14 **R. Alderson** (1997) The Early Christians—a taster, , Day One Publications, Epsom ISBN 0 902 548 743, pp. 23-36.

15 **R. Dawkins** (1978) *The Selfish Gene*, Granada Publishing, p. 2.

16 **See J. M. Frame:** *Apologetics to the Glory of God*, Chapter 4 , Apologetics as Proof: The Existence of God, Presbyterian & Reformed, New Jersey, ISBN 0-87552-243- 2, pp. 92-114.

17 **Alistair MacEwen's** film, *Taking to the Air*: located in Indonesia; producer Malcolm Penny, .8190.

18 **R. Dawkins** (1988) *The Blind Watchmaker*, Harmondsworth, Penguin, p. 5.

19 **F. Hoyle** (1983) *The Intelligent Universe*, Michael Joseph, London, ISBN: 0 7181 2 298 4, Frontispiece.

20 **M. J. Behe** (1996), *Darwin's Black Box: The biochemical challenge to evolution*, Free Press, New York, ISBN 0684827549, p. 251. U.K. Publisher: Simon Schuster.

21 **Ibid,** on back cover.

22 **N. Hawkes** (1997) *An embryonic liar*, The Times, 11/09/97 p. 14.

23 **R. Milton** (1993) *The Facts of Life*, Corgi, ISBN 0 552 14121 6 .

24 **C. Wilson, J. Weldon** (1980) *Occult Shock & Psychic Forces*, Master Books, San Diego, Ca., ISBN O-89051-065-2.

25 **V. H. Ernest** (1970) *I talked with Spirits*, Coverdale Publishers Ltd, Eastbourne, Sussex, ISBN 0 90208 8 17 3, p. 27.

26 **H. A. L. Fisher** (1966) *A History of Europe* (Vol. 1) Collins, Preface.

27 **D. Hume** (1740) Treatise on Human Nature III i. d, Selby-Bigge Edition, p. 470.

28 **S. Johnson** (1997) Review of *Does God Exist?* Prometheus Books : ISBN 0-87975-823-6, in Issue 18 Summer 1997, Philosophy Now, Ipswich.

29 **M. Muggeridge** (1978) *25 Propositions on a 75th Birthday* , New York Times, 24/04/78.

30 **T. Wakeford & M. Walters** (ed.) (1995) *Science for the earth: Can Science Make the World a Better Place?* John Wiley, p. 75.

31 **C. Merchant** (1995) *Physics World*, June 1995.

32 **D. Chapman,** editor (1993*) Who said what?* Chancellor Press, London, p. 319 (ref 13: 613).

33 **H. Dooyeweerd** (1965) *In the Twilight of Western Thought*, The Craig Press, Nutley, NewJersey, Library of Congress No. LC 60-6645, p. vii-viii; See chapters I & II, The Pretended Autonomy of Philosophical Thought, pp.1-27.

Further Reading:

M. J. Behe (1996), *Darwin's Black Box: The biochemical challenge to evolution*, Free Press, New York, ISBN 0 68482 754 9.

Chapter 4

J. M. Frame (1994) *Apologetics to the Glory of God*, P. & R. Publishing, New Jersey, ISBN 0-87552-243-2

F. Hoyle & N. C. Wickramasinghe (1981) *Evolution from Space*, J. M. Dent & Sons, ISBN 0-460-04535-0.

G. R. Lewis (1976) *Testing Christianity's Truth Claims*, Moody Press, Chicago, ISBN 0 8024 8595 2.

J. Rendle-Short (1997) *Green Eye of the storm*, Banner of Truth, Edinburgh, ISBN 0 85151 727 7.

J. Rendle-Short (1991) *Reasonable Christianity*, Evangelical Press, Darlington, ISBN 0-85234-289-6.

L. Samuel (1990) *There is an Answer*, Christian Focus Publications, ISBN 1 871676 06 1.

Key Text:
Psalm 14: 1 *"The fool says in his heart, 'There is no God.' "*

Endnote : 1

Two types of evil are commonly contrasted: moral evil that is the result of deliberate human action, like murder or war; natural evil that is the result of usual or unusual natural occurrences, such as diseases, drought, famines, hurricanes, volcanic disasters, etc. The theological problem of evil is known as an antilogism (a contradiction in terms) that results from assuming three things, only two of which are compatible (dubbed the incompatible triad): the omnipotence of God, the omnibenevolence of God, and the existence of evil. Epicurus set out the problem as follows: Is God willing to prevent it, but not able to prevent evil? Then he claimed that God is not omnipotent. Is God able to prevent evil, but not willing to prevent it? Then God is not omnibenevolent. Finally, is God both willing and able to prevent evil? Then he asked, why does evil exist? To test God by the *"laws of logic"* is condescending to say the least. It is clear that God is above man-made logic. The many attributes of God (love, justice, perfection, etc.) are like the facets of a diamond, each contributing to its brilliance. Even in the natural world there are apparent contradictions in phenomena: Does light travel in straight lines or in waves? The answer is *"both."* Almighty God is both infinite and eternal, so how can we finite beings come to anything like a comprehensive understanding of his qualities and nature, let alone how one quality negates another? The ultimate answer to this problem can best be expressed by the hymnist who asserts: *"Where reason fails, with all her powers, there faith prevails and love adores."*

It is the problem of evil that is the *rock of atheism*. Once this problem rock is climbed by the atheist, he thinks himself unanswerable. In a shrewd analysis, however, Henri Blocher penetrates to the heart of the problem and the Christian answer—the cross of Christ. He concludes: *"Evil is conquered as evil because God turns it back upon itself. He makes the supreme crime, the murder of the only righteous person, the very operation that abolishes sin... No more complete victory could be imagined. God responds in an indirect way that is perfectly suited to the ambiguity of evil. He entraps the deceiver in his own wiles. Evil, like a judoist, takes advantage of the power of the good, which it perverts; the Lord, like a supreme champion, replies by using the very grip of the opponent. .. It is exactly this, the sin of sins, the murder of the Son, which accomplishes this work in a double manner. It provides the opportunity for love to be carried to its very peak, for there is no greater love than to give one's life for one's friends."* H. Blocher (1994) *Evil and the Cross*, Apollos, Leicester, ISBN 0-85111-140-8, p. 132.

Endnote: 2

In fairness to Hall's criticisms of *"Is there a God"*, it is correct to say that Swinburne is not clear about God's omniscience (all-knowing ability) and omnipotence (all-powerfulness). The God of the Bible, is said to know the end from the beginning; we spend our lives before Him, as *"a tale that is told"* (Psalm 90:9). Swinburne thinks it is logically impossible for God to know the future free actions of human beings, and that God is inside time. Hall correctly comments he cannot help feeling this is a post-Holocaust discovery about the nature of God. Swinburne excludes God from knowing about man's future actions, in an attempt to defend God against the accusation that He could have prevented Auschwitz. We have argued above that man being a morally responsible being (See 2 Corinthians 5:10), he cannot blame God for such atrocities as Auschwitz; more likely it is the result of believing in the supremacy of the Master race, which Hitler and Nazis justified on evolutionary philosophy (*"the survival of the fittest"*). R.E.D. Clark (1948) in *Darwin: Before and After*, (Paternoster Press: London), p. 115 says: *"Adolf Hitler's mind was captivated by evolutionary teaching—probably since the time he was a boy. Evolutionary ideas—quite undisguised—lie at the basis of all that is worst in Mein Kampf—and in his public speeches."* Another writer—a staunch evolutionist—Sir Arthur Keith (1947) admitted in *Evolution & Ethics, p. 230*, *"The German Fuhrer ... consciously sought to make the practice of Germany conform to the theory of evolution"* (G. P. Putnam's Sons, New York.) The racism and militarism of Hitler and Mussolini were in large measure results of the philosophical base promulgated in the 19th century by Friedrich Nietzsche and Ernst Haeckel, both of whom were prophets of Darwinism among human societies.

Endnote: 3

Hall in his review correctly notes that Swinburne says in his first chapter that he is defending the God of Western religion (Judaism, Christianity and Islam.) So, in reality, Swinburne often relies more on philosophical arguments, than the clear teaching of God's Word. He also falls into the trap of talking as if God were a *"God of the gaps"*in knowledge, when he uses God of the gap between the physical brain and subjective awareness. Swinburne also suggests that God is inside time, which leads to all sorts of difficulties like if God, time and the world are co-eternals, why suppose that any one gives rise to any other? The Bible says God is outside time and not beholden to it. God is called the Alpha and Omega (beginning and end.)

Endnote: 4

The 'Gaia hypothesis' is associated with James E. Lovelock (1979) *Gaia*, Oxford University Press. It describes how the ecosystem of a planet can be viewed as a single system. Gaia was the Greek earth goddess whose name has been adopted for the theory that the whole planet should be regarded as a living thing. Dawkins' comments, *"All living creatures are Gaia's body parts and they work together as a well-adjusted thermostat, reacting to perturbations so as to preserve all life. ... Gaia has become a cult, almost a religion, and Lovelock now understandably wants to distance himself from this. ... Gaia falsely focuses attention on planetary life as a single unit. Planetary life is a shifting pattern of genetic weather"* from R. Dawkins (1998) *Unweaving the Rainbow*—science, delusion and the appetite for wonder, The Penguin Press, ISBN 0-713-99214-X, pp. 223-224.

Endnote: 5

Nigel Hawkes (science journalist) writes that one of the most famous German biologists of the 19th century—Ernst Haeckel—has been accused of being a scientific fraud, a faker who has muddied the waters of embryology for generations. Dr. Michel Richardson (St. George's Hospital Medical School, London) says: *"This is one of the worst cases of scientific fraud."* Haeckel's drawings in modified form occur in *Gray's Anatomy*, and *Developmental Biology* by Dr. Scott Gilbert (Swarthmore College,

Pennsylvania). His report is in the August '97 issue of the Anatomy and Embryology Journal. Haeckel taught that *"Ontogeny recapitulates phylogeny"*. Richardson explains that this means: *"that ontogeny—the process of development of an individual organism—is a re-run, fast-forward, of the evolution of the species as a whole. In other words, our development in the womb recapitulates the rise of man from primitive creatures to lord of creation."*

Endnote 6:

The Christian philosopher Cornelius Van Til characterised this difference by saying for the atheist facts are *"brute facts"*, the result of chance and contingency, whereas the believer has *"theistic facts"* , that owe their existence to being part of God's created order. The reason non-believers come to some truth is that they are *"rustlers"* who are working in God's universe. As there is 'common grace', man does come to valid truth, but not in an ultimate sense. He discovers facts, but does not realise that they are what they are by virtue of their place in the plan of God. The hymnist captured this thought of seeing reality as part of God's created order when he wrote, *"Heaven above is softer blue, earth beneath is sweeter green, something lives in every hue, Christless eyes have never seen."* See C. Van Til (1963) *The Defense of the Faith*, Presbyterian & Reformed Publishing Co., Philadelphia, Pa. Library of Congress Card Number 55-7140.

Questions for Further Study

1 Why does Hall (the critic) think Swinburne's God *"explains nothing"*?
2 Is the distinction between ultimate and proximate causes important?
3 What point is Sartre making about *"ooze"*?
4 Is axiarchism as innocent as it sounds?
5 What is the problem of evil as stated by Epicurus?
6 How does Augustine's privation argument answer the problem of evil?
7 Why does Hall regard Swinburne's explanation of *"Why God allows evil"* a *nauseating spectacle of specious reasoning"*? Is he right?
8 Why is the existence of "good" a problem for evolutionists like Richard Dawkins?
9 What sort of*"God"* does Huxley recognise and destroy?
10 What is the teleological design argument for the existence of God. Give an appropriate illustration.

11 Both astronomer Sir Fred Hoyle and biologist Dr Richard Dawkins are evolutionists. Do they agree with each other?

12 How does Behe's mousetrap catch both mouse and evolutionist?!

13 *"Man is incurably religious"*. How would you confirm our spiritual makeup?

14 What is the significance of paranormal research?

15 Does Deuteronomy 18: 10-12 discourage Christians from involvement in spiritualism?

16 What is the significance for origins of the phrase, *"It's not fish if my net won't catch it?"*

17 Give an example of how one's starting point influences the interpretation of the same data.

18 What is the significance for humanist ethics of Hume's *"is-ought"* problem, also known as the naturalistic fallacy?

19 What does Moreland indicate is the problem for non-theistic ethical systems?

20 What logical traps have you encountered about God? Which ones are mentioned in this text?

Food for Thought

* "At the beginning of all true theology lies the postulate that God is God—absolute and irresistible. It must be so. Without this we face a closed door: with it we have a key which unlocks every mystery." A. Pink.

* "My observation over the years is that it is people who have not been taught the truth negatively as well as positively who always get carried away by the heresies and cults, because they have not been forewarned and forearmed against them." Dr. D. Martyn Lloyd-Jones

Truth unchanged, unchanging: can we trust the Bible?

"The Scriptures give the key to two kinds of knowledge —the knowledge of God, and the knowledge of men and nature." Francis A. Schaeffer.

If we rely totally on human wisdom, we are still left with no absolutes, uncertainty and unclear paths to truth. There is much evidence that God has not only revealed Himself in nature, but also given His special revelation in the Word of God. The reliability of the Bible is shown not only in archaeological evidence and scientific research, but by the fulfilment of prophecy and the power of Christianity to change lives. The Bible has vindicated itself, despite undergoing more critical evaluation than any other book.

Is God unknown and unknowable?

The Bible proclaims the answers to everybody's greatest problems: the meaning of life and death, problems of eternity, the nature of God himself and how we can know God. But how do we know we can trust the Bible? Although the theist sees God's handiwork in nature, there would be no clear communication of what his past, present and future designs were for humanity. We would still need His own special message to find out the truth about what God is like. This is clear from the Bible's own claims. It says, *"Can you search out the deep things of God? Can you find out the limits of the Almighty?"* (Job 11:7).

The Bible teaches that people cannot understand what God is like, because of their limited power to think, and people's separation from the true and living God. The great Greek thinkers in Athens had many ideas about *"the gods"*. But the apostle Paul said to them that it was their so-called *"Unknown God"* that he had come to tell them about. He explained that the true God made all life and keeps it going, *"For in Him we live and move and have our being" (Acts 17:28)*.

Special Message

The Bible claims to be God's special message (revelation) as recorded by the prophets (Hebrews chapter 1:1). God told these prophets of things which we could not find out unaided—by natural reasoning and logic. Left to our own investigations, God would be unknown and unknowable. We would be left groping around in darkness, with *'the blind trying to lead the blind'*. One person's idea would be as good or as bad as another's! This is the explanation of why there are so many religions in the world. It is a result of people following their own opinion or ideas about God.

The Bible, however, claims to have an authority of its own, to prove that it is true; this quality of the Bible is known as its *"self authentication"*. The Bible's profound teaching, the way it has a single message throughout, clearly single it out as God's book. Scripture does not need to be validated (shown to be true) by any church council. C. H. Spurgeon (a well-known 19th century preacher) said *"the Bible is like a lion—it needs no defence"* all you need to do to demonstrate a lion's power is to let it out of its cage! See Figure 5.1 "Proofs of the Bible's Reliability."

Old Testament Inspiration

The Bible writers themselves claimed that they were writing the Word of God. Phrases like *"God said"*, *"The Lord spoke saying"*, *"The Lord commanded"*, and *"The word of the Lord"* are stated nearly 700 times in the five books of Moses, and more than 2,600 times in the whole Old Testament. The Lord Jesus accepted the inspiration of the Old Testament (Matthew 4:4-10; John 19:28; and Luke chapter 4:16-21). In John chapter 10:35 Jesus Christ said, *"the Scripture cannot be broken"*; in Luke 24:44 Jesus said *"All things must be fulfilled, which were written in the law of Moses, and in the prophets, and in the psalms, concerning me."* This included all three sections of the Hebrew Bible.

New Testament Inspiration

The Old Testament was accepted by Jesus Christ, the Apostles, and also millions today. But it is only part of what God has said to us. The rest is found in the New Testament, and together it makes up one complete message from God to human beings. Peter included Paul's letters with the *"other scriptures"* (2 Peter chapter 3:16) and stated that his and the other apostles' writings should be accepted alongside those of former prophets (see also the Apostle Paul's words in I Cor. 14:37 & I Thes. 2:13).

The Bible's claim for itself is clearly underlined by Paul: *"All Scripture is given by inspiration of God ..."* (2 Tim. 3:16). It also teaches that scripture is complete. The book of Hebrews reads: *"God, who at various times and in different ways spoke in time past to the fathers by the prophets, has in these last days spoken to us by his Son ...."*(Hebrews 1:1,2). It is described as *"the faith which was once for all delivered to the saints"*(Jude 3), not to some guru, prophet or mystic in recent centuries! The implications of this are significant, for if a modern so-called *"revelation"* confirms the scriptures it is unnecessary, and if it contradicts them it is wrong!

The Bible has a "Divine Author"—God

The word *"inspiration"* is used in a rather loose sense today, to mean creativity, ingenuity, invention, resourcefulness or a sudden brilliant idea. The biblical meaning portrays God as the divine influence leading to the writing of Scripture. God over-ruled the writing of the Bible so that the words were at the same time fully human and fully from God. The Bible shows that God used the gifts and writing styles of the various writers in a way that has been compared to pouring water into various shaped containers—that is, each prophet had the same divine inspiration but expressed it in their own different words. The Divine nature of the Bible is also shown by the many truths in God's word which we find difficult to accept, concepts which we would never do justice to, if we were left to develop our own religious ideas. The great scientist and inventor Sir Ambrose Fleming said of the Bible, *"Though written by the pens of men, there is abundant evidence that it is not the product of the human mind."*

The 66 books of the Bible, were written over a period of around 1600 years, yet have an amazing unity. Critics who find *"apparent contra-*

Chapter 5

Figure 5.1

Proofs of the Bible's Reliability

Criteria/Test	Evidence	Comment
Supernatural revelation of Scripture	Complete unity of thought throughout the Bible, though written over 1600 years by different penmen. "Christianity is the revelation of God, not the research of man" James S. Stewart.	The Scripture shows evidence it is not man-made by having thoughts and principles that are alien to man: For instance, God dying to save man; Sin; the Trinity. God's truth always agrees with itself as the same Testator made both Testaments.
Authenticity: the Bible is trustworthy and credible	Christ (recognised universally as a great moral teacher) acknowledged the historicity and truth of the Old Testament, and quoted it as God's word, which he could not have done and maintain his integrity if untrue.	Jesus Christ was either a liar, a lunatic or telling the truth when he claimed to be the Son of God. He has no credibility if he is not who he claimed to be See John 10:35, and Luke 24:44, for Jesus' view of God's word.
Genuineness: written by those who claim to be the authors.	The issue of dating and authorship. The evidence that the Scriptures were written by the person the book states, and at the time indicated. Job is in fact probably the oldest book in the Bible.	There have been many works indicating the reliability of the New and Old Testaments. It was once claimed that Moses could not have written the Pentateuch, as writing was not invented. Later research showed writing goes back a long way, and was around in Moses time. He was trained in the Egyptian Court.
Fulfilment of Prophecy	Detailed Old Testament Prophecies of the Messiah, were met by Jesus Christ's birth, life and death. The prophets were enabled to perform miracles to confirm their message.	Prophecy is being able to forth-tell (preach) and foretell (predict the future). Many instances of both occur in the Bible. The writing on the wall is a graphic example: See details of Belshazzar's Feast, Daniel 5.
The Longevity of the Bible	Voltaire (1694-1788) the French writer boasted the Bible would be extinct by 1850. Despite massive criticism and attack it is still the world's best seller. The preservation of the Old Testament Scriptures was tied up with the history of the Jews.	The Bible has survived by God's providence to the present day, and is recognised as one of the greatest pieces of literature. It's spiritual message has helped millions find meaning and purpose.

Proofs of the Bible's Reliability—cont.

Criteria/Test	Evidence	Comment
Supernatural character and divine mission of Christ	"The deity of Christ is the key doctrine of the Scriptures. Reject it and the Bible becomes a jumble of words without any unifying theme. Accept it, and the Bible becomes an intelligible and ordered revealer of God in the person of Jesus Christ." J. Oswald Sanders. If there were no historical and physical resurrection, then there is no Christianity: I Corinthians 15: 14—17.	It has been said of Jesus of Nazareth: "Nineteen centuries have come and gone. Today he is the centrepiece of the human race and leader of the column of progress. I am far within the mark when I say that all the armies that ever marched, all the navies that were ever built, all the parliaments that have ever sat and all that ever reigned, put together, have not affected the life of man upon this earth as powerfully as has … THAT ONE SOLITARY LIFE." Bishop Phillips-Brooks.
Christianity's influence on the world	Millions of changed lives; the influence on education, hospitals, legislation, and care for the needy.	"Christianity is not merely a programme of conduct; it is the power of a new life." B. B. Warfield.

dictions" ignore the point that all verses in Scripture must be understood in the context of the whole passage in which they were written. Otherwise, anyone can take a phrase or word out—and make it mean anything they want! Also, none of these apparent contradictions affect any Christian doctrine. The idea that there are hidden or coded messages written in the Bible (revealed by computer and statistical selection) with prophetic significance clashes head-on with the principles of Bible interpretation given in the Bible itself, *"comparing spiritual things with spiritual."* The clear fallacy of Michael Drosnin's approach in *"The Bible Code"* becomes evident when we realise that any *"coded messages"* so revealed would depend on which Hebrew versions of the original text were used in such attempts. What do we make of his views? Drosnin claims we are now able to read the Bible *"as it was intended to be read."*[1] This is clearly ridiculous! The assertion that the Bible's message could only be understood at the end of the twentieth century, and only with the aid of high-powered computers would deny the teaching that God's word is plain for all to understand throughout the ages.

Biblical criticism

Negative biblical criticism has conducted a wide-scale brainwashing campaign to the effect that the evidence for the unreliability of the Bible is overwhelming. It is sometimes presented as intellectual suicide to believe in biblical inerrancy or the verbal inspiration of the scriptures. The so-called *"errors"* in the Bible, are very difficult to get your hands on! Basically these *"errors"* are only difficulties masquerading as errors. The French Institute in 1800 listed 82 errors that would destroy Christianity. Today, all these *"errors"* have evaporated with new discoveries, linguistic analysis and further thought. See **Endnote: 1.**

The hub of the problem is: When does a difficulty become an error? In 1850 it was regarded as an error to believe in the existence of the Hittites, but by 1900 this was not so, due to archaeological finds. Thus difficulties, not yet solved, are not inconsistent with an infallible Bible. On the authority of Jesus Christ we have the assurance that any such *"errors"* are more apparent than real. Such confidence is also based on the number of significant reversals.

Genesis, for instance, was once thought a collection of unsubstantiated myths. Moses would not be able to write, the Hittites never existed and so the book was cobbled together. This view was held before the explosion of discoveries in the Middle East. Egyptian and Hittite parallels were found in abundance. The Amarna letters, the Nuzi tablets, and the Ugaritic texts revealed personal names and customs. The higher critical movement's fanciful criteria for discerning literary strands was jettisoned by many. People were able to write well before the second millennium B. C. These facts called for a re-evaluation of the so-called *"errors"* in Genesis.

Respect for the integrity of the Scriptures is shown by Augustine (AD 405) who wrote, *"... I have learned to yield this respect and honour only to the canonical books of Scripture: of these alone do I most firmly believe that the authors were completely free from error. And if in these writings I am perplexed by anything which appears to me opposed to truth, I do not hesitate to suppose that either the manuscript is faulty, or the translator has not caught the meaning of what was said, or I myself have failed to understand it."* [2]

The Bible's amazing predictions.

Some of the greatest *'proofs'* of the Bible's reliability are the detailed predictions in the Old Testament of what the Messiah (the Lord Jesus) would be like, where he would be born, how he would be treated, and how he would die; Isaiah chapter 53 for instance. If you have ever listened to Handel's *Messiah,* you will have heard numerous Scriptures quoted which foretell the coming of Jesus Christ. Many of these prophecies were written hundreds of years before Jesus was born, yet they were fulfilled in the minutest detail. These predictions could in no way be faked afterwards. Take the prediction of Christ's birthplace quoted in Matthew 2:4-6 or how the Roman soldiers would gamble for his clothes when he was crucified—Psalm 22:18 and John 19:24. The destruction of Jerusalem and the temple was prophesied by Christ (Matthew 24:15,16). This actually happened in every detail in AD 70.

The Bible is confirmed by archaeology

The critics have said, *"The Bible is not historically correct"*. At one time, for example, scholars claimed that the descriptions of advanced cities in Genesis were fictitious, but archaeological digs have proved these cities existed beyond doubt. Take *Ur of the Chaldees* , for instance. In 1854 and later, mainly between 1922-34, archaeological evidence was discovered that proved that such cities were part of an advanced civilization. Ur was a Sumerian city state with a population of approximately 500,000. The best evidence came from excavating the Ziggurat at Tell el-Muqayyar (the mound of pitch). This great temple devoted to the moon-god, had cylinders of baked clay with cuneiform writing, and the Royal graves which revealed much of the lifestyle of these ancient peoples.

Some of the remains of Ur can be seen in the British Museum. For example, the *Sacred Goat eating leaves* from one such tomb—a figure made of gold plate, lapis lazuli, and shell, which has been dated at least 500 years before Abraham. As a child Abraham lived either in or near a city called Ur (Genesis 11:31, Nehemiah 9:7), although no direct archaeological evidence has been found to prove Abraham's connection with Ur. Contemporary references to King David have now been found. There is much in archaeology which confirms biblical history. For example see the book *The Bible as History* by Werner Keller (1956) published by Hodder and Stoughton.

The Bible is honest

The Bible never *"covers up"* anybody's sins, in either Old or New Testaments. It tells us people's weaknesses and strengths. It tells us both the good **and** bad news, unlike fiction. The Apostle Peter says: *"For we did not follow cleverly invented stories when we told you about the power and coming of our Lord Jesus Christ, but were eye-witnesses of His majesty"* 2 Peter 1:16. (NIV) Flavius Josephus—a first century Jewish historian born in A.D. 37—has a significant passage in his Antiquities, 18.33 *"Now there was about this time Jesus, a wise man, if it be lawful to call him a man; for he was a doer of wonderful works, a teacher of such men as receive the truth with pleasure. He drew over to him many Jews, and also many of the Greeks. This man was the Christ. And when Pilate had condemned him to the cross, upon his impeachment by the principal* *men among us, those who had loved him from the first did not forsake him, for he appeared to them alive on the third day, the divine prophets having spoken these and thousands of other wonderful things about him. And even now, the race of Christians, so named from him, has not died out.*" Thus even the non-Christian Josephus at points recognised the facts Scripture records. This passage has been challenged as containing "*interpolations*" but all copies of integrity and antiquity possess it. Nobody challenges or doubts the testimony of events recorded by Tacitus (Roman historian, born 52-54 A.D., died after 117 A.D.)) or Pliny (Roman official, 62-113 A.D.) who wrote a letter to the emperor Trajan.

Cornelius Tacitus refers to Christ's death and the existence of Christians at Rome, whom Nero blamed for the Great Fire of Rome. He records, "*Hence to suppress the rumour, he [Nero] falsely charged with the guilt, and punished with the most terrible tortures, the persons commonly called Christians, who were hated for their enormities. Christus, the founder of the name, was put to death by Pontius Pilate, procurator of Judea in the reign of Tiberius ...* " (Annals, XV. 44). Pliny the younger (Plinius Secundus) wrote to the emperor for advice on how to treat Christians. He wrote, "*They affirmed, however, that the whole of their guilt, or their error, was that they were in the habit of meeting on a certain fixed day before it was light, when they sang in alternate verse a hymn to Christ as to a god, and bound themselves to a solemn oath, not to any wicked deeds, but never to commit any fraud when they should be called upon to deliver it up*" (Epistles, X. 96). Other secular sources confirm the historicity of the New Testament accounts.

The Bible's appeal and survival

The Bible is still the world's most popular book. It has been the world's best seller for centuries, and translated into more languages than any other book. It remains the most attacked book in history, but it still stands triumphant over all attempts to destroy it. The Bible is the first religious book to be taken into outer space (on microfilm). It was the first book read in space describing the origin of the earth. The American astronauts read Genesis chapter 1:1—" *In the beginning God ...*" Just think: Voltaire, the great French thinker, boasted that the Bible would be extinct by 1850! All the New Testament books are now generally admitted by academics to be written in the first century. Some of these scholars are radical in their theology (e.g. Adolf Harnack; John A. T. Robinson—of the *"God is dead"* controversy), but despite this they have been conservative in their historical judgements. Robinson claimed that the New Testament documents were probably written before A.D. 70. [3]

Taste and see ...

We sometimes say *"the proof of the pudding is in the eating"*. There is the story of the tramp who called out to the preacher, *"Christianity has been around for 2,000 years, and look at the state of the world!"* The preacher replied, *"Water has been around for 2,000 years—and look at the state of your neck!"* When the message of the Bible—salvation and new life through faith in Jesus Christ—is put into practice, instead of just being admired as a good ethical code, its power can be seen and felt. The proof of Christianity has been seen in millions upon millions of truly changed lives. Thousands of good causes to improve the state of society—including hospitals, education, care of the needy—were all started by Christians.

The divine authority of the Bible is found within the Bible itself—its profound teaching, its consistent and unique message, its integrity plainly mark it out as God's book. If the message changes lives, and it is clearly not fiction, it is surely worth some of your time to read this *"Book of books"*, before you dismiss it as a book of outdated myths. C. H. Spurgeon told of a poor woman who was challenged by an agnostic to prove that the Bible was the Word of God. She pointed to the sun and said, *"Can you prove that there is a sun in the sky?"*. The unbeliever said, *"Of course, the proof is that it warms me and I see its light"*. *"That is it,"* she replied, *"and the best proof that this Book is the Word of God is that it warms and lights my soul!"*

Conclusion: the Word alone

Whilst this appeal to subjective experience is worthwhile, it should be remembered that truth is addressed to the whole person: heart (emotions) mind (rationality) and will (volitional). The great Christian philosopher Herman Dooyeweerd has said: *"Human reason is not an independent substance: much rather it is an instrument. The I is the hidden player, who avails himself of it. And the central motive that rules both human thought and the human ego itself, is of a central religious nature.*

The question: 'What is man? Who is he?', cannot be answered by man himself. But it has been answered by God's Word-revelation, which uncovers the religious root and centre of human nature in its creation, fall into sin and redemption by Jesus Christ. Man lost true self-knowledge since he lost true knowledge of God. But all idols of human selfhood, which man in his apostasy has devised, break down when they are confronted with the Word of God, which unmasks their vanity and noth-ingness. It is this Word alone, which by its radical grip can bring about a real reformation of our view of man ... and the temporal world; and such an inner reformation is the very opposite of the scholastic device of accommodation." [4]

Scholars of the higher critical movement have thought it necessary to *"accommodate to the findings of scientific research"* when what is in doubt is their ability to comprehend that a Supernatural God can do amazing things. The miraculous element that they find most offensive, is the very raison d'etre for the Christian faith. For a message which can be fully understood by modern man is not the Christianity of the New Testament. Take away the fact of the sign miracles performed by Christ or his resurrection, and then the Christian faith has no more claim to solve the world's problems than any other teaching or philosophy.

References:

1   **M. Drosnin** (1996) *The Bible Code*, Weidenfeld & Nicholson, p. 25.
2   **P. Schaff** (1996) *The Nicene and Post-Nicene Fathers First Series* Vol. 1,
    The Confessions & letters of Augustine, Ages Software, Albany, Oregon, p. 697.
3   See **J. A. T. Robinson** (1976) *Redating the New Testament*, S. C. M. Press, London.
4   **H. Dooyeweerd** (1965) *In the Twilight of Western Thought*, The Craig Press,
    Nutley, New Jersey, Library of Congress No. LC 60-6645, pp. 149-5.

Further Reading:

C. Blomberg (1987) *The Historical Reliability of the Gospels*, I.V.P., Leicester, ISBN 0-85110-774-5.

J. McDowell (1979) *Evidence that demands a verdict*, Here's Life Publishers, Inc., ISBN 0- 918956-57-9.

R. Pache (1974) *The Inspiration and Authority of Scripture*, Moody Press, Chicago.

E. J. Young (1972) *Thy Word is Truth*, Banner of Truth, London (now Edinburgh).

Endnote: 1.

Bible dates particularly in the Old Testament have often proved a puzzle. Professor Edwin Thiele has discovered the basic methods employed by early Hebrew scribes in calculating and recording dates. By following these methods he produced a pattern of Hebrew chronology that not only agrees with the Biblical account but also with the historical dates obtained from the records of Israel's neighbours. This helped to resolve the apparent conflict of the dates of the ancient Babylonian and Assyrian empires, and the Hebrew Kings. See **Edwin R. Thiele** (1965) *The Mysterious Numbers of the Hebrew Kings*, Paternoster Press, Exeter, Devon.

Key text

2 Tim 3:16 *"All Scripture is given by inspiration of God, and is profitable for doctrine, for reproof, for correction, for instruction in righteousness."*

Questions for Further Study

1 Would it be possible to find God without an inspired revelation?
2 How do we know Jesus Christ trusted the entire Old Testament?
3 It has been said, *"A half truth masquerading as the whole truth, is an untruth."* How would this apply to the Old and New Testaments? How do we know the apostles Peter and Paul accepted the New Testament letters as scripture?
4 Why is 2 Timothy 3: 16 a pivotal verse for one's approach to the Bible?
5 How would you argue that "new revelations" are unnecessary?
6 In what way would you use the illustration of filling water vessels to explain the nature of revelation, and to show such inspiration is not some kind of mechanical dictation from God to man.
7 Do you think Ambrose Fleming, a Christian man of science, was correct to say there

is abundant evidence the Bible is not just human ingenuity?

8 It is often said, *"a text without a context, is a pretext"*. How do we correctly interpret Scripture?

9 How would you argue Drosnin's Bible Code is fallacious?

10 What happened to the claimed 82 Bible errors listed in 1800?

11 How would listening to the Messiah help you explain fulfilled prophecy?

12 List three fulfilled New Testament prophecies.

13 What archaeological evidence confirms the existence of advanced cities (like Ur) in ancient times.

14 What grounds are there for accepting the integrity of the Bible?

15 Do secular historians record Christ's existence?

16 What are the amazing facts about the Bible?

17 Do you think the Bible is a "Wonderful book"? If so, why?

18 By when were most of the New Testament documents written?

19 Why does man need God's Word-revelation?

Food for Thought

* "The Bible is truth given by God. The writers themselves claim that this truth was received by them, that is was given to them. They do not say that after much research and endeavour and seeking they arrived at it, and shouted their 'Eureka'." D. Martyn Lloyd-Jones, *The Approach to Truth: Scientific and Religious.*

6 : Science or Scientism?

"My suspicion is that the Universe is not only queerer than we suppose, but queerer than we can suppose." J. B. S. Haldane

Some scientists today are totally committed to empiricism (e.g. logical positivists). They believe if something cannot be defined scientifically and verified by experiment, it is insignificant or inconsequential. Science, however, has no in-built value system, it cannot determine its own worth and at best discovers only relative truth. The nature of true science presupposes a universal law giver, who has made such research valuable. It is at this foundational level that there is a "Christian" view of science. The valid discoveries scientists make are "thinking God's thoughts after Him" but rely on the scientific method. To be truly scientific, events or experiments must be repeatable. The role of science and scripture is reviewed, arguing that scientists must admit the possibility of change and re-evaluation of their theories or models. The Big Bang origin of the universe is explained and evaluated in the light of Hawking's and Dawkins' comments. Paradigm shifts and their implications help illuminate the creation versus evolution models. The desire of some scientists to achieve finality and authority in their pronouncements can lead to a false deification of science, so that it becomes scientism rather than true science. The Christian view of science is contrasted with the intellectual schizophrenia exhibited by some modern scientific philosophy.

Science fact and Fiction
The ability of modern science and the media to create *"realistic simulations"* of *"lost worlds"* or use virtual reality to simulate actual conditions (like weather systems) has incredible possibilities. It can help people see how to react as if they were in an actual situation (such as piloting a plane, or learning surgery) but without any damage! Such technology helps to blur the line between scientific fact and fiction. Living in a technological

and scientific age has led some thinkers to a philosophy of total commitment to empiricism. This affects their view of how we know things and what can be believed. (See **Endnote** 1)

Logical positivists, such as the late Bertrand Russell, thought that if science cannot give the answer then it was a non-question. Science is given pride of place and is regarded as the only valid source of knowledge. Science is thought to be able to answer everything. Logical positivism is the belief that something is nothing but the scientific description of it. For instance: *"We are nothing but atoms and molecules."* Yet even common sense says the whole is more than the sum of its parts! Bertrand Russell pontificated: *"Whatever knowledge is attainable, must be attained by scientific means; and what science cannot discover, mankind cannot know."*[1] Richard Dawkins assumes: *"Truth means scientific truth"*[2] which results in science becoming the ultimate test of belief. This is not true science, but scientism. The evolutionary theory per se cannot be used to prop up metaphysical systems, despite the claims of scientists like Dawkins. Science is no more and no less than a human attempt to describe the relationships that exist between material components of the Universe. (See **Endnote** 2)

Logical positivists

Russell's and Dawkins' views are derived from their holding to a logical positivist philosophy. This believes in direct observation so that ethical or theological statements become meaningless. For instance belief in God would only be acceptable if you could find a scientific test. However, science itself is based on certain assumptions that cannot be verified by direct observation. For example, the belief that natural laws do not change over time. Thus *"those things only are meaningful that can be proved by direct observation"* is not true by definition or even meaningful in its own terms. In contrast, Professor Behe proposes an *'open approach'* in science. He says: *"In a very real sense, the separateness of the spheres of science versus philosophy and religion is as it should be."* He continues: *"To a large extent people of different philosophical and theological bents can also agree on scientific theories, such as gravitation or plate tectonics or evolution, to organise the data (even if the theories are ultimately incorrect.)"* Behe goes on to advocate tolerance of pluralistic approaches to science: *"But the fundamental philosophical principles that underlie reality and the theological principles, or lack of principles that can be garnered from philosophy and historical experience are at root chosen by the individual. A man or woman must be free to search for the good, the true, and the beautiful."*[3]

From a Christian viewpoint, science is founded upon religious and philosophical assumptions, and the "two spheres" cannot be separated. Despite the fact that a theory can organise data, if that theory is wrong, it will pervert the data. If it is true that man has been given free choice, it does not mean any one theory is as good as another. This is a basic assumption of most postmodern pluralism. As scientists often claim to be *"neutral"* in their scientific endeavours, Behe reports an alarming comment of Dawkins showing that such claimed neutrality is often a myth: *"Richard Dawkins has written that anyone who denies evolution is either 'ignorant, stupid or insane (or wicked—but I'd rather not consider that.')" Dawkins has claimed that Darwin made it possible to be an "intellectually fulfilled atheist."* Professor Behe comments: *"The failure of Darwin's theory on the molecular scale may cause him to feel less fulfilled, but no one should try to stop him from continuing his search."*[4] It is interesting to note here, that there is a strong probability—i.e. good evidence—that Charles Darwin (1809-1882) himself regretted publishing his ideas. His book on the *Origin of Species by means of Natural Selection* (1859) is dubbed, *"the book that shook the world."* There is some evidence Darwin may have converted to Christianity in 1881. In his lifetime he wrote, *"in my most extreme fluctuations I have never been an atheist in the sense of denying the existence of a God."* (See E. K. Victor Pearce (1998) *Science* , Volume 1, Eagle Publications, ISBN 0—86347 263 X, p. 155, 162-3 and this issue is dealt with in detail by Malcolm Bowden (1998) *True Science Agrees with the Bible*, Sovereign Publications,Bromley, Kent, ISBN 0 9506042 4 0, pp. 259-276.) Certainly Darwin was open-minded enough to give financial support to the South American Missionary Society—for around 15 years.

Clearly, if there is no God, then Richard Dawkins is free to pursue his naturalistic theories. However, if the biblical God exists (see Romans chapter 1), then any scientist who holds down (verse 18) or *"suppresses"* the truth (as one holds down someone beneath water to force him to

Figure 6.1 Sample of Pioneer Scientists, also professing Christians

Charles Babbage 1792-1871
Babbage was a mathematician and inventor. He designed the first automatic computer with storage and retrieval of data. He contributed to the Bridgewater Treatises, a series of apologetic writings, including a mathematical analysis of Biblical miracles.

Sir William Herschel 1783-1822
A keen astronomer, who discovered the planet Uranus. He thought that, 'the undevout astronomer must be mad'.

Francis Bacon (1561-1626)
The father of the scientific method with its systematic method of investigation and experiment. He understood that 'There are two books laid before us to study ... first, the volume of the Scriptures, which reveal the will of God; then the volume of the Creatures, which express His power.'

Johannes Kepler (1571-1630)
Kepler formulated the three laws of planetary motion. Kepler believed science was 'thinking God's thoughts after Him.' He looked for order in complexity. He correctly claimed the earth went around the Sun. In so doing, he undermined the established church view based on Greek tradition, not the Bible.

Robert Boyle (1627-1691)
Boyle is known as the founder of modern chemistry. He was also a linguist and studied the Bible in its original languages. He was offered the Presidency of the Royal Society in 1681, but declined it. He wrote a Discourse of Things Above Reason (1689).

Joseph Lister (1827-1912)
Established antiseptic surgery. He invented the carbolic steam spray, which saved many lives. Lister noted that he was 'a believer in the fundamental doctrines of Christianity.'

Michael Faraday (1791-1867)
Faraday was the founder of electro-magnetic theory. His studies were motivated by a desire to find the laws of God that governed the universe. He declined the Presidency of the Royal Society.

Samuel Morse (1791-1872)
The inventor of the electric telegraph. Morse's first transmitted message was "What hath God wrought!" Morse was a strong supporter of Sunday Schools and mission work.

These pioneers of science all had an unshakable faith in the God of the Bible and were professing Christians. They made tremendous contributions to scientific advance, believing the Bible encouraged them to strive for wisdom, truth, knowledge and understanding of the works of God. Further reference to similar pioneer scientists is found in Men of Science—Men of God, by H. M. Morris (1990) Master Books, El Cajon, CA 92022, ISBN 0-89051-080-6. Contemporary scientists (21 in number) are found in Scientists Who Believe (1986) edited by E. C. Barrett & D. Fisher, Scripture Press Foundation, Bucks, HP6 6JQ, ISBN 0 94651509 3.

drown) despite God clearly revealing the truth about himself through creation (including molecular genetics!) (verse 20) will ultimately experience the *"wrath of God"* and must be opposed with the gospel of Christ (verse 16). It must also be remembered that those who approve of those who do such things are included in God's anathema (verse 32). Calvin used the term science to cover systematised knowledge both in the natural sciences and humanities as well. Indeed, he would include the sciences of theology and philosophy. He noted that these *"scientiae"* are designed to glorify God, for *"in attesting of His wondrous wisdom, both the heavens and the earth present us with innumerable proofs … proofs which astronomy, medicine and all the natural sciences are designed to illustrate"* (Institutes 1: 5: 2).

Textbook of science?

Whilst the Bible does not provide a detailed scientific explanation of everything in the Universe (in the often quoted phrase *"is not a textbook of science"*), it is still correct when it touches upon matters of science. For instance, in *Psalm 8* David marvels at the vastness of the Universe in relation to humankind, long before anyone had invented the radio-telescope or landed on the moon! Science can never be really certain about origins. To be *"scientifically proved"* an experiment must be repeatable. No human can claim to have seen the origin of the universe—let alone be able to repeat it, and therefore no one has any right to say they have disproved the Bible.

Professor G. Clark (philosopher) has pointed out: *"Finally, to show the uselessness of science outside its own restricted sphere, science cannot determine its own value. No doubt, science enables man to dominate nature. By science, bombs are made, and cancer may soon be cured. Most people think that bombs and medicine are good to have. But there is not an experiment that proves their goodness. They are undoubtedly 'good for' something; they are effective means to an end. But can experimentation demonstrate that either the destruction of cities or the extension of life is good? The value of science depends on the value of life; but the value of life, when suicide is a possible choice, and therefore the value of science itself, must be determined by some sort of general philosophy, of which science is neither the whole nor the base, but only a subsidiary part. And it is my conviction that the best general philosophy, indeed the only position that satisfactorily manages all these problems, is the revelational philosophy of Christian theism."* 5

Absolute and relative truth

The scientist does not claim to have absolute truth (which is infallible, and divinely revealed). Scientists recognize that what (s)he believes is at best relative truth. (**See Endnote: 3**) No law or principle of science can be regarded as absolutely proved. Science deals with changing truth or relative truth which is altered as the boundaries of knowledge are pushed out by new discoveries. The Bible deals with divine truth which is known as unchanging, or absolute truth.

The Bible clearly shows its divine inspiration. The oldest book in the Bible, *Job*, says *"He hangs the earth upon nothing"* (Job chapter 26:7). There is no primitive idea of the earth being supported on the back of elephants standing on a giant turtle! Or take the rules set down on cleanliness given in Deuteronomy 14:21 and 23:13, long before people understood anything about invisible germs that cause disease. This kind of evidence points towards the divine authorship of the Bible—as such knowledge of the earth's shape or need for hygiene rules had yet to be discovered or understood.

Scientific theories are simply the best representation of reality we have, given the present level of knowledge. Sir James Jeans cautioned, *"Science should leave off making pronouncements: the river of knowledge has too often turned back on itself."*6 Science enables us to understand the world better, and so harness its potential for our own uses. Despite this, Erwin Schrodinger states: *"I am very astonished that the scientific picture of the real world around me is very deficient. It gives a lot of factual information, puts all our experience in a magnificently consistent order, but it is ghastly silent about all and sundry that is really near to our heart ...... it knows nothing of beautiful and ugly, good or bad, God and eternity. Science sometimes pretends to answer questions in these domains, but the answers are very often so silly that we are not inclined to take them seriously."*7

Science can never pontificate about origins. Christian men and women of science are convinced that this is God's Universe they are investigating. Some wonder if there is a *"Christian"* form of science. Historian of science, R. Hookyaas explains that to look for such a thing is rather like a man who looks for his spectacles while they are already on his nose! Modern science and technology are to a great extent the fruits of Christianity. The scientific method is the same for either Christians or non-Christians. The success of modern science is, however, due to its borrowed capital. The belief in a God who created and designed an ordered universe (which can be studied by the scientific method) prompted men like Isaac Newton (thought by Einstein to be the greatest scientist) to search for certain scientific laws to explain this order. Thus science must find its ultimate roots in biblical truth. See **Figure 6.1, Scientific Pioneers**—to note just a few of many scientists who based their scientific outlook on man's spiritual mandate to subdue the earth.

Big Bang and scientific models

Today many scientists think that a sound description of the Universe from the time when it was only a fraction of a second old to the present day, is that the Universe was an incredibly dense mass, so small that it could pass through the eye of a needle! From that point it expanded very rapidly in what is commonly called the *"Big Bang"*. Astrophysicists tell us that within the first thousand seconds of the expansion, hydrogen and helium were formed. Over the next billion years, clouds of hydrogen gas collapsed under gravity to form galaxies of a hundred billion stars. Stars continued the process of *"creation"* as they progressed from birth to death.

According to the currently accepted big bang theory, the universe originated from 10 and 20 billion years ago, and has been expanding ever since. Cosmologists tell us that the future of the universe is uncertain! There are at least three possibilities: the expansion may be finite (**closed universe**) with the universe eventually contracting back in upon itself. Again, the expansion might be unlimited (**open universe**)—in which case the universe will continue expanding forever. The borderline case between these two possibilities is known as a **flat universe**, balanced on a gravitational knife edge between the two possibilities—teetering on the brink of being open and closed. (**See Endnote: 4**) One simple way to understand the concept of an expanding universe is to draw dots, representing galaxies on a balloon. As the balloon is inflated, each dot moves away from all the others. To a person viewing the universe from a galaxy, all other galaxies would seem to be receding. The distant galaxies seem to be moving away quicker than the nearer ones, which is known as Hubble's Law. Some cosmologists think that this expansion will continue for ever, whereas others think at a certain point the universe will begin contracting under its own gravity in a *"big crunch"*.

A Brief History of Time

In modern times another distinguished theoretical physicist, Stephen Hawking—of Cambridge University, in his *A Brief History of Time* seeks to give a scientific understanding of the origin of the Universe, but does not answer the question "Why?" Hawking has tried to unite general relativity with quantum theory. His research indicates that general relativity, if true, supports the big-bang theory of the creation of the universe. Hawking argued initially that the big bang arose from a singularity, or a point of infinite distortion of space and time. Later he refined this concept by viewing all such theories as secondary attempts to describe a reality in which ideas like "singularities" have no meaning. Also, a concept of the universe where space and time form a closed surface without any boundary. He suggested, in other words, that the universe had no cause in space or time. Quantum theory deals with events that do not have causes, so applying this to the Universe removes the need for a first cause.

Hawking's model of the universe has important philosophical implications. He is saying that it is possible to develop a mathematical model that describes the Universe completely in terms of the known laws of science, without any need to invoke special conditions even at the moment of creation. It is thought by cosmologists, that quantum physics is the key to unlock the last secrets of the universe and to explain both its beginning and end. John Gribbon (Science writer) makes this quite clear: *"Our search for the Big Bang, and back of the Big Bang to the moment of creation itself, is over. Hawking's universe holds out the prospect of combining General Relativity and cosmology in one grand theory of creation, and tells us that we already know all of the fundamental laws of physics. There is no need to invoke miracles, or new physics, to explain where the Universe came from. Hawking himself foresees an 'end to theoretical physics' in the sense that a satisfactory unified theory of everything, perhaps based on N = 8 supergravity, may be in sight and could be reached before the end of this century. There would still, of course, be plenty of work for physicists left to do, such as filling in the details of the evolution of the Universe. Perhaps it would be more accurate to say that Hawking has already indicated an end, not to physics but to metaphysics. It is now possible to give a good scientific answer to the question 'Where do we come from?' without invoking either God or special boundary conditions for the Universe at the moment of creation. As of the Vatican conference of 1981, it is the metaphysicians who are out of a job. Everything else shrinks into insignificance alongside such a claim and the end of the road for metaphysics certainly seems to be a good place to end this book."*[8]

Despite this, Hawking desires to discover a *"theory of everything"*, which might provide answers to the *"Why?"* questions. Stephen Hawking comments: *"If we do discover a complete theory, it should in time be understandable in broad principle by everyone, not just a few scientists. Then we shall all, ... be able to take part in the discussion of why it is that we and the Universe exist. If we find the answer to that, it would be the ultimate triumph of human reason—for then we would know the mind of God."*[9] This comment clearly implied that Hawkings thinks we have no way of knowing the *"mind of God"* now!

Professor Richard Dawkins picks up this theme of physicists and their *"mystical beliefs"*. He comments: *"Modern physicists sometimes wax a bit mystical when they contemplate questions such as why the big bang happened when it did, why the laws of physics are these laws and not those laws, why the universe exists at all, and so on. Sometimes physicists may resort to saying that there is an inner core of mystery that we don't understand, and perhaps never can; and they may then say that perhaps this inner core of mystery is another name for God. Or in Stephen Hawking's words, if we understand these things, we shall perhaps 'know the mind of God'.*

The trouble is that God in this sophisticated, physicist's sense bears absolutely no resemblance to the God of the Bible or any other religion. If a physicist says God is another name for Planck's constant, or God is a superstring, we should take it as a picturesque, metaphorical way of saying that the nature of superstrings or the value of Planck's constant is a profound mystery. It has obviously not the smallest connection with a being capable of forgiving sins, a being who might listen to prayers, who cares whether or not the Sabbath begins at 5pm or 6pm, whether your bow is accurately aimed towards Mecca, whether you wear a veil or have a bit of arm showing; and no connection whatever with a being capable of imposing a death penalty on His son to expiate the sins of the world before and after he was born ."[10]

Dawkins is correct in his view from a logical viewpoint, as this view of God is only the projection of man's mind—a *"god of the gaps"*. He further cautions against tying the big bang theory with what he terms the *"myth"* of Genesis: *"The same is true of attempts to identify the big bang of modern cosmology with the myth of Genesis. There is only an utterly trivial resemblance between the sophisticated, esoteric conceptions of modern physics, and the creation myths of the Babylonians and the Jews that we have inherited."*[11]

Knots untied, or knots tied tighter?

Is the Big -Bang theory the way God did it? John Whitcomb (Professor of Old Testament) warns us: *"Time and time again, Christians have been pressured into adopting some popular scientific theory only to discover, to their sorrow and embarrassment, that they have succeeded in 'harmonizing' Scripture to a scientific concept that was proven to be erroneous after all. As someone has well said, the person who becomes wedded to the scientific cosmology of one generation will find himself widowed in the next. Man's understanding of the universe continues to change as he learns more and more of its intricate and marvellous structure; but God's Word never changes, for it is the direct product of an infinite and unchanging God .*"[12] Dr. Whitcomb has hit the nail on the head, for those who would tie the Gordian knot of Scripture and a specific scientific model of origins. It is impossible to tie together absolute truth (which is supernatural) with relative truth (with its scientific explanations) without generating grave problems. It is rather like trying to tie together steel cable and a silk thread! This is not contrasting true and false, scripture and science, but saying how can an essentially supernatural explanation tie in with a naturalistic scientific one?

An instance of this is given by Professor Neil Turok (a colleague of Stephen Hawking at Cambridge) who explained their latest theory that the universe began as an *"instanton"* an exploding cocktail of space, time, matter and gravity. He suggests, *"Many people ask whether this has implications for the existence of a creator or divine intervention. Personally I don't think it does. But if a divine being wanted to create a universe, the simplest way to do it would be to use our instanton ."*[13] The fallible scientific deductions which we make from our fallible scientific observations form knowledge that is *"relative"* in the sense that it is discovered by fallible creatures, and as such does not carry a guarantee of truth from the all-knowing and truthful God. Although we strive for comprehensive scientific knowledge it is never attainable. For every question scientists answer, the more they realise there are new questions to be answered. There is another layer of truth to be uncovered. Whitcomb (whilst clearly aware of the dangers) does not deny the possibility of using Scripture (absolute truth) to build a basic foundation of the earth's history (e.g. the creation model) which may have scientific observations constructed upon it. Indeed, Whitcomb elsewhere (e.g. *The Genesis Flood*) takes precisely this approach of combining the absolute with the relative in a *"creation model"*.

Dr Whitcomb (as a theologian) is merely challenging the right of science to pontificate about origins. He thinks that relative scientific knowledge should not be allowed to shape the absolute, so that harmonious interpretations are found. He agrees it is possible to have a relationship between absolute and relative knowledge. This is the reason there is a distinction between Creation (based on pure Scripture) and creationism (mixing science and Scripture) and accounts for problems of whether the Big Bang, Plate tectonics, Black holes, etc. are valid, when they are primarily scientific rather than Scriptural explanations of phenomena.

Certainly there are grounds for challenging the accepted scientific status quo, but this can also be done by exposing the false naturalistic assumptions of secular scientists, and by evaluation of any scientific model to see if it is internally coherent, alongside alternative explanations. After all, scientists mainly replace their speculative theories whilst adding to the overall data. The view of the objectivity and autonomy of observational evidence for scientific theories has itself been challenged, as facts are selected by scientists as significant, if they confirm their presuppositional frame of reference.

Paradigm shifts

What does one do, for example, if one has irrevocably tied Scripture to a specific scientific viewpoint (e.g. Big Bang) if new and incompatible data is discovered, or a major *"paradigm shift"*? The term *"paradigm"* is a hotly contested term, which has been applied in all sorts of ways that the originator (Kuhn) never intended, and which (arguably) are neither credible nor based upon evidence. The paradigm is one (debatable) way of interpreting the history of science. A paradigm is a set of universally recognised scientific achievements that for a time provide problems and solutions to a body of users. The paradigm is a body of presuppositions which make science possible. Without paradigms all data are equally relevant and equally meaningless. A paradigm is an accepted model or pattern which establishes what shall be regarded as science. The paradigm refuses to tolerate data which do not conform to the presuppositions. A paradigm is thus a criterion for choosing problems, and paradigms are inescapable for man.[14] (**See Endnote: 5**)

Dead men do not bleed

In a somewhat amusing story John Warlock Montgomery tells how prejudice can so colour our perceptions that we cannot see the wood for the trees, and this clearly has a relevance for scientific investigation and paradigms! *"Once upon a time there was a man who thought he was dead. His concerned wife and friends sent him to the friendly neighbourhood psychiatrist. The psychiatrist determined to cure him by convincing him of one fact that contradicted his belief that he was dead. The psychiatrist decided to use the simple truth that dead men do not bleed. He put his patient to work reading medical texts, observing autopsies, etc. After* weeks of effort, the patient finally said, 'All right, all right! You've convinced me. Dead men do not bleed.' Whereupon the psychiatrist stuck him in the arm with a needle, and the blood flowed. The man looked down with a contorted, ashen face and cried: 'Good Heavens, Dead men bleed after all!'"

Montgomery goes on to comment astutely: "This parable illustrates that if you hold unsound presuppositions with sufficient tenacity, facts will make no difference at all, and you will be able to create a world of your own, totally unrelated to reality and totally incapable of being touched by reality. Such a condition (which the philosophers call solipsistic, psychiatrists call autistically psychotic, and lawyers call insane) is tantamount to death because connection with the living world is severed. The man in the parable not only thought he was dead, but in a very real sense, he was dead because facts no longer meant anything to him."[15]

Objectivity and relativism

Science writer Peter Lipton says: "The objectivity of evidence has been rejected on the grounds that scientific evidence is inevitably contaminated by scientific theories. It is not just that scientists tend to see what they want to see, but that scientific observation is only possible in the context of particular theoretical presuppositions. Observation is 'theory-laden.' .... If the nature of the evidence changes as scientific theories change, and the evidence is our only access to the empirical facts, then perhaps the facts change too. This is relativism about science, whose most influential recent proponent is Thomas Kuhn. ... Although metaphysically radical, Kuhn's account of science is in one respect epistemologically conservative. For him, the causes of scientific change are almost exclusively intellectual and internal to a narrow community of scientific specialists.

There are, however, other recent forms of relativism about science that reject this internalist perspective, insisting that the major causes of scientific change include social, cultural, and political factors that extend well beyond the confines of the laboratory. Since there is no reason to believe that these highly variable factors are conducive to the discovery of the truth, this 'social constructivist' view of science is perhaps even more hostile to scientific realism than is the Kuhnian position."[16] Lipton does not, however, define what he means by *'scientific realism'*. He possibly means that if a theory leads to correct predictions, or enables an experiment or machine to work, then it is pragmatically valid, and scientifically real—in that down to earth engineering sense.

Present 'state of play'

Peter Lipton concludes: *"Scientific realists have not taken challenges lying down. Some have accused the relativists of adopting what amounts to a self-refuting position. If, as claimed, there is no such thing as truth, then that claim cannot be true either. Realists have also questioned the philosophy of language that lies behind Kuhn's claim that successive theories refer to different entities and phenomena, and also argued that the social constructivists have exaggerated the long-term influence of noncognitive factors on the development of science. But the debate over whether science is a process of discovery or invention is as old as the history of science and philosophy, and there is no firm resolution in sight. Here, as elsewhere, philosophers have been much more successful at revealing difficulties than at resolving them. Fortunately, an appreciation of how scientific practice resists explanation may itself illuminate the nature of science."*[17]

Eileen Barker (sociologist and Dean of London School of Economics) showed optimism that science will attain this elusive ideal of *"the truth"* She stated: *"It is hard not to believe that modern science is moving towards a greater understanding of our origins. The theoretical rigour and practical impact of much modern knowledge makes it ridiculous to adopt an utterly relativistic approach to science. We can see more areas in which old ideas have been replaced by new ones so that it looks as though we are progressing towards 'the truth'."* [18] Barker then cautioned, *"However, it should also be recognized that, when we look at the many social uses to which the concepts of science are put, there is no guarantee that there will be a steady convergence towards truth. At the popular, and perhaps not infrequently at the academic level, the creation of knowledge may be supported or rationalized by scientism rather than by empirical fact, and then we shall observe not a convergence towards one clear truth but rather a divergence of beliefs which bear more relationship to the needs, interests and circumstances of those who adopt them than they do to any objective reality in the natural world. If we are to understand what is accepted as scientifically proven truth in any particular context, and the ways in which such truth is used for the furtherance of people's ideological interests, we shall need an improved sociology of knowledge as well as a clearer understanding of the epistemological status of the differing claims. The debate between evolution and creation science provides just one area within which the phenomena of social adaptation, curiously mixed with the scientific quest, are manifested. Perhaps through the pursuit of such darknesses we shall, eventually, glimpse more light."*[19]

Pressure to conform

Dr. Whitcomb criticises those who neglect these issues and other epistemological considerations. He continues to challenge those scientists who hold to a great divide between the light thrown on origins by Scripture and scientific truth: *"It is not surprising that Christians who prefer to accept the Biblical doctrine of origins find themselves under continual pressure, not only from secular scientists, but also from evangelical scientists who adhere tenaciously to the double-revelation theory."*[20] The term *"double-revelation theory"* refers to those who hold to God's revelation in nature and scripture as two completely different autonomous spheres. This is usually typically signified by the phrase : *"Scripture tells us the 'Why?' of creation, while science tells us the 'How?'"*

Whitcomb illustrates this by referring to Kulp's objections. *"For example, Dr. J. Laurence Kulp, ... feels that it is the height of presumption for Christians to call into question a theory of the origin of the universe that the majority of modern scientists accept: It may be theologically undesirable for those who hold a particular doctrine of creation to accept the "hot hydrogen hypothesis" of the origin of the universe, but certainly it is not for a theologian to reject the hypothesis that is held in one form or another by practically all scientists in cosmology on scientific grounds .... Apparently we are to let the theologians pontificate all knowledge of the physical world and dare not investigate any of it. The first stage of all scientific investigation is guessing (forming hypotheses) prior to testing. Why should the first stage of the created universe be any less subject to study than any other part of history? How the acceptance of a particular theory of the first stage of the universe involves one in total evolution is not understandable."*[21]

Evolutionary versus Creation models

Nevertheless, Cosmology is a different kettle of fish from the rest of physics, in that it deals with a unique event which happened in the past. It goes without saying that astronomers cannot get a Universe into their laboratory and set off a Big Bang to study it! Galileo noted that the purpose of the Bible is to *"teach us how one goes to heaven, not how heaven goes"*. There is a need for scientific discovery—including outer space—but due to the nature of true science, and despite scientists' desire for certainty, science can never pontificate about origins. Patrick Moore comments: *"On the other hand, this does not prove that the universe began with a 'big bang' and is now evolving toward eventual death. It has been suggested that the universe is in an oscillating condition, and that the cycle has been repeated many times. At present, the galaxies are in a state of spreading-out (assuming, of course, that we accept the evidence of the red shifts in their spectra), but it may be that in the future this mutual recession will cease, and that the galaxies will come together once more before embarking upon a new phase of expansion. But we are still uncertain of our ground, and the discovery of the quasars has shown again how little we really know. Quasars, indeed, may provide us with vital clues, whether they really are immensely remote and super-luminous (as is the official view so far) or whether they will turn out to be relatively local. Far from saying the last word, we cannot be sure that we have said even the first. It seems that our own galaxy, at least, must die; but men of the Earth will have vanished from the scene long before the end of the story. The Sun will eventually become more luminous, and there must come a time when our world will be too hot to support life. Even if it is not destroyed, it will become a scorched globe devoid of air and water, and all living creatures will have perished from its surface."*[22]

The same problem pervades the geological arena. Geologists can fail to emphasize the problems facing historical geology, especially the non-repeatability of pre-historic events.[23] One can agree with those who believe in general in the uniformity of natural laws, but not necessarily in the uniformity of rates of erosion or deposition—a point recognised by Dr S. Gould, Harvard Professor of Geology.[24] As Historical Geology allows an exceptionally high proportion of hypotheses which concern the very constitution and structure of its explanations, great humility is called for: science observes, records and studies but cannot proceed with certainty from effects to causes.

Apotheosis of science?

Why should naturalistic scientists get so excited, if creationists using scientific evidence propose a different model of origins? It has been such apparent conflicts (e.g. between the Catastrophists and Uniformitarian geologists) that have sparked off new research, and enabled new lines of investigation, as long as both parties are prepared to modify their interpretation in the light of new evidence. Both are working under different presuppositions. The creationist knows that ultimately there is a God behind it all - *"through faith we understand that the worlds were framed by the word of God"* (Hebrews 11:3)—whereas the secular scientist has faith in the uniformity of natural law, eternity of matter, and that given enough time, blind evolutionary "forces" can account for our present Universe and its life-forms. Some scientists claim that creation is not scientific, and therefore cannot be true.

Richard Dawkins has said: *"The alternative hypothesis, that it was all started by a supernatural creator, is not only superfluous, it is also highly improbable..... Even if the postulation of such an entity explained anything (and we don't need it to), it still wouldn't help because it raises a bigger mystery than it solves. Science offers us an explanation of how complexity (the difficult) arose out of simplicity (the easy). The hypothesis of God offers no worthwhile explanation for anything, for it simply postulates what we are trying to explain. It postulates the difficult to explain, and leaves it at that. We cannot prove there is no God, but we can safely conclude that He is very, very improbable indeed."*[25] If, however, creation really occurred, these scientists categorically rule out the acceptance of what is true, simply because it is considered to be *"unscientific"*. In accord with their belief that science will explain everything, they rule out the possibility of all they know they cannot explain. This must surely be a case of the *"apotheosis of science"*—making a god of science itself. Those—like Dawkins—who believe a creator God is improbable, do not have problems with believing in life, and yet, as we have argued elsewhere, that is 'highly improbable' (see chapter 2, and textbooks like *Mathematical Challenges to the Neo-Darwinian Interpretation of Evolution*, edited by P. S. Moorhead and M. M. Kaplan (1967) Wistar Institute Press.)

Catastrophists lay empirical foundations

Some evolutionary geologists I have read talk in disparaging terms of alternative models: *"What creationist method has ever accurately located oil traps, gas, minerals, etc.?"* Such comments hardly show an understanding of the issues mentioned here. We have already maintained that the scientific method itself depends on a God of order behind the universe. Furthermore, it was the catastrophists and creationists who first helped pioneer geological science. This includes, William Buckland (1784 -1856) who held the chair of geology at Oxford, Adam Sedgwick (1785-1873)— Professor of Geology at Cambridge and the so-called "father of modern palaeontology" George Cuvier (1769 -1832)—who was a catastrophist. It was, as Stephen Gould (Harvard Palaeontologist) admitted, the catastrophists who were the *"hard-nosed empiricists of their day."* Gould comments, for instance, on Charles Lyell's weaknesses as one of the *"uniformitarian advocates"*: *"Charles Lyell was a lawyer by profession, and his book is one of the most brilliant briefs ever published by an advocate ..... Lyell relied upon true bits of cunning to establish his uniformitarian views as the only true geology. First, he set up a straw man to demolish ..... In fact, the catastrophists were much more empirically minded than Lyell. The geologic record does seem to require catastrophes: rocks are fractured and contorted; whole faunas are wiped out. To circumvent this literal appearance, Lyell imposed his imagination upon the evidence. The geological record, he argued, is extremely imperfect and we must interpolate into it what we can reasonably infer but cannot see. The catastrophists were the hard-nosed empiricists of their day ......"* [26] Again, while criticising certain Christian groups Gould praises the work of the great scientist-theologians of past centuries. He admits that they had *"a willingness to abandon preferred hypotheses in the face of geological evidence. They were scientists and religious leaders."* [27]

The uniformitarian system (based on the principle *"the present is the key to the past"*)has proved so sterile that geologists are increasingly being forced to rely on neo-catastrophic thinking. [28] However, if the rock strata must be explained by catastrophic phenomena which are inaccessible to observation or measurement, and which are incommensurate with present processes, then historical geology in its interpretations is highly speculative. This is one of the major reasons geologists are keen to avoid the catastrophic explanation. Typical is the reaction of geoscientist B. W. Brown.

Brown has warned, *"Of late there has been a serious rejuvenation of catastrophism in geological thought. This defies logic; there is no science of singularities. If catastrophe is not a uniform process, there is no rational basis for understanding the past. For those who would return us to our Babylonian heritage of 'science' by revelation and possibility, we must insist that the only justifiable key to the past is probability and the orderliness of natural process; if uniformity is not the key, there is no key in the rational sense, and we should pack up our boots and go home."* [29]

The late Professor Derek Ager, (Palaeontologist, University of Swansea) sought to reconcile both views within a uniformitarian framework. He claimed that geological history was rather like the life of a soldier, with long periods of boredom and short periods of terror! This resulted in the "gaps" in the geological record being longer than the shorter periods of sedimentation.

A geomagnetic survey will reveal the presence of any magnetic anomalies—which help to locate oil traps; the use of micro-fossils can help to indicate the proximity of oil—but it does not necessarily prove the evolutionary tenets of the mud-logger; mineral lodes and deposits can be detected by geochemical methods, aerial surveys and geological mapping. The success of these methods depends on the validity of the scientific method, not the underlying evolutionary presuppositions or conceptual framework of the researchers. Indeed, phenomena can be accurately described and located long before their current explanation is accepted. One only has to think of *turbidites* (slurry deposited by fast flowing density currents)—correctly described in terms of their lithology (rock and particle content) long before they were interpreted as resulting from deposition by rapid density currents in the sea.

A Christian view of Science

Scientific activities must be engaged in, as part of man's general 'end' - *"To glorify God and fully to enjoy him for ever"* (Westminster Larger Catechism). Science is a purposeful activity both because humans have been made lord over creation, and because God reveals his glory through creation. As John Calvin, the Reformer said: *"Astronomy is not only pleasant, but also very useful to be known: it cannot be denied that this art unfolds the admirable wisdom of God. Wherefore, as ingenious men are to be honoured who have expended useful labour on this subject, so they who have leisure and capacity ought not to neglect this kind of exercise."*[30]

The fundamental assumptions of science—such as the possibility of observing reality—are valid because God has created the cosmos in such a way as to render them valid. Thus science is both purposeful and possible. One may engage in science and discover truths without the aim of glorifying God, but to do so is to defeat the object: *"To be so occupied in the investigation of the secrets of nature, as never to turn the eyes to its Author, is a most perverted study; and to enjoy everything in nature without acknowledging the Author of the benefit, is the basest ingratitude."*[31]

If one takes the position that science is dependent for its purpose, aims and methods upon God, then if God supernaturally reveals something about the cosmos, scientists ought to listen! God has made such supernatural revelations in the Bible, and if a scientist rejects those revelations, then that scientist is likely to go as wrong in science as he/she has already gone in religion! This argument applies whether one is studying cosmological history or the distribution of winds off Crete (Acts 27:14). However, it is doubly important when one is studying cosmological history, as one's conclusions are entirely dependent upon one's starting assumptions, and there is no way of verifying those starting assumptions within science, so that theories of cosmological history cannot be verified scientifically.

Calvin maintains that we must take the explanations that God has supernaturally given us and believe them, in faith, since we cannot scientifically verify them. Any other starting point for students of cosmological history is pointless: *"The Apostle [asserts] that through no other means than faith can it be understood that the worlds were made by the word of God (Hebrews, 11:3) … It is vain for any to reason as philosophers on the workmanship of the world, except those who, having been first humbled by the preaching of the Gospel, have learned to submit the whole of their intellectual wisdom (as Paul expresses it) to the foolishness of the cross (I Corinthians 1:21)."*[32] See **Endnote: 6** on Calvin's view of Science.

So is there no room left for science in cosmological history? Yes there is! The Bible only deals with cosmological history insofar as it is necessary for the purposes of redemption, leaving more to be discovered than there will be time on earth to discover! There is abundant material in the cosmos and methods of interpreting that material that are valid in the context of the Biblical revelation, so that there is the possibility of investigating cosmological history. There are the same aims as for any scientific endeavour (see above), with the additional one of showing how accurate the Bible is. Thus, based upon the Bible, the field of cosmological history is a wonderful one to be involved in, whether as a researcher or as a layman, whether in geology, palaeontology or palaeoclimatology!

Double-minded?

Modern atheistic science is schizophrenic! Why? It operates on the basis of two mutually exclusive paradigms. Firstly, it assumes, whilst seeking to deny it, God's eternal decree—that is, a created order, whereby, instead of brute meaningless factuality (where facts come out of a chance universe), God's law establishes and undergirds all reality. Scientists do come to valid conclusions in their research, largely because the metaphysical assumptions that underpin their observations and their reasoning based upon those observations are legitimate: God has created the universe and reality in such a way as to make them legitimate.

Secondly, modern science assumes the independence (autonomy) of man and his thinking from God, and that man's knowledge and discoveries are the sole source of law and meaning in an ultimately meaningless world. In terms of autonomy (man's desire to be independent from God) such a philosophy refuses to attribute any goal or purpose to the universe. The danger of extending science into an all-embracing philosophy, and extrapolating from it to explain and dogmatise about prehistory is surely the point at which science has ceased to be science: it has become scientism. It is also clear that where its philosophical and metaphysical extrapolations or theories are regarded as being as valid as its empirical counterparts or foundations, this must be exposed and declared only as scientific speculations or opinion.

Conclusion

As Mike Fuller concludes in answer to the question: Is science an ideology? *"The overall conclusion seems to be that all forms of knowledge, including scientific knowledge, are 'ideological' in the sense that there is no neutral, objective body of knowledge that is not infected by the purpose-relative concepts of a group of inquirers."*[33] Nevertheless, science is successful because it works! As Max Perutz (Nobel prize winning biologist) commented, *"The bulk of scientific knowledge is final. If it were not, jet planes could not fly, computers would not work and atom bombs fail to explode."*[34]

References

1   **B. Russell** (1997) *Religion & Science*, O.U.P., Oxford, pp. 243.

2   **R. Dawkins** (1991) The Independent, 23/12/91.

3   **M. J. Behe** (1996), *Darwin's Black Box: The biochemical challenge to evolution*, Free Press, New York, ISDN 0 68482 754 9, p. 250. Quote taken from R. Dawkins (1989) New York Times, April 9, sec. 7, p. 34.

4   **Ibid,** p. 251.

5   **G. H. Clark** (1964) *The Philosophy of Science and Belief in God*, The Craig Press, Nutley, New Jersey, Library of Congress Number: 64-25833, p. 95.

6   **James Jeans,** *The Mysterious Universe*, Ch. 5.

7   **E. Schrodinger** (1954) *Nature and the Greeks*, C, U. P., Cambridge.

8   **J. Gribben** (1986) In Search of the Big Bang, Corgi, The Guernsey Press Co., ISBN 0 552 13146 6, pp. 391-2.

9   **S. W. Hawking** (1988) *A Brief History of Time*, Bantam, London, p. 175.

10 R. Dawkins (1992) *A scientist's case against God*, (a speech by Professor Dawkins at the Edinburgh International Science Festival on 15th April, 1992), *The Independent,* 20 April, 1992, p. 17.

11 **Ibid.**

12 **J. C. Whitcomb** (1971)*The Origin of the Solar System*, Presbyterian & Reformed Publishing Co, Philadelphia, p. 27. Library of Congress Card Number 64-66003.

13 **N. Turok** (1998) "The beginning of everything", *Weekend, The Daily Telegraph*, Sat. March 14, 1998, p. 2.

14 **T. S. Kuhn** (1964) *The Structure of Scientific Revolutions*, University of Chicago Press, Phoenix Books, Chicago.

15 **J. W. Montgomery** (1967) *The Altizer-Montgomery Dialogue* , Inter-Varsity Press , pp. 21-2.

16 **P. Lipton** (1997) *Philosophy of Science*, Microsoft, Encarta, 97 Encyclopedia.

17 **Ibid.**

18 **J. Durant (ed.)** (1985) *Darwinism and Divinity*, Basil Blackwell, Oxford, ISBN 0 631 14188, p. 201.

19 **Ibid.**

20 **Whitcomb,** op. cit., p. 27.

21 **Ibid.**

22 **P. Moore** (1974) *The Amateur Astronomer*, Lutterworth Press, London, ISBN 0 7188 1815 6, pp. 206-7.

23 **E. C. Powell** (1973) "The Challenge of Historical Geology" , *Creation Research Quarterly,* March, Michigan, pp. 230-7.

24 **S. J. Gould** (1974) *Catastrophes and Steady State Earth* , Natural History, Feb., pp. 16-17. See also: S. J. Gould, (1965) "Is Uniformitarianism Necessary?", *American Journal of Science,* vol. 263, March, pp. 223—227.

25 **R. Dawkins** (1992) *A scientist's case against God*, (a speech by Professor Dawkins at the Edinburgh International Science Festival on 15th April, 1992), The Independent, 20 April, 1992, p. 17.

26 **S. J. Gould** (1974) Ibid.

27 **S.J. Gould** (1988) *"Creationism: Genesis vs Geology"* in the Flood Myth, edited by Alan Dundes, University of California Press, Berkeley, CA, p. 434.

28 **D. V. Ager** (1973)*The Nature of the Stratigraphical Record*, Macmillan, London.

29 **Brown, B. W.** (1974) *Induction, Deduction and Irrationality in Geologic Reasoning,* Geology, vol. 2, Sept. p. 456.

30 **J. Calvin** (1554) *A commentary on Genesis,* Banner of Truth, Edinburgh, p.86.

31 **Ibid.,** p. 60.

32 **Ibid.,** p. 63.

33 **M. Fuller** (1996) *Are Scientists Objective?* Philosophy Now, Issue No. 15 , Spring/Summer, Ipswich, p. 12.

34 **M. Perutz** (1994) The Times Higher Educational Supplement, November 25th, 1994.

Further Reading:

I.T. Taylor (1991) *In the minds of men: Darwin and the New World Order,* TFE Publishing, Toronto, M4Y, ISBN 0-9691 788-3-2.

G. A. Kerkut (1960) *Implications of Evolution,* Pergamon Press, Oxford, ISBN 0 08 09249 7.

J. Mervis & R. Hairman (1994) *A Brief History of Time: An Interactive Adventure,* CD-ROM, Creative Technology, Crunch Media Corporation & Apollo Partners Ltd, 17133110007.

Endnote 1

Jurassic Park a reality?

A view popular amongst the young and espoused by the tabloid papers is that science can do anything—even recreate a dinosaur! The idea behind the film *Jurassic Park* of extracting DNA from a mosquito which had sucked dinosaur blood and had then been preserved in amber was hotly contested by scientists. In the story DNA had been injected into frogs and then given birth to live dinosaurs! Scientists from the Natural History Museum (London), have done tests on more amber specimens (claimed to be 30 million years old) and is unable to substantiate the claim. DNA is an unstable molecule and could not be successfully extracted from the specimens. Those who claim it could, used only 12 specimens. Scientists who could not succeed in gaining any DNA examined about 55 specimens. Amber does preserve the morphology of insect specimens in great detail, even down to the hairs on their legs or their eyes. However, it seems that amber does let certain gases through it (i.e. it is porous) and so it let agents of DNA decay get into the amber, which allowed the DNA structure to degenerate. This report dashed the hopes of anyone who would like the fantasy of *Jurassic Park* to become a reality!

Born-again mammoths

New Scientist reported another venture to obtain DNA from frozen mammoths in Northern Siberia (Sakha). *"The search is part of a bizarre effort to recreate the species from mammoth sperm using IVF [In Vitro Fertilisation] techniques. The overall project is the brainchild of Kazufumi Goto, a veterinary scientist from Kagoshima University in Japan"* A. Coghlan (1997) *Born Again Mammoths* New Scientist, 20 September, 1977, No. 2100, p. 25. Goto is convinced that woolly mammoths can be recreated by injecting DNA from mammoth sperm preserved in the permafrost into eggs of African elephants. This permafrost preservation of DNA seems unlikely. Other breeders are highly sceptical of Goto's project, as DNA in frozen tissue tends to get broken up into fragments. It is empirical evidence that must decide whether a scientific theory is credible. Some scientists, however, rely solely on such scientific knowledge to determine truth.

The oldest known specimens that have given consistent DNA results are for the Siberian woolly mammoths dated by scientists at 50,000 years old (done by various researchers). The permafrost does allow the preservation of the DNA molecules. The claimed successful results of DNA from the amber insects could have resulted from contamination, or possibly this group of scientists gained the only ten valid specimens. It would take only one insect (e.g. a cockroach or fruit fly) to enter a lab to spread enough DNA material to produce *"results"*. These findings were reported in the Proceedings of the Royal Society: Authors: J. J. Austin, R. A. Forty, A. J. Ross, & R. H. Thomas (1997) Problems of reproducibility—Does geologically ancient DNA survive in amber-preserved insects? Proceedings: Biological Science Series, B Volume, 264, No. 1381, 22nd April, 1997. These scientists were unable to find any insect DNA in 15 specimens in amber dated as millions of years old. Science must be able to reproduce the results to give credibility to a claim (source: BBC Science Now, Sat. 19/04/97).

Endnote 2

Bertrand Russell proclaimed that man is the product of causes which had no prevision of his emergence; that his hopes and fears are the accidental collocations of atoms; that no heroism or intensity of thought can preserve an individual beyond the grave; that all human labour, inspiration, and genius are destined to extinction and will be buried beneath the debris of a universe in ruins. And with finality he concluded, *" ... all these things, if not quite beyond dispute, are yet so nearly certain, that no philosophy which rejects them can hope to stand"* B. Russell (1957)*Why I am not a Christian*, George Allen and Unwin, New York, p. 107.

Endnote 3

The distinction between relative truth and absolute truth is made clear by Professor John Klotz (1965) in *Genes Genesis and Evolution* (Concordia Publishing House, St. Louis, Missouri, LC No: 55-6434, p.3). "Only the Bible claims infallibility for itself. The scientist, *"says that what he presents is at best relative truth. Mavor, for instance, points out that no law or principle of science can ever be regarded as absolutely proved. All laws and principles, he says, are subject to modification with the accumulation of more data and the increase of knowledge ....This relativity of scientific truth is inherent in the tools and methods with which the scientist must work (pp. 3-4)"*.

Endnote 4
Stellar evolution

Despite this, current scientific theory is unable to describe adequately the expansion of the Universe. Unfortunately for the theory of stellar evolution, the picture is not becoming simpler as more research is done. Instead, the complexity of the physical universe multiplies as each new discovery is made. Gamow's *"big bang"* theory could not explain the origin of most of the elements! Scientists estimate that hydrogen and helium do in fact make up about 99 percent of the matter of the universe. This leaves cosmologists with the problem of building the heavier elements. Several scientists hold to the opinion that some of the heavier elements were built by the capture of neutrons. However, since the absence of any stable nucleus of atomic weight 5 makes it improbable that the heavier elements could have been produced in the first half hour in the abundances now observed, they would agree that the lion's share of the heavy elements may well have been formed later in the hot interior of stars.

There are dissenting voices to the Big Bang Theory amongst astronomers. David Darling (astronomer) wrote: *"Don't let the cosmologists try to kid you on this one. They have not got a clue either ... 'In the beginning,' they will say, there was nothing—no time, space, matter, or energy. Then there was a quantum fluctuation from which -whoa! Stop right there. You see what I mean? First there is nothing, then there is something—and before you know it, they have pulled a hundred billion galaxies out of their quantum hats"* (*"On Creating Something From Nothing"* New Scientist, volume 151, September 14, 1996, p. 49). Five notable astronomers raised objections to the Big Bang theory and concluded: *"The above discussion clearly indicates that the present evidence does not warrant an implicit belief in the standard hot Big Bang picture."* Later they add: *"Cosmology is unique in science in that it is a very large intellectual edifice based on a very few facts"* (Arp, Halton C., G. Burbridge, F. Hoyle, J. V. Nartikar and N. C. Wickramasinghe, *"The Extra-Galactic Universe: An Alternative View,"* Nature, volume 346, August 30, 1990, pp. 810 & 812.

Endnote 5

Kuhn sets out to show in his work, *The Structure of Scientific Revolutions* (1970) that it is impossible to separate scientific knowledge and reasoning from its historical development. History displays a variety of traditions or *'paradigms'* in which men are bound by shared presuppositions or underlying principles. These determine the way we see the world. Kuhn has been criticised for his key concept of paradigm as being too all embracing, and therefore liable to lead to confusion and philosophical obscurity. As a result, Kuhn had *Second Thoughts on Paradigms (1977)* and sought to clarify exemplars and paradigms. Exemplars are concrete problem situations accepted within the scientific community; and disciplinary matrixes are the more generally shared elements which characterise the scientific community, such as symbolic generalisations, models, values and metaphysical principles.

Derek Stanesby points out, *"although Newton and Einstein each employed the same term 'mass', they interpreted it in entirely different senses and produced theories which picture the world in entirely different ways. Furthermore, since the exemplars indicate the sort of questions and answers that are appropriate to the community sharing those exemplars, there will be disagreement between communities with different shared exemplars concerning the relevant questions and answers. That is, the shared exemplars will determine the scientific values adopted by a scientific community. The import of this sociological analysis is that not only can there be no neutral observation language common to all scientific investigators, but there are no objective 'facts' because they too are determined by the exemplars"* D. Stanesby (1985) *Science, Reason & Religion*, Croom Helm, London, ISBN 0-7099-3360-6, p. 141.

Endnote 6

Dr Nigel Lee (1969) produced a short essay *Calvin on the Sciences*, published by Sovereign Grace Union, England.

Key Text:

Psalm: 19:1 *"The heavens declare the glory of God; And the firmament shows his handiwork."*

Questions for Further Study

1 Albert Einstein said, *"The whole of science is nothing more than a refinement of everyday thinking."* What has increased the popular misconception that science can do practically anything?
2 What is the major teaching of logical positivism?
3 Richard Dawkins said, *"Science replaces religion. It is the grandiose vision".* What is scientism?
4 Why does Behe recommend an open-minded approach to science.
5 Is the Bible a textbook of science?
6 Can science determine its own value?
7 What is the distinction between relative and absolute truth?
8 Historian of science R. Hookyaas claims the scientific method implies a created Universe. To look for a distinctive Christian approach is like looking for one's spectacles whilst wearing them! Do you agree?
9 When is the significance of Stephen Hawking's latest application of quantum theory to the Universe's origin?
10 What does Dr. Dawkins warn us about regarding: (a) physicists' mystical beliefs and (b) whether the Genesis account resembles the conceptions of modern physics?
11 Does Dr Whitcomb think it wise to marry Genesis to the Big Bang theory?
12 How does science progress?
13 What would happen to science if there were no paradigms?
14 What lessons did you learn from the *"Dead men do not bleed"* parable?
15 What is the double-revelation theory?
16 What is Patrick Moore's view of the future of the galaxy?
17 What is the significance of the fact: *"Science observes, records and studies but cannot proceed with certainty from effects to causes."*
18 What is the difference between the creationist and evolutionist models of origins?
19 Why is catastrophism so unpopular in geological circles?
20 What is a Christian view of science and its value?
21 Why is modern atheistic science schizophrenic (double-minded)?
22 John Gribben (Science writer) reports a physicist as saying, *"There is speculation.*

Then there is wild speculation. Then there is cosmology," in his book *Companion to the Cosmos* (1997) published by Phoenix. Do you agree, with the physicist?

Food for thought:
"The supreme achievement of reason is to bring us to see that there is a limit to reason." Blaise Pascal

"Science without religion is lame, religion without science is blind."
Albert Einstein (1879-1955) German born US physicist: *Out of My Later Years.*

Only One Way?

"A half truth masquerading as the whole truth is an untruth."

Another key feature of the search for truth is whether any one path or many paths lead to religious truth. The synthetic approach to truth is examined, demonstrating that it can only appear valid at a very superficial level. Ultimately the issue arises by what standard we are judging, and the fact that Jesus Christ claims to be the exclusive way to God, is advocated. He was either a lunatic, a liar, or he was telling the truth when he claimed to be the way, the truth and the life.

Information age

Today we live in an age that is afraid of extremes and exclusivism. Never before has it been possible for peoples of different backgrounds (ethnic, social, etc.) to rub shoulders and communicate with each other on such a scale. It is well expressed in the concept of the *"global village"* where we can know what is happening in another remote part of the planet in 'real time'—as it happens—and through the media and particularly the 'world wide web' exchange topical data at a phenomenal rate. The problem nowadays is often not too little information, but *"infoglut"*, the availability of so much data—we can hardly hope to process it all!

This great exchange of cultures and beliefs in the *"information age"* has led to an increasing tendency to *"pluralistic beliefs"* and *"indifference"* to religion. People feel it is too narrow to claim, any one party or sect has *"the truth"*, so the policy of *"live and let live"* seems the best to generate peace. Anyway, people have always found greatest satisfaction in the immediate—sense gratification, whether it be food or *"wine, women and song"*. The diversity of religious opinion leaves others to effectively say *"why bother?"*; *"Religion—no thanks"* and *"Let's eat, drink and be merry, for tomorrow we die"*. However, everybody has a belief system, which affects the way they behave. Even if we claim to have no beliefs, we have by that very position committed ourselves to a belief system of no commitment! We are all incurably religious *"made in the image of God"*, but how can we know which faith to follow?

Proverbial elephants

Confronted with a choice of religions, conventional wisdom has the following analogy: Three blind men feel an elephant, one its trunk, another its tail, and the last one of its legs. Their descriptions of each part are diverse and different, nobody would guess they were all parts of the same animal! The proverb or moral is simple; all are dealing with the same reality, but appear to be dealing with completely different entities! So with religion—and God in particular—there may be many different approaches, but all deal with the same ultimate reality. In a nutshell, this view says *"all religious roads lead to Heaven."* But Jesus would have called this a case of *"the blind leading the blind"*.

This viewpoint, however, epitomised for instance in the Bahai faith (which believes in a universal religion based on the essence of all the great religions), seeks to find elements of truth in any religion. As Dr. William Edgar (Professor of Apologetics) states: *"Yet a third person may have something else in mind when asking the question of the truths of other faiths. One common presupposition behind the question is that at bottom all religions are the same; specifically that there is one great Truth (capital T) and many little truths (small t) leading to it. Each religion may have its particular set of rituals, symbols, and holy persons, but the adherents will eventually find a universal truth that transcends all the particular symbols and practices. This approach has serious flaws, the main one being that it lumps all religions into one paradigm. All are said to begin at the same level, and all will reach the same place. But a careful look at different world views makes it impossible to be so categorical. Try looking for a basic commonality in world-views. It is not a belief in God because not all world-views believe in God—Confucianism is agnostic; Zen Buddhism atheistic. Nor is it an eschatology—a vision for the end of the world. Marxism's vision is based on historical materialism but refuses the label religion. Mahayana Buddhism believes in abandoning any utopian ideas and opting for the sunyata, or ultimate void. The list continues. When all is said and done, what finally matters is one essential question: Is it true?"* [1]

The heredity factor

Professor Richard Dawkins in his case against God, throws all religion into the same basket, despite the differences we have noted above. He strongly objects to what he calls the *"heredity factor"* in religion. Other things being equal, people will tend to follow the faith of their fathers. He says, *"As a Darwinian, something strikes me when I look at religion. Religion shows a pattern of heredity which I think is similar to genetic heredity. The vast majority of people have an allegiance to one particular religion. There are hundreds of different religious sects, and every religious person is loyal to just one of these. Out of all the sects in the world, we notice an uncanny coincidence: the overwhelming majority just happen to choose the one their parents belonged to. Not the sect that has the best evidence in its favour, the best miracles, the best moral code, the best cathedral, the best stained-glass, the best music: when it comes to choosing from the smorgasbord of available religions, their potential virtues seem to count for nothing compared to the matter of heredity. This is an unmistakable fact; nobody could seriously deny it. Yet people with full knowledge of the arbitrary nature of this heredity, somehow manage to go on believing in their religion, often with such fanaticism that they are prepared to murder people who follow a different one. Truths about the cosmos are true all around the universe. They don't differ in Pakistan , Afghanistan, Poland or Norway. Yet we are apparently prepared to accept that the religion we adopt is a matter of an accident of geography."* [2]

Clearly, there is an element of truth in Dawkin's criticisms of world religions. As far as biblical Christianity is concerned, people do change their initial beliefs radically: For instance, the disciples of Jesus changed from orthodox Judaism to Christianity, despite the social stigma and persecution associated with such a change. The Bible itself gives many examples of families where some believed the faith of their parents, and others who did not. Esau and Jacob are typical of this: Esau despised the faith of his father, but Jacob became a true believer. The Christian church has millions upon millions of examples of those who have changed from a life of unbelief and degradation, to the Christian faith. St. Augustine of Hippo would be one classic example, as would the Apostle Paul who as a Jew was an ardent persecutor of those early Christians—before his conversion. The history of the church is littered with examples of twins, one who became a Christian and the other who remained indifferent.

However, Dawkins cautions, *"If you ask people why they are convinced of the truth of their religion, they don't appeal to heredity... Nor do they appeal to evidence. There isn't any, and nowadays the better educated admit it. No, they appeal to faith. Faith is the great cop-out, the great excuse to evade the need to think and evaluate evidence. Faith is belief in spite of, even perhaps because of, the lack of evidence."*[3] This runs completely counter to the claims of Christianity to be based on historic fact, and evidence. There have been rationalistic lawyers, and archaeologists who have set out to disprove the Christian faith, but have been overwhelmed by the evidence in its favour.[4]

The Christian faith is robust enough to undergo any amount of analysis: *"Christianity lays open its claim to every one that asks a reason for the hope which it inspires, and declines no species of a fair investigation"*. It argues that without God's special revelation, it is sadly only *"the blind leading the blind."* Although non-Christian faiths all contain some elements of truth or other features which can be called *"good"* in a limited sense, they are still—as systems—false, because they give wrong answers to the most important and ultimate questions of life. Yes, it is a knife edge between *"truth and error"* and we need to be confident, that if theistic beliefs are valid then there must be a *"correct answer"*. The real world is not like some religious version of *Alice in Wonderland*, where *"all have won and all shall have prizes"*; some religions are saying diametrically opposed things, so they cannot be synthesised!

Ultimate questions

The vital questions to be concerned about are:

◆ **1**: What is the nature of God?

◆ **2**: What is the relation between God and the Universe?

◆ **3**: What is the real reason for the problems we face in this world?

◆ **4**: What must a person do to be saved?

◆ **5**: What is the real meaning of death? and
◆ **6**: What comes after death?

Such questions as these are given poor or untrue answers by all non-Christian religions. No other religion sees people's need as it really is. That we are dead in sin, cut off from fellowship with God, they will not readily admit. Only Bible-based Christianity deals with our desperate need, as rebels against God—in moral and intellectual revolt against Him. Other religions offer us advice—some good, some not so good. Christianity brings us good news—the Gospel, the message of Jesus Christ, the Son of God; Christianity brings the offer of an absolutely free salvation from a gracious God, who has done for people what they could not do for them-selves. In essence, *"The distinction between Christianity and all other systems of religion consists largely in this, that in these others men are found seeking God, while Christianity is God seeking after men"* said Thomas Arnold.

All tarred with the same brush

As members of the human race, we are like a person who has fallen into a deep pit. Efforts to escape from such a hole are doomed to failure; we are all tarred with the same brush. No-one is perfect. What typical advice do the world religions give? The Confucianist says, *"Why did you fall into the pit? A wise person takes care where they are walking. In future, be careful where you are going!"*—but you are still left helpless in the pit. The Taoist priest says, *"You must burn incense and win the favour of the spirits"*. This does not help rescue you from the pit. Next, the Buddhist monk says, *"Your trouble is that you want to get out of the pit. All our human misery comes from desire, we want things we cannot have. Rid yourself of such evil desires and you will get peace. Try to develop a detached attitude so that you will not worry whether you get out of the pit or not!"* The Mullah (Muslim priest) advised, *"Don't despair, there is life on the other side, and if you try to please Allah in this life—who knows—you might get there. Say your prayers daily and help the poor, fast in Ramadan."* Other religions say, *"Live a good life, and God will be pleased with you!"* But

God's standards are perfection and that none of us can obtain. We cannot pull ourselves up by our own bootstraps, to reach God's standards.

The only answer

The Christian believes it is the Saviour, Jesus Christ, who alone is able to reach down and rescue the captive. Bishop Phillips-Brooks, referring to the impact of the Lord Jesus Christ said: *"Nineteen wide centuries have come and gone. Today he is the centrepiece of the human race and leader of the column of progress. I am far within the mark when I say that all the armies that ever marched, all the navies that have ever built, all the parliaments that have ever sat and all that ever reigned, put together, have not affected the life of man upon this earth as powerfully as has ... THAT ONE SOLITARY LIFE."*[5] The Christian message tells of a gracious God who is rich in mercy, not willing that any should perish, that takes man out of the fearful pit and who puts such sinners upon a great secure rock—whom the Bible calls the Lord Jesus Christ. The psalmist says, *"He also brought me up out of a horrible pit, Out of the miry clay, And set my feet upon a rock, He has put a new song in my mouth—Praise to our God"* (Psalm 40:2-3).

A hard-hitting message

Only biblical Christianity recognises the real fallen state we are in. It alone tells us of the hopelessness of all human schemes of salvation by our own efforts, good works or achievements. Also, only Christianity has the almighty power of the Holy Spirit by which a man is born again and his will renewed and his character changed. People are changed, re-directed from sin and self, and made right with God. The Bible alone has the full authority of *"Thus says the Lord"* to back up its message.

God is not the author of confusion and He cannot lie. Modern ideas that anything goes would undermine the vital Bible truth that Jesus Christ is the only Saviour of the world, *"the light of the world"*. The apostles declared, *"Salvation is found in no-one else, for there is no other name under heaven given to men by which we must be saved"* (Acts 4:12). The greatest missionary of all time—the apostle Paul—did not pussyfoot around either when it came to those who denied the true gospel: (*"As we have said before, so now I say again, if anyone preaches any gospel to you other than what you have received, let him be accursed")* (Galatians 1:9). Of course, we should also be loving and tolerant towards those outside the church who disagree. Man-made religion is a quest for the values of the ideal life, or *"People's recognition of a controlling superhuman power entitled to obedience, reverence and worship."* Christianity differs from all other religions. Christianity is about our relationship to the Lord Jesus Christ, and not primarily a set of rules and regulations to earn our way to heaven.

Jesus—the only way?

"How can one Jew save the world?" a Chinese student asked me once. Christianity is the message of Jesus Christ and Him crucified as the Lamb of God, who takes away the sin of the world. But how can a Rabbi be *"the door to God"* or a tan-coloured person be the Saviour of blacks? To represent women? To represent the abused? To represent the oppressed? How is this possible? The Bible says God does not want to punish any other creature for human debt, as no creature can bear the burden of God's eternal wrath against sin. The Westminster Catechism summarises: *"What sort of mediator and redeemer must we seek?"* Answer: *"One who is a true and righteous man and yet more powerful than all creatures, that is, one who is at the same time true God."*

Christ was the God-Man—this was God's solution, as there was *"no other good enough to pay the price of sin."* Jesus as a priest (as the book of Hebrews calls him) is one who bears people's burdens, makes intercession, and becomes the only substitute for sin: see Hebrews 2:18; 4:15-16. Dr Edgar summarises: *"Because Christ is unique, so He is the way to deal with adversity. We do not escape trials as Christians, but we do have a singular way to endure them and know that our high priest will ultimately remove every hardship and injustice. As the great singer Blind Willy Johnson says in one of his songs, "Take your burden to the Lord and leave it there. Leave it there. Leave it there."*[6]

Dr. Edgar continues, *"Thus Jesus is able to represent every kind of human being. It may seem strange to modern ears to hear that a person from a particular culture and race, a specific economic and social back- ground, a male and a celibate, could represent rich and poor, men and women, African and Asian. But if the idea of representation is at all valid, the person who is my priest is necessarily different from me but can understand me because he has experienced the same sorts of difficulties I have. Jesus therefore cannot be our representative if he is only a spirit or a philosophical abstraction; he must be a human who can empathize with the circumstance of so many different people."*[7]

Countless religions?

The Bible explains the origin of false religions in Romans chapter one, one of the most profound chapters in the Bible. *"Professing themselves to be wise, they became fools .... who changed the truth of God into a lie, and worshipped and served the creature more than the Creator"* (Romans 1: 22-25). Human beings preferred to imagine that they were independent of God, and could set their own standards of conduct and truth. They would make up their own way to God—if there is one—rather than accept God's Word.

Anything goes?

Jesus as the world's greatest teacher did not claim that there are many roads to Heaven. When he said, *"In my Father's house are many mansions"* (John 14:2), he was not teaching *"anything goes in religion"* but that there is plenty of room in heaven for all true believers. Jesus commented immediately before these words to His disciples, *"You believe in God, believe also in me"*. Jesus made it clear in this very passage that it is only through faith in Him we can be saved. Jesus said, *"I am the way, the truth and the life, no one comes to the Father except through me"* (John 14:6). Such claims make it very clear that Jesus spoke with authority and stated truths no other prophet can equal. He was either the greatest liar that ever lived, or He spoke the truth. Jesus also said, *"I am the door [entrance], if anyone enters by me, he will be saved ..."* (John 10:9). Notice Jesus did not say that he was one of many doors into heaven!

Lewis' challenge

C. S. Lewis commented: *"I am trying here to prevent anyone saying the really foolish thing that people often say about him: 'I'm ready to accept Jesus as a great moral teacher, but I don't accept His claim to be God.' That is the one thing we must not say. A man who was merely a man and said the sort of things Jesus said wouldn't be a great moral teacher. He'd be either a lunatic—on a level with a man who says he's a poached egg—or else he'd be the devil of hell. You must make your choice. Either this man was and is the Son of God, or else a madman or something worse …. But don't let us come up with any patronising nonsense about his being a great human teacher. He hasn't left that open to us."*[8]

Some may still feel uneasy about the exclusive claims of Christianity. After all, people from other faiths are so sincere and devout. Isn't that what matters? Here, we have to be honest with ourselves. *"Does the wrong train get you to the right place so long as you believe sincerely that you are on the right train? Will poison taken from a bottle at night do you no harm so long as you sincerely believe you are taking the medicine your doctor prescribed? It is right to have a high regard for sincerity and to dislike humbug and hypocrisy. But we need truth as well as sincerity, facts as well as faith."*[9]

By what standard?

Numbers do not decide truth. Jesus said, *"Enter through the narrow gate. For wide is the gate and broad is the road that leads to destruction, and many enter through it. But small is the gate and narrow the road that leads to life, and only a few find it"* (Matthew 7:13-14). What point is there in believing something that will lead you to your doom? It's no comfort to know that everybody else tells you not to worry. How do you know that you can trust Christ? You can trust Him because He speaks with authority, as the Son of God. He is not like us who change our opinions from day to day, or scientists who revise their theories as knowledge advances. Jesus is the way, the truth and the life.

Josh McDowell (Christian Apologist) gives the following illustration, why Jesus is to be preferred to other religious leaders: If we were lost in a dense forest on a hike, and noticed two human forms ahead, we would run to catch up. *"We notice that one has on a park ranger uniform, and he is standing there perfectly healthy and alive, while the other person is lying face down, dead. Now which of these two are you going to ask about the way out? Obviously the one who is living. When it comes to eternal matters, we are going to ask the one who is alive the way out of the predicament. This is not Muhammad, not Confucius, but Jesus Christ. Jesus is unique. He has come back from the dead. This demonstrates He is the one whom He claimed to be (Romans 1:4), the unique Son of God and the only way by which a person can have a personal relationship with the true and living God.*"[10] So what's the Christian message all about? It is summed up simply as follows: *"There's a way back to God from the dark paths of sin, there's a way that is open and you may go in, at Calvary's Cross is where you begin, when you come as a sinner to Jesus."*

References:

1   **W. Edgar** (1996) *Reasons of the Heart*, Hourglass Books, Baker Book House, Grand Rapids, ISBN: 0-8010-5138X, p. 88.

2   **R. Dawkins** (1992) *A scientist's case against God*, (a speech by Professor Dawkins at the Edinburgh International Science Festival on 15th April, 1992), The Independent, 20 April, 1992, p. 17.

3   **Ibid.**

4   **F. Morison** (1967) *Who moved the stone?* Faber & Faber, London.

5   **Schools Council** (1977) *"How others see life"* Journeys into Religion, Granada Publishing Ltd, ISBN 0 247 12758 2, p. 21.

6   **W. Edgar** (1996) op. cit., p. 92

7   **Ibid.**, pp. 92-3

8   **C. S. Lewis** (1960) *Mere Christianity*, Macmillan Publishing Co., New York, pp. 40-41.

9   **L. Samuel** (1990) *There is an answer*, Christian Focus Publications, ISBN 1 87167606 1, p.154

10 **J. McDowell** (1980) *Answers to Tough Questions about the Christian Faith*, Scripture Press, Bucks, ISBN 0-9456515-51-4, p. 52.

Further Reading:

J. McDowell (1990) *Christianity : A Ready Defence*, Here's Life Publishers, ISBN 1 872059 56 2.

J. G. Vos (1965) *A Christian Introduction to the Religions of the World*, Baker Book House, Michigan, ISBN 0-8010-9261-2.

Resources:

Answers to questions Muslims ask: http://www. answering_islam.org.uk
http://www.jsmith@debate.org.uk

Key Text:

John 14: 6 *"I am the way, the truth and the life, No one comes to the Father except through me"* .

Questions for Further Study

1   Why is there increased indifference and pluralistic beliefs in todays society?
2   What is the proverb of the blind men and the elephants supposed to teach?
3   What approach to truth is the Behai faith typical of?
4   What evidence suggests all religions are not part of the one great Truth?
5   How would you answer Dawkins' criticism that religion is largely inherited?
6   What are the ultimate questions we should ask?
7   Many admit they are not perfect. If we assume we are in a pit, what advice would be given by various leaders to get us out?
8   Is anything unique about the Christian message, if so—what?
9   Is the *"anything goes"* philosophy to finding God, condemned in Scripture?
10 What Bible references best explain the origin of false religions?
11 C. S. Lewis made a perceptive challenge regarding Jesus Christ. What was this?
12 How would you indicate to a friend that sincerity is not enough when it comes to finding truth?
13 What fact above all other indicates that Jesus Christ is unique?
14 Dr David Bellamy—the well known botanist and broadcaster said: *"On my travels I can now worship with and so learn from the teaching of the world's religions, all of which hold the sanctity of life in all its forms as a central part of their belief "* (*The Times:* 28/09/1996, p. 8). Describe how you would deal with this position.

Food for Thought

* *"If you want to know what God has to say to you, see what Christ was and is."* C. H. Spurgeon.
* *"No religion has ever been greater than its idea of God."* A. W. Tozer.

Vanity of Vanities

"It is always a relief to believe what is pleasant, but it is more important to believe what is true." Hilaire Belloc

There is a need for justice in all societies. A valid concept of justice, as C. S. Lewis realised, depends ultimately on God's justice. Without any such ultimate judgement as Hell, Christianity is reduced to a system of ethics. Humanistic concepts of Hell are examined, but found to fall far short of the Bible's teaching. Not only does God reluctantly inflict Hell, in his Son, he suffers it. Thus the incarnation, the Cross and Resurrection presuppose the reality of Hell and evil.

Punishment—the missing ingredient

We are altogether incapable of estimating God's justice and standards. Like the lumberjack, cutting the logs all askew because his cutting saw is set at a wrong angle, we do not realise our views are out of line. Arthur W. Pink reminds us: *"We are ourselves so infected and affected by sin that we are altogether incapable of estimating its due merits. Imagine a company of criminals passing judgement on the equity and goodness of the law which had condemned them! The truth of the matter is—and how often is it lost!—that God is not to be measured by human standards."* [1]

John Benton has stated this matter clearly, *"'How can he? How can a God of love send people to Hell?' This is a most serious question and one which is frequently asked. Usually it is a very honest question. People find it genuinely difficult to reconcile the idea of God's love with that of eternal punishment. Not surprisingly, emotions can run high. Confronted with the teaching concerning judgement, some people angrily reject the God of the Bible. He is accused of being callous, belligerent and primitive. The final irony occurs when the Bible itself is condemned as 'unchristian' because of the teaching of God's wrath. In our politically correct days, some people like to think only good things happen after death. But the strength of feeling on this subject is understandable. Heaven and hell are the most serious and solemn matters we can ever contemplate and to raise such serious matters causes people to question at the deepest possible level the way that they are living their lives."* [2]

Ultimate justice

Every person, to some degree, recognises evil, disapproves of it and agrees that it should be punished. Even a thief, for instance, will report his own stolen car to the police! As a result of this inherent sense of justice, every society sets up its own justice systems, with verdicts and sentences. Therefore, we cannot sit in judgement on the concept of justice. Such judicial systems are only valid to the degree in which they reflect a divine one. C. S. Lewis (Oxford Professor of English) was originally an atheist because of all the injustice in the world. He came to realise the problem: *"Where did he get his idea of justice from in the first place?"* How could he call a line crooked unless he had some idea of a straight line? What are we comparing this universe with when we call it unjust? Lewis concluded that injustice in the world pointed to the One who set the standard of justice. None of us have the right to send another person to prison either in our own name, or even the state's. It can only be done in God's name. If there were no judgement in the world, there would be no courts. If we see the need for punishment and prisons, then God must believe in justice and ultimately Hell itself.

A greater moral sense than Christ?

Those who regard the whole idea of Hell as completely repulsive, betray the fact that they think that their moral sense is more acute than that of Jesus. Not only does this imply Christ was misguided about theoretical theology, but that he had a blatant inability to detect immorality, and thus this would prove to be a fatal flaw in his authority. The term *"hell"* occurs 54 times in the Bible, so it is **not** an insignificant term. The idea of a just God implies Hell, as Geoffrey Gorer says, *"If there is no belief in hell the concept of judgement also becomes meaningless; and then all that is left of Christianity is a system of ethics."* To our minds the concept of Hell is both unpleasant and to be avoided; no one in their right mind would wish to discuss such a topic in a cold dispassionate way. Christians have been accused of developing appalling theologies which make God into a sadistic monster. It is argued by such critics that Hell should be seen as *"nothingness"* or *"non-being"* but not as eternal torment.

Watered down views

It is thought by some that the idea of Hell is outmoded. This is one of many *"reductionist"* views, which seek to reduce the significance of Hell to a limited concept of annihilation, and this has been extended further by those who reduce it to a phenomenon in this life only. Jean Paul Sartre (the French existentialist) for instance said, *"Hell is other people"*. Another Frenchman, George Bernanos (priest and mystic) defined Hell as *"not to love anymore"*. Philo of Alexandria wrote *"Hell is the life of the wicked"*. Swedenborg (Swedish philosopher) taught Heaven or Hell are states of consciousness not *"places"*.

Unfortunately such theories are the end result of rejecting the Bible as God's revelation. Truth is being decided on human reasoning alone—or access in Swedenborg's case to claimed *"special revelations"*. These views do not square with Jesus' teaching on the worthless servant thrown into darkness where there will be weeping and gnashing of teeth. Bible-believing Christians cannot just rip out pages of the Bible that are unpalatable or unfashionable to the modern mind (see Matthew 25: 31-46). God's standard is perfection, and as a just God, he must deal with sin. God's wrath is not just a threat to mankind. It signifies a hatred of evil. Would God be just if he let Hitler, Stalin and Pol Pot be snuffed out, never to be punished for the evil they committed?

That we are not to take justice into our own hands as individuals is justified by the Apostle Paul on the grounds of God's ultimate justice: Romans 12:19b states, *"Vengeance is mine; I will repay, says the Lord."* [3] The state, in contrast, is said by the apostle to have the "power of the sword." The word used for the latter object is not dagger, but gladius or sword. The Roman power is symbolised in the Apocalyse with the great sword. It is a symbol of the magistrates power to punish. Romans 13: 3-4 says, "For rulers are not a terror to good works, but to evil. Do you want to be unafraid of the authority? Do what is good, and you will have praise from the same. For he is God's minister to you for good. But if you do evil, be afraid; for he does not bear the sword in vain; for he is God's minister, an avenger to execute wrath on him who practises evil."

To gloss over the Bible's teaching on justice, is also to deny Jesus' clear message—no other prophet spoke as much on Hell. It was Jesus who referred to: Dives opening his eyes in Hell, the place of outer darkness, and who spoke of the place of weeping and wailing and gnashing of teeth. The Hebrew word "Gehenna"("hell") means shame, disgrace, sin, guilt, judgement and punishment. Gehenna was the name of the rubbish tip outside Jerusalem where the bodies of executed criminals were burnt, which Jesus used as an analogy of hell. The word is by far the most vivid in teaching the reality of eternal punishment.

John Blanchard points out regarding *"Gehenna ... [it] may surprise many people, ... that eleven out of the twelve times that it occurs it is Jesus who uses it. Nor does he mince his words. He speaks about a person's whole body being 'thrown into hell'* (Matthew 5:29), of those who will be *'thrown into the fire of hell'* (Matthew 18:9), and of hypocrites being *'condemned to hell'* (Matthew 23:33). When sending out his twelve apostles on their first mission Jesus warned them of the persecution they would face and added, *'Do not be afraid of those who kill the body but cannot kill the soul. Rather, be afraid of the One who can destroy both soul and body in hell'"* (Matthew 10:28). Whatever *'hell'* means, Jesus taught that going there is a worse fate than being murdered. Elsewhere he spoke of it as being a place *'where the fire never goes out'* (Mark 9:43) and where *'their worm does not die'"* (Mark 9:48) 4 that is, their conscience does not die.

Consistent message

The apostle Paul says those who do not obey the gospel of our Lord Jesus Christ ... *"shall be punished with everlasting destruction from the presence of the Lord and from the glory of his power, when he comes in that day, to be glorified in his saints" (Christians)* (2 Thess. 1: 9,10). Hell is a place devoid of peace and happiness. The teaching on Hell is one proof that the Bible is not a man-made book, for which one of us would want such a place of torment? Some other religions have derived their notions of it from this source. It hardly helps make Christianity a desirable product, if it were engineered by humans! The Bible does not cover up the truth, or present it to us in a *"sugar-coated"* pill to make it sweeter. **See Endnote:** 1

The authors of the *Westminster Catechism* summarise the teaching of Scripture thus: *Question 29: "What are the punishments of sin in the world to come?"* Answer: *"The punishments of sin in the world to come, are everlasting separation from the comfortable presence of God, and most grievous torments in soul and body, without intermission, in hell-fire for ever."* 5 No wonder the discussion of God's existence generates so much opposition.

Scripture tells us that God does not rejoice in the death of the wicked. God does not judge in malice, but fairly, patiently and his verdict will be equitable. Once sin became a reality—through mankind's rebellion (Romans 5 :12-15), then the existence of Hell and pain in God followed. The fact that sin inflicts pain on God, includes the pain of having to prepare a place of outer darkness, and having to condemn people to it. Even God himself protests: *"Why have you put me in this impossible position of having to condemn you?"* In Christian theology, there is the corresponding thought that God is not simply the one who inflicts Hell, but in his Son, the one who suffers it.

For as the Apostles' Creed states : *"He descended into Hell"*, which means that Christ on the Cross *"endured in His soul the torments of a condemned and ruined mankind"*. It was His devastating cry on the Cross, *"My God, my God, why have you forsaken me?"* (Matthew 27:46) as Christ suffered the loss of God's love, and His self image was reduced to one thing—sin. He became the banished one, cursed by God. God the Father could not even look on him. This was clearly His divine mission. Jesus' first recorded words were, *"Why is it you have sought me? Did you not know that I must be about my Father's business"* (Luke 2: 49). His last recorded words on the cross, were that He had accomplished what He came to do, *"It is finished."* He suffered the agonies of Hell, to save a people for Himself, *"that whoever believes in Him should not perish but have everlasting life."*

Where is Hell?
In the New Testament, Hell is referred to as the place of outer darkness, or

as John says *"outside."* But we may ask, *"outside what?"* Clearly we are talking of another *"spiritual realm"*, but having said this, it is probable it will be outside the cosmos, or *"the new heaven and new earth"*, that the Bible promises. Hell is no part of the ordered cosmos, as like sin itself, it is lawless, loveless and without light. Hell is the place of lawlessness, hopelessness, and demonic malevolence to which God has confined it. Some have likened it to a Black Hole, which is *"outside"* but such physical analogies may confuse rather than assist us in understanding it.

Professor Louis Berkhof (theologian) commented: *"In present day theology there is an evident tendency in some circles to rule out the idea of eternal punishment. ....The Bible also speaks of a 'furnace of fire', Matt. 13:42, and a 'lake of fire,' Rev. 20: 14,15, which forms a contrast with the 'sea of glass like unto crystal', Rev. 4:6. The terms 'prison,' 1 Pet. 3:19, 'abyss', Luke 8:31, and 'tartarus', 2 Pet. 2:4 are also used. From the fact that the preceding terms are all local designations, we may infer that Hell is a place. Moreover, local expressions are generally used in connection with it. .."* [6] Nor is the New Testament alone in its teaching. Two significant passages in the Old Testament (amongst others) make it clear there is *'life after death'*. Firstly, Isaiah 26:19 *"But your dead will live; their bodies will rise."* Secondly, Daniel 12: 2 *"Multitudes who sleep in the dust of the earth will awake: some to everlasting life, others to shame and everlasting contempt."*

The problem of evil and Hell

Rejection of the view that God would send anyone to Hell has led some to reject the idea of any *"Hell"* or to re-define it as annihilation. Matthew 25: 41 says: *"Then He will also say to those on the left hand, 'Depart from me, you cursed, into the everlasting fire prepared for the devil and His angels'.* Later in verse 46 it says: *"And these will go away into everlasting punishment, but the righteous into eternal life."* Augustine of Hippo commenting on Matthew 25: 41, 46, over 1,500 years ago stated: *"To say that life eternal shall be endless [but that] punishment shall come to an end is the height of absurdity."* [7] So the idea of annihilationism (when it's over, it's over) is ruled out. Such nebulous views seem more influenced by a society where even *"rats have got rights"* and demands are made for humane treatment of oysters! Such a society does not understand God's justice nor the clear teaching of Scripture.

Other viewpoints

Some have suggested the concept of Hell be abandoned as *"medieval superstition"*. Certainly Dante's grotesque visions of the *Inferno* were fuelled more by classical mythology and his own imagination than by Scripture. Some teach a state of purgatory (a state between heaven and hell). This idea is still believed in by the Roman Catholic Church. F. J. Sheed (a Catholic Apologist) seeks to justify it thus: *"Be wary when an objector says that some doctrine or practice of ours is not in Scripture— wary of accepting his statement, still warier of producing texts to prove him wrong."* [8] He goes on to admit, *" ... such texts as are usually quoted to establish purgatory's existence turn out to be not as compelling as we might wish."* [9] Sheed therefore tries to justify it on the basis of church tradition, passed on (he claims) but not recorded by the apostles. Professor Berkhof states clearly: *"The doctrine finds absolutely no support in Scripture, and moreover rests on false premises such as (a) that we must add something to the work of Christ; (b) that our good works are meritorious in the strict sense of the word ...."* [10]

Conclusion

Apart from Scripture teaching the existence of Hell, there is the bigger problem of the reality of evil. How could a just God ignore man's inhumanity to man? The incredible and endless list of gruesome events that are scarcely mentionable for their wickedness and horror. How could God permit Auschwitz? Surely, Hell is part of the solution, not part of the problem. Could we believe in a God who ignored Auschwitz? There must be some ultimate justice if God is truly just. Again, does not the mission of Christ need the reality of Hell as its backdrop? What immense problem or emergency could have called for *"God to be contracted to a span, and incomprehensibly made man"*? What emergency could have necessitated the enfleshment of God? It was because there was no one else good enough to pay the price of sin, He only could unlock the gates of Heaven and let us in. As Vernon Higham wrote:

"Great is the gospel of our glorious God,
where mercy met the anger of God's rod;
A penalty was paid and pardon bought,
And sinners lost at last to Him were brought."

Christ came to suffer, the just for the unjust, to bear our sins lest we perish. But Jesus, the eternal Son of God, warned us of the threat of Hell. *"It is better for you to enter life maimed than with two hands to go into Hell, where the fire never goes out."* These warnings mean that despite the fate of the wicked, it need not be your fate. Jesus also promised: *"Whoever hears my word and believes him who sent me has eternal life and will not be condemned; he has crossed over from death to life"* (John 5 : 24). C. H. Spurgeon (preacher) said: *"He who does not prepare for death is more than an ordinary fool. He is a madman."*

References:

1   **A. W. Pink,** *Eternal Punishment*, Keiner Publications, Swengel, Pa 17880.

2   **J. Benton** (1985) *How can a God of love send people to Hell?* Evangelical Press, ISBN 0 85234 216 0, pp. 8-9

3   See also: Deuteronomy 32:35; Hebrews 10: 30-31.

4   **J. Blanchard** (1993) *Whatever happened to Hell?* Evangelical Press, Darlington, ISBN 0-85234-303-5, p. 42.

5   Supporting References: 2 Thess. 1:9; Mark 9: 43, 44, 46, 48; and Luke 16: 24.

6   **L. Berkhof** (1994) *Systematic Theology*, Banner of Truth, Edinburgh, p. 735.

7   **Augustine,** *City of God*, Book 21, Chapter 23, Ages Software, p. 990.

8   **F. J. Sheed** (1977)*Where will you spend eternity?*, Sheed and Ward Ltd, London, ISBN 0 72207 808 0, p. 59.

9   **Ibid.**

10   **L. Berkhof** (1994) Ibid, p. 687.

Further Reading:

Eryl Davies (1991) *An Angry God?* Evangelical Press of Wales, Bridgend, Mid Glam., ISBN 1-850449-096-1.

William Hendrickson: (1980) The Bible on the Life Hereafter, Baker Book House, ISDN 0-8010-4189-9

Key Text:
Hebrews 9:27: *"It is appointed unto men once to die, but after this the judgement."*

Endnote: 1

Michael Watts writing on *"Why did the English stop going to Church?"concluded— somewhat reluctantly—that C. H. Spurgeon was right in his future predictions. He says, "Yet, a hundred years after the Down Grade controversy, I have to confess that both in his interpretation of history, and in his prognosis for the future, it was Spurgeon, not Clifford* [President of the Baptist Union in 1888] *, who was right. The English churches of the late eighteenth century, did indeed abandon 'the faith which was once delivered to the saints'. That is why they have been so singularly unsuccessful in retaining the adherence of English men and women. The Tracterian leader Edward Bouverie Pusey once commented that nothing keeps men from the pleasures of sin 'but the love of God or the fear of Hell', and that it is 'the fear of Hell' that drives people back to God'. The English churches by and large ignored his advice, and as a result English men and women stopped attending their services."* **M. Watts** (1995) *Why did the English stop going to Church?* Dr Williams Trust, London, WCIH 0AG, ISBN 0305-3962, p. 14.

Questions for Further Study

1   According to Arthur Pink are we in a good position to judge God's view of justice?
2   How do people show they recognise the need for justice?
3   What did C. S. Lewis come to understand about the concept of justice?
4   If we are critical of God's need to punish, then we imply Christ was misguided in his theoretical theology. Is this possible?
5   What reductionist views have been proposed on the nature of "Hell"?
6   Would God be just if he let Hitler, Stalin and Pol Pot be snuffed out, never to be punished for the evil they committed? See Romans 12: 19b *"Vengeance is mine; I will repay, says the Lord."*
7   Where is Hell, and is it a location?

8 How does Augustine of Hippo show annihilation is not a biblical option? This is with reference to Matthew 25: 41, *"Then He will also say to those on the left hand, 'Depart from me, you cursed, into the everlasting fire prepared for the devil and His angels'.* In verse 46 it says: *"And these will go away into everlasting punishment, but the righteous into eternal life."*

9 Is there any clear biblical support for the idea of purgatory?

10 Does the mission of Christ need the reality of Hell as its backdrop?

Food for thought:

* *"Those who will not deliver themselves into the hand of God's mercy cannot be delivered out of the hand of his justice."*Matthew Henry.

* *"There are no personal relationships in hell"* C. S. Lewis.

* *"Punishment, that is the justice of the unjust."* Augustine of Hippo.

* *"If I profess with the loudest voice every Bible doctrine except the one truth which Satan is attacking today, I am no soldier of Jesus Christ."* Martin Luther.

* *"*Apart from God and immortality, human life, in all its departments and issues, must be regarded as a failure. 'All is vanity.'"* T. H. Leale.

* *"*Vanity of vanities: the idea denoted by this frequent word is transitoriness, swift passing away; rather than nothingness. Things may be very transient, yet very important - like the present human life, which St. James pictures as 'a vapour that soon passes away', James 4:14." O. Zockler on Ecclesiastes 1:2.

Tragedies—why?

"We can sometimes see more through a tear than through a telescope." Anonymous

When considering the reasons for tragedies, pain and suffering we note that life in this world is a vale of tears affected by mankind's rebellion against God. Evolutionists have to accept suffering as part of the way the world is, as a part of life. Dr Brand realised that pain is -in one sense—a good thing, as it gives warning of something wrong. Christians have proved that even in suffering they can glorify God, e.g. Joni (paralysed after a dive) and Tony (facing terminal cancer). It is through suffering that Christ offers redemption, and ultimate hope in this life and the next.

The problem of pain

Those who listen to *Thought for the Day* must be struck by the recurrent theme of, *"Why is there suffering in this world"*? One flower tribute to the sixteen children and one teacher who died at Dunblane, Scotland—at the hands of a crazed gunman—simply asked on the attached card *"why?"* The Bible teaches we are part of a fallen world. Even so, when we see such depraved acts we find it hard to accept how people can really stoop so low as to murder the young and innocent. Tragedies, sadly, are not new. We remember the sinking of the Free Enterprise, the Lockerbie air disaster, and the massacre of the young children at Dunblane—followed by another gunman tragedy in Port Arthur, Tasmania. Then the bombing in Oklahoma City ..... Hurricane Mitch creating havoc in central America, with ten thousand killed, one million left homeless, and several economies set back 30 years; war and bloodshed in Sudan, as one of many places. In addition, people everywhere have serious health problems and worries that may be *"life-threatening"* , or may have lost loved ones in road accidents.

As G. A. Studdert Kennedy has pronounced, *"If anybody is not disturbed by the problem of pain, it is for one of two reasons: either because of hardening of the heart or else because of softening of the brain."* Pain and suffering encompass so many things. Broadly speaking there is psychological, physical and/or spiritual pain, or any combination of these. Pain includes: injury, hurt, sprain, strain, heartache, anguish, despair, sickness and grief. The list is endless. Sophocles (496-406 BC) wisely pointed out that the troubles hurt most when they are self inflicted. Some of our problems are a direct result of our wrong actions or choices. This is true personally, nationally and internationally. Wealthy nations have been known to destroy food and drink— rather than donate it to the poor and needy. Rightly, this world has been called a *"vale of tears"*. The Bible says, *"Man is born to trouble as the sparks fly upward"* (Job 5:7). As sure as the physical law operates that hot smoke and sparks rise in a fire, so we can be certain that troubles will affect us in this life. As others have put it, *"Life is not a bowl of cherries"*.

Jesus' answer

We deeply sympathise with those who suffer and have suffered in this manner. Our thoughts and our prayers go out to those concerned. How can they ever fully recover from such senseless bereavement or pain, the bomb or the bullet? Why does God allow these things to happen? The same question was asked of the Lord Jesus Christ. Dr Luke records the incident of the Galileans whose blood Pilate mixed with their sacrifices, and the eighteen who met a violent death when the tower of Siloam fell on them. *"Why was this?"* people asked him. *"Were these people worse than others?"* Jesus dealt with the problem by pointing out that this tragedy was not a direct result of their sin, but a result of sin in general (see Luke 13 verses 1 to 5). We live in a fallen world. We have lost paradise, and suffer the consequences of people turning away from God. If people refuse to acknowledge God, and gratify their own lust at the expense of other people, is God to be blamed? The Bible teaches the responsibility of people for their actions. The same goes for *"wars and rumours of wars"* as Cordell Hull commented, *"War is not an act of God but a crime of man."*

Evolutionary perspectives on suffering

The fundamental question: *"Why is there suffering?"* usually refers to human suffering. It is often directed at an illness or loss suffered by the questioner. For the evolutionist, some aspects of suffering are the products of natural selection. Pain, for instance, is essential for survival. Dr Mike Appleby (biologist) points out, *"The evolutionary approach does not yet explain all aspects of suffering but our understanding of evolutionary psychology and evolutionary medicine is expanding rapidly. Nevertheless, a response from the evolutionary perspective to the question 'Why is there suffering?' doesn't necessarily satisfy the questioner, any more than does a straightforward cause-and-effect answer ('Your mother has cancer because she has smoked all her life')."*[1]

This approach—claims Appleby—is a pre-Darwinian question. The latter may be put in the form, *"Why is the world the way it is?"* Often the query took the form, *"Why did God make the world this way?"* In a highly derogatory remark Appleby says, *"The evolutionary perspective on the world is that the world is not arbitrary and events are not the whims of a capricious God. Understanding of evolution helps us see that suffering is part of life. How could there be an evolved world without suffering ."*[2] Appleby then reports the reaction of Professor Richard Dawkins as given on the BBC's *The Moral Maze* programme: Dawkins said: *"'Why' questions are non-questions except in certain special senses. If I ask the question 'Why do birds have wings?' I can give an answer to that in a Darwinian sense: it's a very special kind of 'Why'. If I ask the question 'Why does so-and-so whom I love have cancer, why did it have to happen to that person?', that's the kind of question that religious people might ask—'Why me? Why me, God?'"* [and at this point the interviewer interpolated *"Or why is there suffering?"*]—*"that is a silly question that has no answer. You will get nowhere if you try to ask questions like that—you simply have to accept that you have cancer and that's that."*[3]

In fact it is not just religious people who ask such questions and dismissing them as silly was probably not the most sensitive way to alert people to the supposed error of their ways. Furthermore, as Appleby notes, by *"silly"* he apparently means *"irrational"*—people who ask *"Why me?"* questions are being irrational because they are failing to take into account their knowledge of the world and its evolutionary history. What is even more questionable is Dawkins' implication that such so-called "irrationality" is wrong and his "rationality" is right.

God is at work

The Bible assures us there is an answer to pain, suffering and ultimately death itself... but often our thinking is too human-centred, rather than God-centred, to fully appreciate it. Let us remember that the world would be in an even worse condition, if God did not restrain evil in some measure. God makes the sun shine on both the just and the unjust. His restraining grace holds back the torrent of evil that would soon overwhelm us. The Lord in His kindness exercises a general goodness toward all His creatures. *"The Lord is good to all, and His tender mercies are over all His works."* Is therefore *"pain"* in any sense good?

Much of the research and advances in treating Leprosy has been brought about by Christian missionary doctors. Foremost amongst these has been Dr Paul Brand. He established that the terrible disfigurement associated with Leprosy is not caused by the bacterium but by the patient. The bacterium destroys the pain sensors at the end of the nerve cells. Any damage, any disease, any accident, occurring to the leper is all hidden. Dr Paul Brand says if there is one thing he could give lepers, it would be to give them back their sense of pain. *"Thank God for pain!"* Brand declares with conviction, *"I cannot think of a greater gift I could give my leprosy patients."*4 Even in this area, so commonly held up as a challenge to a loving God, Brand sees reason for thoughtful gratitude.

A Wounded Creation

We have already indicated that the woes of this world are a result of sin. There is a dark side to the natural world too, just as there is to human beings. In this physical realm we are often subject to unexpected danger, as TV programmes like 999 so graphically illustrates. The point is well illustrated by the amazing story of American Joni Eareckson Tada, when as the result of a diving accident at the age of seventeen she was left totally paralysed. She had to struggle to accept her handicap, and find the meaning and purpose of her life. Joni learned to face sickness and pain drawing on her faith in God, and an awareness of His presence.5 Another significant example of courage, similar to Joni's, was found in Tony Tindall, who was told as a young man of twenty one that he had cancer. It was through facing the *"Big C"* that Tony found his faith in God. Yet he was able to endure the agony of pain relieved only by increased doses of morphine and heroin, the prospect of decreased mobility and, indeed death itself, and yet to say that he was happier and more fulfilled than ever.[6]

God's involvement

The Gospels declare a God who is anything but isolated from His creatures. The gospel of Jesus Christ is the amazing news of a God who was *"Our God contracted to a span, incomprehensibly made man"* as one hymn puts it. It is about Jesus, the eternal Son of God, who left the courts of Heaven, to come to planet earth: *"out of the ivory palaces into a world of woe"*. At the announcement of His coming, Herod passed a law to massacre all baby boys, in an attempt to kill Him. But Mary and Joseph escaped to Egypt. Why did the God-man Jesus come? He was the only perfect one who had come to suffer and give His life as a ransom for many to be saved. On the cross Christ's last words were, *"It is finished"* as He bore the punishment from God the Father for our sin. Sin is living life as if God did not exist, ignoring Him. As the living creator God, He deserves our love and thanks for all He has done.

The suffering Saviour

The Bible teaches that God has come to us in our grief. God himself—in the person of His Son, has entered into and participated in the suffering of the human realm. Christ's death was not just another death. By shedding His blood, He atoned for the sins of those who would turn to Him. Those who would ask forgiveness for their own sin, and who would *"believe on the name of the Lord Jesus Christ"*. Jesus was prophesied by Isaiah as *"a man of sorrows, and familiar with suffering .... Surely He took up our infirmities, and carried our sorrows, yet we considered Him stricken by God, smitten by Him and afflicted. But He was pierced for our trans-gressions, He was crushed for our iniquities ..."* (see Isaiah 53: 1 to 7). People are often willing to talk about the deaths of other people, but never their own. The emphasis that Jesus brings out in Luke 13, when he speaks so solemnly about these tragedies, is that we too must die, and are we prepared? The great matter is to be ready when death comes—death is the one appointment we will all keep.

The problem of pain

The Bible records a dramatic scene when the overwhelming questions raised by the problem of pain were asked of God himself in the book of Job. Job was robbed of his wealth, his ten children, and finally his health. No one is sure of the exact nature of his illness, which resulted in him being covered head to foot in boils. There have been suggestions it was elephantiasis, erythema, or smallpox. His state was so gross, even his wife told him to curse God and die. The long speech God gave in reply has endured as one of the great nature passages of literature—a celebration of wildlife and weather—mountain goats, ostriches, wild horses and snowstorms. To the problem of pain God gave no direct answer. He challenged Job: *"If I as creator, have produced such a marvellous world as this, which you can see for yourself, cannot you trust me with those areas you cannot comprehend?"*

Job and his companions all agreed on the doctrine of the sovereignty of God (that God controls all things), but they were inconsistent in their faith in that they approached the problem of suffering from a human-centred point of view. They thought that God's dealings with people were determined in terms of man's justice or injustice, and that Job's sin or righteousness was the determining fact in the course of events. They believed God's dealings with Job were to be understood merely in terms of Job's inner life. God made known this way of thinking is wrong and insisted that the only valid standard is a God-centred standard.

The only measure by which things in heaven and earth can be judged is the Lord and His purpose, the Sovereign God Himself. Job could not claim of any event in the course of his life that this event was wrong because it affected him adversely, since all events in the life of Job could only be judged in terms of one standard, the purpose of the sovereign Triune God. When Job recognised these things to be the correct interpretation, the Lord blessed the last part of Job's life, more than the first part. Once again, Job returned to the wisdom of his original reaction, *"The Lord gave, and the Lord has taken away; blessed be the name of the Lord "* (Job 1:21).

Similarly the tragedies in Jesus' time were the talking point with all. People were asking *"Why?"* Jesus did not directly answer their question. His response was, *"What about you? ... Unless you repent, you too will all perish"*. It is often through sorrow that we see the folly of this passing world. It is at such times we may look seriously at our lives, and come to thank God for every day He gives us. A hymn expresses so well the Christian response to trouble and grief:

When through the deep waters I cause thee to go,
The rivers of woe shall not thee overflow;
For I will be with thee, thy troubles to bless,
And sanctify to thee thy deepest distress. 7

The lesson Jesus pointed out was that this is a passing world. There are *"no gains, without pains"* in this life. We live in a *"paradise lost"* and the only way to see a *"paradise regained"* is to trust in Him, as our redeemer, who pays our debt of sin, and gives us a place in heaven—if we trust in Him (John 3: 15, 16).

References:

1   **R. Appleby,** *Darwin was my grandmother,* Philosophy Now, Issue No. 18, Summer 1997, Ipswich. ISBN 0961-5970, p. 20.

2   **Ibid.**

3   **Ibid.**

4   **A. Spangler & C. Turner** (editors) (1991) Heroes, IVP, Leicester, ISBN 0—85110 862 8, p. 14.

5   **J. Eareckson** (1996) *The Joni Story,* Marshall Pickering, ISBN 0-551-03065-8.

6   **V. Wood** (1988) *Tony,* Mayflower Christian Books, Southampton, ISBN 0 907821 05 7.

7   **Robert Keen** (1787)*"How firm a foundation, ye saints of the Lord,"* Hymn: 307, Baptist Hymnal (1933), Psalms and Hymns Trust, London, W. C. 1.

Further Reading:

H. M. Carson (1979) *Facing Suffering,* Eurobooks, Welwyn, Herts, ISBN 0 906 56 601 0.

C. S. Lewis (1942) *The Problem of Pain,* Fontana.

D. M. Lloyd-Jones (1986) *Why does God allow War?* Evangelical Press of Wales.

Key Texts:

Job 38: 2 *"Who is this who darkens counsel By words without knowledge?"*

Job 38: 4 *"Where were you when I laid the earth's foundation? Tell me , if you understand."*

Questions for Further Study

1 If this is God's world, why does he allow tragedies? (See Luke 13 : 1-5).
2 What is the evolutionary explanation for pain and suffering?
3 Is Dr Richard Dawkins' response to suffering, realistic or dismissive?
4 Does God restrain evil in this world?
5 What case studies show how marvellously people with pain can still glorify God in their affliction?
6 Why is Christ known as the "Suffering Saviour"? (See Isaiah 53).
7 Can you think of any biblical reasons why people feel death is wrong? (SeeGenesis 2: 17).
8 What ultimately is a greater tragedy than loss of life in this world?
9 What Scripture, hymns or poetry have given you comfort in times of trouble, bereavement, etc?
10 How would you answer the criticism that Christianity is offering, *"pie in the sky when you die"*- that is, a better life after death. Would such a perspective help those who are suffering now?
11 C. S. Lewis said: *"God whispers to us in our pleasures, speaks in our consciences, but shouts in our pains; it is his megaphone to rouse a deaf world."* What does C. S. Lewis mean when he says that pain is God's megaphone [or loudspeaker]? See Food for Thought.
12 The loss of the Titanic in 1912 has remained one of the world's greatest maritime disasters. The orchestra continued to play popular tunes, to the very end. The hymn*"Nearer, My God, to Thee"* is believed to have been one of the last pieces of music to be played before the ship took its final dive. Do you think that this "unsinkable ship" is a modern parable, and if so how?

Food for Thought
  * "As lately I lay very sick, so sick that I thought I should have left this world, many cogitations and musings had I in my weakness. Ah! thought I, what may eternity be? What joys may it have?" Martin Luther.

It ain't necessarily so: can we accept miracles?

"He that will believe only what he can fully comprehend must have a very long head or a very short creed."
Charles Caleb Colton

In this section, we look at the meaning of the term "miracle", and seek to clarify this concept. Then, we progress to the question of evidence for miracles; we examine in detail the views of the philosopher Hume (one of the chief opponents of the idea of miracle). The different classification of miracles is explained, viz. "miracles of creation" and "miracles of providence". The issue of whether miracles are physically possible is discussed and the credibility of the witnesses to miracles is reviewed. The biblical picture is of a God who controls all natural forces; a miracle, then, is a particularly significant act of God, not a particularly supernatural one—as God is sustaining the whole universe continuously. If miracles like the resurrection of Jesus Christ are not a fact, Christianity has no unique message.

Miracles: introduction

"It ain't necessarily so, the things that you're liable to read in the Bible, they ain't necessarily so." These pithy words were written by George Gershwin, for his *Porgy and Bess* opera (1935). The sentiments expressed in this song encapsulate so much of the modern approach to miracles. The latter viewpoint claims that miracles were written into the Gospel accounts to inculcate religious truths—rather than to record historical events. Thus the significance of the miracle, they claim, lies in its meaning rather than the event itself. It shows only that God directs and intervenes in human affairs. We shall examine in detail this minimalist view, putting it in context with its related concept of rejection of the Bible's teaching.

Semantics

What is a miracle? The word, from Latin, literally means *"an object of wonder"*, that is attributed to a special divine intervention or to supernatural forces. Theologically it is sometimes defined as an event in nature produced by God, who **suspends** His laws of nature in order to produce a (usually) beneficial effect for humans. This definition already suggests a system running—like a clock (the world)—independently of the watchmaker (God). This is a **deistic interpretation** of a miracle. It contradicts the clear teaching of Scripture that *"God sustains all things by the word of His power"* and that *"in Him we live and move and have our being"*. In reality, the biblical miracle is not a *"suspension"* of natural law as God is upholding the whole of reality all the time. Instead, it is a time when the laws of nature are *"superseded at a particular point by a higher manifestation of the will of God."*[1] Writers have used the concept of *"miracle"* so loosely that it ceases to have meaning: For instance, *"A thousand miles of miracles in China (Burkhardt)"* almost implies everything was a miracle in China, so that one could be forgiven for thinking that nothing was!

Like many issues the acceptability of miracles depends not only on your original assumptions and definitions, but also on metaphysical issues. Some sceptics argue that nothing can happen without a cause; furthermore nothing happens that cannot happen, and when what was capable of happening has happened, it cannot be interpreted as a miracle. This sort of definition tells us nothing about the possibility of a miracle, merely that the term miracle can be so defined as to be logically incoherent, like a *"square circle"*.

Foundational beliefs

In our naturalistic secular culture, the belief in miracles is highly questionable because many believe everything that happens in the universe follows the laws of science. Our scientific culture excludes the supernatural. In contrast, the Christian believes that as God created the universe to start with, there is no problem in accepting that He can continue to cause things to occur that would not normally happen. As has been argued elsewhere in this book, no one approaches the issue of

Figure 10 . 1 Miracles under the Microscope

Definition	Deist's conception	Theist's conception
(i) General definition: "an object of wonder"	Miracles occur where there is a "suspension" of natural law; miracles in this scheme are 'proofs of God'. Belief in God depends on reason rather than revelation.	A miracle occurs where natural laws are "superseded" by a higher manifestation of the will of God.
(ii) Vague definitions: "Everything is miraculous" e.g. '1000 miles of miracles.'		
(iii) Logically incoherent: "Nothing happens that cannot happen," renders idea meaningless; e.g. a square circle. Comment "The miraculous is absolutely basic to Christianity." E. H. A.	The world is like a clock, made by the watchmaker (God) who left it to tick on its own. God has to poke his finger into the mechanism to effect a miracle. Notion of miracle attacked by David Hume.	The whole of creation and its laws are sustained by God. This means God can cause miracles by imposing His will on Nature. Colossians 1:16 teaches God sustains all things by the word of His power.

miracles with a completely open mind.

The argument over miracles is not so much a matter of assessing whether the evidence for a given miracle is strong or weak, but a matter of your foundational beliefs. A person's worldview will determine what conclusion they arrive at, whether they are "for" or "against". In the following discussion we hope to show that a belief in materialism or naturalism as the total system is drastically flawed. Furthermore, there is sufficient evidence to show that God has intervened in the world, and so challenge the assumption that only the natural world exists. We begin, however, by looking at the philosopher Hume's views, as he still encapsulates a lot of the animosity shown, by some modern scientists, against the possibility of miracles occurring. David Hume (1711-1776) was a Scottish philosopher who is considered to be one of the greatest sceptics in the history of philosophy.

Evidences

In his Essay entitled *"Of Miracles"* (1741) Hume claims: *"The Christian religion not only was at first attended with miracles, but even at this day cannot be believed by any reasonable person without one. Mere reason is insufficient to convince us of its veracity: and whoever is moved by faith to assent to it, is conscious of a continued miracle in his own person, which subverts all the principles of his understanding, and gives him a determination to believe what is most contrary to custom and experience."* Hume declared that, *"no human testimony can have such force as to prove a miracle and make it a just foundation for any such system of religion."* [2] It is argued by Hume and others that the question *"Has a miracle ever occurred?"* is impossible to answer in principle', as it is impossible to provide sufficient evidence for a miracle. See **Figure 10 .1 "Miracles under the Microscope."**

Hume's criticisms

Hume's arguments are still widely respected in philosophy departments today, despite the fact that his reasoning fails to distinguish between the deist and theist conceptions of God. His argument is directed at the deist, who looks for miracles as a proof for the supernatural. Deism is the belief in the existence of a supreme being arising from reason rather than revelation; reason is in harmony with revelation (or revelation must conform to reason). In contrast, theism is the world-view that asserts the reality of a personal infinite Creator, who is both immanent in His creation and transcendent to it. It is the deist, primarily, not the theist who is implicated in Hume's criticisms, although Hume himself does not appear to distinguish between the two positions. For the deist, a miracle is the point at which the remote watchmaker *("God")* puts his "finger" into the clockwork of the universe and makes something happen.

The Biblical theist relies on the Bible's own description of miracles. If God upholds all things by the word of his power, then a miracle is no more spectacular, or supernatural, than what are usually known as the *"laws of nature"*. The Bible says that without God's constant and continuous intervention, this universe would degenerate into chaos! So Hume may be showing an atheistic bias, by being uncritical about arguments that prove what he wanted to prove, i.e. there is no Supernatural God sustaining nature, therefore no possibility of such a God intervening in the world or universe for that matter!

Another tack

Another way to criticise Hume's views is to point out first that his argument is only valid if one first assumes that miracles do not happen: if miracles do not happen, then miracles do not happen to people, and so the only people who believe in miracles (the people who believe that a miracle has happened inside themselves) experience the *"subversion of all the principles of their understanding"*, and there is no solid evidence for miracles. However, if one leaves open the question of whether miracles do happen, then Hume's argument falls apart: if miracles may possibly happen, then miracles may possibly happen to people, and the people who believe in miracles (the people who believe that a miracle has happened inside themselves) may possibly not be deluded, and may possibly provide solid evidence for miracles.

Second, Hume assumes that it is possible to verify things using *"mere reason,"* as opposed to *"faith"*. As we argued in chapter 6 *Science or Scientism*, any scientific exercise requires basic faith assumptions, and the relevant question is not whether faith is involved, but whether the evidence upon which the faith is based is sound. Third, Hume makes a very general statement: *"Whoever is moved by faith to assent to [a miracle] is conscious of a continued miracle in his own person"*. The Bible flatly contradicts this: many people witnessed Christ's miracles without experiencing regeneration (e.g. John 6: 66; Matthew 28:11-15).

Possibility of miracles

Many laugh at the possibility of miracles. As God established the laws, He is able to change or suspend them if He desires. To say miracles are impossible is actually to deny that God exists. Thus the basis for believing in the miraculous goes back to the biblical conception of God. If the main premise of theism is accepted, *"In the beginning God"* (Genesis: 1:1), then the rest should not pose any problems. Naturally in the system of theology and apologetics the doctrine of God is of fundamental importance. We must first ask what kind of a God Christianity believes in before we can really ask with intelligence whether such a God exists. If it is true that God exists, with the communicable and incommunicable attributes that the Bible claims for him, then one may say with certainty that miracles are theoretically possible. This cannot be done if creation is not taken as the starting point.

The answer as to whether miracles do happen, with respect to God, is contained in his incomprehensible and inscrutable will; with respect to man, it is contained in the Bible (as God's declaration of his past, present and future actions), and in man's experience (e.g. Peter walking on the water). Whether God has adequate reason to suspend his ordinary laws is not a legitimate subject of human discussion, and the relevant evidence is in the Bible and experience. The question therefore is not whether miracles can happen, but whether they do happen. The answer depends on whether God has adequate reason for superseding His ordinary laws or not, and also upon whether there is sufficient evidence that God has done so. There have been two major types of miracle recognised: those called *"miracles of creation"* and others, known as *"miracles of providence."*

Miracles of creation

Miracles of creation involve a new act of creation (be it energy, matter, or order) that none other than a Creator God can do. The act of creation *"ex nihilo"* is clearly such a miracle! Despite this, a learned Professor who attended a conference on *Evolution and Creation*, objected to the idea that God could say *"hey presto"*—as it were—and an elephant occur. What was his problem with such a concept, when dealing with a God who is said to be able to do far exceedingly above what we can ask or think? *"What would happen to the particles so displaced?"* he queried. We see immediately the fallacy of his criticism: using the normal laws of physics or nature as a yardstick to measure what the creator of those laws could, or could not do. A miracle is by definition a unique event. Although a miracle is not necessarily without precedent—II Kings 4:35, for example, is a precedent for Matthew 9:25. It is impossible to account for it as we do other events. If an event happened which defies explanation, we still have to admit to the fact that it occurred. It is only "impossible to account for miracles as we do other events" in a limited sense: miracles cannot be accounted for in scientific terms, but they can be in teleological terms; e.g. Luke 5:24. This miracle was designed to show Jesus could forgive sins.

Other *"miracles of creation"* are the great *"sign miracles"* like turning the water into wine, the feeding of the five thousand, and the raising of Lazarus from the dead. These were to confirm that *"Jesus is the Christ, the Son of God, and that believing you may have life through his name"* (John 20: 31). The miracle of regeneration, whereby a person by believing on the Lord Jesus receives assurance of forgiveness and everlasting life (2 Cor. 5:17).

Miracles of providence

The second type of miracles are those of providence. Here there is no direct divine intervention in natural laws but a special ordering of the manner or time of occurrence of a particular event or process. In miracles of providence there is no supernatural *"opposition"* of natural laws, as there are in miracles of creation. Such miracles include: the Philippian earthquake (Acts 16:26), the drought of Elijah (lasting three and a half years) recorded in 1 Kings 17, and many other miracles. Such miracles may involve a *"rare event"* but sometimes (if it is not clearly revealed in Scripture) only God knows whether he specifically intervened to create these conditions. Archie Poulos has, in support of providential miracles, said this: *"It is worth adding a comment on another misunderstanding of biblical miracles. That is, miracles in the Bible are not always presented as necessarily violating natural laws or being without secondary causes. For example, the miracle of the parting of the Red Sea is said in Exodus 14:22 to have been accomplished "with a strong east wind". While this event was certainly very unusual, it involved natural elements; the real miracle was in the purpose and timing of the event. The Bible does not present God as outside and remote from the world, [as the Deist believes] with miracles as evidence of supernatural intervention. The biblical picture is of a God who controls all natural forces; a miracle, then, is a particularly significant act of God, not a particularly supernatural one. Indeed, in the Bible the very natural/supernatural distinction on which Hume based his argument is overturned. The 'supernatural' event is accomplished by natural means."*[3]

Poulos' comments can be criticised, however. Firstly, what is a *"particularly supernatural"* act of God? Either it is natural or it is supernatural, it cannot be particularly supernatural! Second, it is only from the Bible that it is possible to hold a natural/supernatural distinction! If there is no God, then there is no supernatural against which to set the natural. Yet God does exist, and He created an orderly cosmos governed by natural laws which God may (supernaturally) override (miracles of creation) or use to achieve ends which demonstrate the existence of the supernatural (miracles of providence). Finally the parting of the Red Sea involved God holding back a wall of water, which rushed in to drown all the Egyptian army so can hardly be classified as a miracle of providence. Rather it was a miracle of creation, as God created a wall of water and dry path through the river, by a strong east wind. God then told Moses to stretch his hand over the sea, *"and the waters returned and covered the chariots, the horsemen, and all the army of Pharaoh that came into the sea after them"* (Exodus 14 :26-28). The alternative idea—that the water was so shallow the Israelites crossed over safely, is also made nonsense of by this graphic account. Shallow water does not engulf and drown a whole army!

Logically or physically impossible?

Whilst some agree that miracles are logically possible, they may claim there is no way of showing that nature could not produce the 'miraculous' events unaided. As miracles involve God's overriding normal laws by His supernatural power, how can we know that nature could not do these unaided? Then, it is argued, how can we be certain that any event is an act of God, could it not be something nature could bring about without God's help? Something like this viewpoint may have been in the minds of the Epicurean philosophers who heard the apostle Paul preach about the resurrection of Jesus. Was this a new potentiality of man? *"We want to hear you again on this subject,"* said some (Acts 17:32). Antony Flew presented this argument as follows: *"The natural scientist, confronted with some occurrence inconsistent with a proposition previously believed to express a law of nature, can find in this disturbing inconsistency no ground whatever for proclaiming that the particular law of nature has been supernaturally overridden. On the contrary, the new discovery is* *simply a reason for his conceding that he had previously been wrong in thinking that the proposition thus confuted, did indeed express a true law; it is also a reason for his resolving to search again for the law which really does obtain."*4

Occam's Razor

Flew's claim that there are *"no grounds whatever"* to accept supernatural intervention is very questionable. To re-define a natural law to accommodate the *"new potentiality"* may involve too many *"twists and turns"*, too many random adjustments to our definitions of scientific laws. This is where the principle of simplicity comes into play. This principle of simplicity is known as Occam's Razor. It states that the simplest explanation is the one most likely to be true, to depict reality as it is. Roger White correctly points out: *"... to salvage the natural law requires just too many ad hoc adjustments. For example, the natural law that people die and stay dead may be amended by the clause 'except when the person's name begins with the letter J, he claims to be God and founds a major western religion.' Then the scientist may proclaim, 'So there, it is not really a miracle after all, for it fits well with the laws of nature!' In practice, of course, a competent scientist will find it extremely difficult to make such a bizarre amendment; or to amend such general laws at all, without overturning a vast amount of well-established theory."*5

White comments later from a philosophical viewpoint: *"The focus on violations of physical law and divine intervention seems misguided. First, given the statistical nature of modern physical theories it is not clear that "miraculous" events do strictly contradict physical laws—but this renders such events not the least bit less astonishing. A person rising from the dead, or water turning into wine, is highly unusual and amazing however you describe it. Second, it is not clear what is the relevance of the notion of divine intervention. On one view of the relation between God and creation, God is continually controlling and sustaining every part of creation. On this view every event is an act of God. All talk of "overriding of laws" or "interventions into the natural order" assumes a conception of God and the world which has little relevance in this context. The laws of nature, whatever else we might say about them, can be seen as descriptions of the regular ways in which God acts as opposed to all the other ways in which he acts. God does not have to poke his fingers into the natural mechanisms of the world to perform a miracle, he merely acts in a way different from the usual course for a specific purpose ."*[6]

Clearly one may question White's choice of words, as it is more than highly significant when supernatural acts occur. God expressly orders supernatural acts in order to declare to humans that He is doing important things in the *"time-space continuum"* with regard to his redemptive and revelatory plans. Again, to refer to someone rising from the dead as merely an astonishing instance of a statistical theory seems grossly inadequate.

Quality of witnesses

The final plank in Hume's argument on accepting whether a miracle may have occurred depends on the credibility of the witnesses to that miracle. The aspect Hume emphasised was that the Biblical miracles were not recorded by *"men of good sense"*, but by *"unlearned and ignorant men."* He believed a wise man proportions his belief to the evidence. A careful study shows, however, that the accounts in the Bible are **not** written as a superstitious reaction to a clever trickster called Jesus Christ. The reactions of the people in Bible times were as sceptical and surprised as in modern times. The Bible records that Thomas (a close follower) doubted the resurrection. Matthew records of Jesus: *"When they saw him, they worshipped him; but some doubted"* (Matthew 28:17). The people living at the time knew that men born blind do not see immediately (John 9:32) that five loaves and a few fish cannot feed 5000 people (John 6: 14), and that men do not walk on water (Matthew 14: 26). Luke was a doctor, and Paul trained under the learned Gamaliel—so not all were *"ignorant fishermen"*. To imply any group is lacking in common sense is also stereotyping those with practical skills and knowledge, but who are still intelligent!

Naturalistic explanations need more faith!

The people living in those days were as sceptical as we are today. The supposed *"explanations of the miracles"* often beggar belief! Descartes attempted a rationalistic explanation of the feeding of the 5000 by saying that the crowd were shamed into providing food hitherto concealed! Jesus supposedly walking on a hidden sandbank (not water) or getting the crowd of 5000 to share their food, do not tie in with the facts! Even Old Testament events such as Elijah getting God to set light to the altar and sacrifice (saturated by gallons of water!) is supposed to have been done by Elijah knowing of a secret location where marsh gas was emitted! (While being watched by hundreds of people?!) It was the unavoidable, inescapable and irrefutable facts that caused both followers and sceptics to believe miraculous happenings, and to be willing to die for proclaiming what they had witnessed. Jesus was never asked if he performed miracles, but by what power and authority he did them. Peter at Pentecost (in front of a hostile crowd) was able to claim: *"Jesus of Nazareth, a man approved of God among you by miracles and wonders and signs, which God did by him in the midst of you, as you yourselves know"* (Acts: 2:22).

Uncomfortable truths

The obsession with proving the supernatural continues to the present. The television is used as a testing ground for spiritual beliefs, including shows on the theme of *"Strange but true"* or the paranormal. Kirsten Birkett sums up the position thus: *"If a miraculous event can be proved to have happened, then religion is true, if it can be proved to be false, then religion is not true—all at no moral cost to us. The Bible, however, is not impressed with such games. It recognises there is no such thing as an unbiased observer, dispassionately weighing up evidence. Popular obsession with the spectacular has very little to do with God, who is not a sideshow special but a ruler who requires a response from us. Perhaps that is why it is so much easier to argue about proving, or disproving, miracles; looking at the Bible for what it says is far too uncomfortable."*[7] In fact, if Christianity is not a religion or faith of miraculous events it has no more claim to our attention than any other belief or philosophy! White rightly states: *"The question of whether or not, given certain definitions of terms, the bodily resurrection of Jesus is labelled a 'miracle' is insignificant—you can call it a 'banana' if you wish—what is interesting is did it actually happen? And this cannot be answered by playing with words."*[8] Paul, the apostle, made it plain, *"If Christ has not been raised, your faith is futile"* I Corinthians 15: 17.

References:

1   **L. Berkhof** (1994)*Systematic Theology*, Banner of Truth, Edinburgh, p. 177.
2   **D. Hume** (1962) *On Human Nature and the Understanding*, Collier books, New York, p. 133.
3   **A. Poulos** (1997) *"Addendum: miracles as evidence for Christianity"*, Kategoria, Issue 5, Autumn 1997, Kingsford NSW 2032, Australia, p. 32.
4   **A. Flew** (1972) *"Miracles"*, Encyclopaedia of Philosophy, vol. 5, p. 349.
5   **R. White** (1997) *"Miracles and rational belief"*, Kategoria, Issue 5, Autumn 1997, Kingsford, NSW 2032, Australia, p. 11.
6   **Ibid,** pp. 13-4.
7   **K. Birkett** (1997) Editorial, Kategoria, Issue 5, Autumn 1997, Kingsford NSW 2032, Australia, pp. 6-7.
8   **R. White** (1997) op. cit., p. 10.

Further Reading:

R. D. Geivett & G. R. Habermas (1997) *In Defence of Miracles*, Apollos.
C. S. Lewis (1960) *Miracles,*, Fontana.

Key Text:
Luke 16: 31: *"If they do not hear Moses and the Prophets, neither will they be persuaded though one rise from the dead"*.

Key Terms:
Deism: The belief in the existence of a supreme being arising from reason rather than revelation.

Immanence: A state of being present or dwelling within. In modern pantheism, God or the Absolute is completely within the world and identical with it. According to Deism, God is essentially absent from the world. According to theism, He is both immanent (in presence and activity) and transcendent (in essence) with respect to the world. Mysticism in its broadest sense assumes the mutual immanence of the human and the divine.

Ockham's Razor (or Occam's Razor): The principle of simplicity or ontological economy, usually defined as 'Entities are not to be multiplied beyond necessity'. The principle implies: Firstly, that of two or more possible explanations for phenomena choose the one that (i) explains what is to be explained with the fewest assumptions and explanatory principles; and (ii) explains all, or most, of the facts that need explaining as satisfactorily as any of the other theories. Secondly, the simplest explanation is the one most likely to be true.

Theism: The world-view that asserts the reality of a personal infinite Creator, who is both immanent in His creation and transcendent to it. See "immanence."

Questions for Further Study

1 Is a miracle a *"suspension of natural law"*, or a *"time when the laws of nature are superseded"*? Does it really matter which?

2 What is the *"semantic trap"* reasoning (or intellectual conundrum!) used by sceptics to disprove miracles; how would you disprove it?

3 What was the Scottish philosopher David Hume's view of the possibility of a miracle?

4 How does the deistic view of God as some kind of *"remote watchmaker poking his finger into the mechanism of nature"*, affect the issue of miracles?

5 Does Hume distinguish between deistic and theistic world views, and is this important anyway?

6 Does Hume leave open the argument that miracles can happen to people?

7 Did all the people who witnessed Christ's miracles *"have faith"* ?

8 How would you distinguish between *"miracles of creation"* and *"miracles of providence"* ?

9 What was the reaction of the Epicureans to Christ's resurrection? (Acts 17:32)

10 How does Occam's Razor undermine Flew's claim that there are no grounds whatsoever for supernatural intervention, as laws can be redefined to accommodate new data or possibilities?

11 Why does God not have to *"poke his finger"* into the natural mechanisms of the world to perform a miracle?

12 How would you show that Jesus was no clever trickster or magician?

13 Were all the witnesses to miracles *"unlearned and ignorant men?"* What does the latter phrase mean?

14 How do natural explanations of miracles sometimes *"beggar belief"*?!

15 What is the significance of the bodily resurrection of Jesus, to Christianity? (Note further discussion of this is given in **Appendix 1**, ***Nice One, Cyril.***)

Food for thought:

  * *"The miraculous is absolutely basic to Christianity." Prof. E. H. Andrews.*

  * *"Miracles are not meant to be understood, they are meant to be believed." Dr D. M. Lloyd- Jones.*

Evolution—on the rocks?

"The fossil record is highly imperfect from a Darwinian point of view, not because of the inadequacies of geologists, but because the slow evolutionary connections required by the theory did not happen."
Fred Hoyle & N. C. Wickramasinghe (still both committed evolutionists).

Fossil series are claimed to be the best evidence of micro-evolution, particularly in invertebrates like trilobites, ammonites (related to the pearly nautilus) and sea urchins. Despite these "proofs" there are several methodological problems: the unrepeatability of the timescale invoked, the so-called "species problem" and the issue of whether these case studies took place in a closed biological system. The overall picture is one of "missing links" for macro-evolution, as Hoyle (astronomer) claims the evolutionary record leaks like a sieve.

Evolutionary trends

Evolution in a fossil series? This is often claimed to provide the *"best"* evidence that evolution has occurred in the past. Fossil series are groups of fossilised creatures or animals which it is claimed show some development (transformation) over time in their shape or form, like the famous horse series. Most commonly, invertebrate creatures (those without backbones) are used to show how a species has changed over time. These include such well known fossil creatures as the trilobites, ammonites and echinoids (sea urchins).

A species is said to be the smallest natural group of animals or plants. For example, roach form one single species of fish; among many others. Generally speaking, all the members of a species look and behave alike in every important respect, and can interbreed among themselves. Breeding between members of different species does not usually occur in nature. These small changes (micro-evolution) that may be seen in fossil series are thought to take place over thousands of years. Professor A.S. Romer, former Harvard Zoologist, raises a vital question for geo-scientists, *"Is evolution true? The answer depends upon what is considered by the questioner as valid evidence. Obviously no one can go back through the ages and furnish birth certificates for each of the countless generations of individuals in every animal series. But it can be said that all the known facts of palaeontology are consistent with the theory of evolution and impossible of rational interpretation on any other basis."* [1]

Despite Romer's claims, it is exceedingly difficult to establish supposed evolutionary trends in any series of fossils distributed throughout the rock strata of the geologic column. In fact, Professor Romer's statement gives the real truth away. Ask for any vigorous scientific tests to be applied, or for alternative explanations of the data to be considered, and one will generally be sadly disappointed.

Horse evolution

It has been noted by Richard Milton (science journalist) that, *"Anyone educated in a western country in the last forty years will recall being shown a chart of the horse evolution from 'Eohippus', a small dog-like creature in the Eocene period 50 million years ago, to 'Mesohippus', a sheep-sized animal of 30 million years ago, eventually to 'Dinohippus', the size of a Shetland pony. This chart was drawn up in 1950 by Harvard's Professor of Palaeontology George Simpson, to accompany his standard text book, 'Horses', which encapsulated all the research done by the American Museum of Natural History in the previous half century. Simpson plainly believed that his evidence was incontrovertible because he wrote, 'The history of the horse family is still one of the clearest and most convincing for showing that organisms really have evolved ... There really is no point nowadays in continuing to collect and to study fossils simply to determine whether or not evolution is a fact. The question has been decisively answered in the affirmative.'* [2] This is an amazing claim, when one thinks that even today, there are small circus horses right up to giant cart horses, that if they were buried and fossilised—could be readily arranged in an evolutionary sequence. Alternatively, think if all of today's dog species were buried and their remains dug up—again, it would be possible to arrange these bones in some evolutionary sequence from Pekinese to Great Dane, when in fact they could all interbreed and co-existed together.

Such possibilities Simpson does not recognise, but he did admit that the chart he had constructed contained major gaps that he had not included. Milton continues, " ... *a gap before 'Eohippus' and its unknown ancestors, for example, and another gap after 'Eohippus' and before its supposed descendant 'Mesohippus'. What is it, scientifically, that connects these isolated species on the famous chart if it is not fossil remains? And how could such unconnected examples demonstrate either genetic mutation or natural selection?*" [3]

Micro-evolution and macro problems

Admittedly palaeontologists have got some insurmountable problems. A brief synopsis of these problems can be illustrated by studying invertebrate series found in the fossil record, which are considered to provide some of the best lines of evidence for micro-evolution. Our critique assumes for convenience the validity of the geologic column, although even this may be open to criticism.

The Question of Time

◆ 1. Firstly the timescale invoked for a new species to develop is not available to us, so that experimental verification of inferred change is impossible. The lack of intermediate fossil forms, linking one group to another, has led fossil experts to suggest that change took place rapidly—leaving little evidence. Today, however theorists state that evolution is taking place so gradually that it is not observable. It seems that palaeontologists, *"Look their problems straight in the face—and pass on!"*

What is a Species?

◆ 2. Secondly, a more important problem is that to establish change in a creature one must first be able to identify and classify what the relationships are between the various groups. Today, for instance, biologists and zoologists establish limits for various groups by breeding tests, sterility being evidence of non-compatibility. John Imbries, writing on the species problem with fossil animals says, *"What is a fossil species? How can a fossil species be recognised .... The concept of fossil species held by most palaeontologists is largely an inference, an inference based both on observed structure of living species and on a theoretical model of the evolutionary mechanism."* [4]

Splitters and Lumpers

With fossil forms it is mainly the outward shape (morphology) that is used to classify the creatures. In practice some specialists concentrate on differences in forms (dubbed "Splitters") whilst others ("Lumpers") emphasize their common characteristics. Archie Hills (former Coalboard Geologist) has commented, *"It is certainly true geologists have gone too far in establishing sub species and species amongst fossils. This is due to a failure to see that these sub species have far more in common with each other than they do by way of differences. For instance it is quite unreasonable to give a fossil a new sub species name merely because of the presence of some minor detail in its ornamental morphology."* [5] Specialists not only classify creatures into different groups, but the same fossil may be given a different name when studied in another geographical locality.

◆ 3. An Open or Closed Biological System?

Thirdly it is only possible to prove changes in and between groups of living creatures if there is a controlled or *"closed"* biological system. An ideal example today would be a fish tank, where various species could be put in, so any resultant offspring would be attributable to the original fish breeding. When it comes to a body of water open to the sea, or the ocean itself, however, how can it be established beyond doubt that A and B bred to produce C, when another related creature D may have swum into the area, and successfully bred with the parent stock? Professor Middlemiss, Palaeontologist, when discussing the fossil Ammonite development admits this very problem, *"The British area .... was invaded several times during the Jurassic by fresh groups of families coming from outside."* [6]

Ammonite Development

The nearest surviving relative of the Ammonite is the pearly Nautilus, a creature with a chambered shell. The course of evolution in the ammonoid stock is through *"development"* occurring mainly in its dividing chamber wall, and different shaped coiling of the shell. If you imagine a round coiling tube with a series of fitting discs in it, (shaped like tiddly-winks) this would be equivalent to the dividing walls spaced out in the ammonite shell. The discs would have holes in the middle to enable a central tube (or siphuncle) to connect to the other chambers. See **Endnote 1** for further information on ammonites.

The Pattern

◆ **A:** Even if the supposed changes in the ammonites shell shape and dividing wall structure were proved, the degree of variation demonstrated would be minimal. For in this case we have the whole history of the group laid bare for inspection. They begin as ammonites, became enormously diversified, then disappear without being anything but ammonites.

◆ **B:** The primitive ammonoid, *"Goniatite"* had a simple shell division (or septal wall). It is like the disc (dividing wall) having a simple bend in it. *"Ceratites"* had a slightly more crinkled septal wall, and finally *"Ammonites"* proper had a very corrugated and crenulated septal wall. This simple pattern however, is in fact more complicated, as Professor Middlemiss admits, *"It should be noted, however, that it is a dangerous over-generalisation simply to state that, 'simple sutures are earlier, more complex sutures are later', as is sometimes said."* 7 The suture is the growth line, formed where the internal shell wall met the surface of the shell.

◆ **C:** The classic pattern of ammonoid development is not clear cut, as after the so-called development of the true ammonite (with a corrugated shell wall) the *"ceratites"*. If having a stronger shell wall was evolution, why should some species devolve to a simpler form? (This problem of becoming simpler from a more complex form is also found in other fossil groups including the graptolites).

◆ **D:** Coiling and uncoiling of the ammonoid stock is sometimes inferred to be due to evolutionary change. Here, however, we again encounter difficulties. Professor A. G. Fischer, in the authoritative textbook, *Invertebrate Fossils*, says, *"The uncoiling of the ammonoids in late Mesozoic times has been cited as a sign of decadence of these cephalopods towards the close of their reign. This seems doubtful when we remember that uncoiled ammonoids occurred in the Triassic, and that partly uncoiled or entirely straight nautiloids flourished alongside coiled forms through most of the Palaeozoic."*[8] This indicates that little significance can be attached to coiled or uncoiled forms as regards survival value, or a clear-cut evolutionary pattern.

◆ **E: Sexual Differences: Ammonite Dimorphism**
Whilst discussing change in form, it is an amazing fact that Ammonites have only relatively recently been analysed from the viewpoint of the differences between male and female forms. If the pearly Nautilus is taken as a clue to their variation in shape, the male nautilus has a larger shell known as the *"macroconch"*, and the female a smaller shell *"microconch"*. If this difference between the sexes (sexual dimorphism) was applied to classifying ammonites, Middlemiss admitted, it would be extremely inconvenient, as for a start the number of ammonite species would be drastically reduced! Until recently male and female ammonites were *"regarded as different species and in many cases different genera"*. Since the mid 1950's there have been renewed attempts to detect dimorphism in ammonite shells (by experts like J. H. Collomon) although this assumes the adult ammonite stage can be identified and defined.

The ammonite fossil series does not exist in entirety in one geographical locality. The typical *"Ceratites"* intermediate form (which some regard as a "dead-end") is found in the Muschelkalk (Middle Trias) of Saxony in Germany, for example, whilst the first and last stages are present in the U.K. An alternative explanation of the ammonoid stocks variation would be that these creatures were made to live in different environments, and the strength of their dividing shell walls was related to the depth at which the creature could survive. Ammonites with the more corrugated and arched shell walls would be better able to withstand the pressure of greater depths of water, so that the different septal walls probably had a functional or ecological significance rather than an evolutionary one.

Trilobites

Another extinct fossil group belonging to the Arthropods are the trilobites, which were crudely a sort of marine version of the common woodlouse and these were both well developed and varied. They crawled along the sea floor muds, or burrowed into them. Trilobites appear without former trace in the Cambrian rock layers, and are said by geologists to have a *"cryptogenic" (hidden)* origin. As no primitive prototype of the trilobite has been found, palaeontologists have built up what one might call an *"identi-kit trilobite"* made up of what fossil experts think are primitive characteristics. In an amazing confession of circular reasoning Professor Moore (referring to such a made-up prototype) states, *"No known fossil approximates the form described other than partially, but we may construe deviations from it as marking evolutionary trends."*[9]

Most experts think primitive trilobites are those which possess worm-like features, such as numerous segments. However, many multi-segmented forms could also *"roll-up"* which is supposed to be an *"advanced"* characteristic. Another problem for those experts who think annelid-type (worm-like) features are primitive is that they imply agnostid trilobites (a blind form with only two body segments, and head plus tail approximately the same size) were more advanced than other forms which had compound eyes (similar to those found in bees today)! One study of a trilobite genus also showed that the trilobite *Phacops "had better vision than some of its living relatives today"* (K. M. Towe (1973) Science, Vol. 179). It could be argued that the trilobites were adapted for living in different conditions and that these different characteristics have not got any evolutionary significance at all, but are related to the trilobites' *"life style"*. Some probably burrowed into the sediment (those with streamlined shape and no eyes) floated or swam through the water (those with a large area of spinose skeleton, and eyes beneath body) or survived in darker deep regions (those with large eyes). See **Endnote 2**, for further details.

Echinoids—the sea urchin "micraster".

Perhaps it is the *"sea-urchin"* or *"sea-egg"* that provides palaeontologists with a claimed classic example of micro-evolution, parallel to the modern biologists' dark and light peppered moths in importance. Dr Rowe (1899) studied over 2000 fossil sea urchins found in the Middle and Upper Chalk. He noted and measured various deviations in certain selected character-istics which he interpreted as evolutionary change over time. Professor J. F. Kirkaldy (formerly Head of Geology at Queen Mary College, London) summarises thus, *"Exceptionally one can find examples of evolutionary series showing the transformation of one species to another. Such a series is shown by those common fossils of the Upper Chalk, the Micraster ..... there is sufficient general correspondence for it is possible to divide the micraster lineage into a number of arbitrarily defined species ....."* [10]

Dr Rowe showed that successive changes in a number of the characters of the micrasters test were regular, when the population as a whole were studied at various levels in the chalk. Professor M. R. House reminds us that, *"at any one level, any individual might be primitive in certain char-acters whilst being advanced in others."* [11] Experts deviate over the supposed lineage pattern of this echinoids evolution—some believing new stock came into the area to breed with the original micraster stock thus raising the problem of unclear biological relationships. An alternative explanation of the micraster series is that they were one highly variable species. See **Endnote 3** for further details on echinoids.

Conclusion

The criticisms and issues raised, namely the question of timescale, whether the evolution occurs in a closed biological system, plus the problem of defining a fossil species—are applicable to all fossil groups be they invertebrates (such as bivalves, brachiopods, corals, graptolites) or vertebrates (humans or horses.) The existing variability within species (including both sexual dimorphism and ornamentation), plus the progressive destruction of their ecological niches—during the formation of the strata and the process of sedimentation—are able to provide an alternative interpretation of the fossil types, that are found in *"fossil series"*. Clearly the Zoologist, Douglas Dewer's claim is still valid today:

Chapter 11

*"It is not possible to arrange a genealogical series of fossils proving .....
that any species in the past has undergone sufficient change to transform it
into a member of another family."*[12] It certainly seems evolution may be in
trouble (i.e. 'on the rocks') rather than providing evidence for step-wise
change in any fossilised life-forms in the rock strata.

References:

1. **A. S. Romer** (1971) "Palaeontology" *Encyclopaedia Britannica*, 200th edition,
   William Benton Publisher, London, p. 150.
2. **R. Milton** (1995) *Scientific Censorship and Evolution*, www. lauralee. comm/ milton.ht
3. **Ibid.**
4. **J. Imbrie** (1957)"The Species Problem with Fossil Animals" in the *Species Problem*,
   ed. Mayr, E., American Association for the Advancement of Science,
   Washington D. C. Publication No. 50, p. 127.
5. **A. C. Hills** (1977) Personal Communication.
6. **F. A. Middlemiss** (1971) *A Guide to Invertebrate Fossils*, Hutchinson,
   Educational, London, p. 93.
7. **F. A. Middlemiss** (1971) Ibid, p. 92.
8. **R. C. Moore** (ed) (1952)Fischer, A. G. "Cephalopods" *Invertebrate Fossils*,
   Mc Graw-Hill Book Co Inc. p. 386.
9. **R. C. Moore** (ed) (1952) Ibid, "Trilobites" p. 92.
10. **J. F. Kirkaldy** (1970) *Fossils in Colour*, 2nd revised edition, Blandford Press,
    London, p. 27.
11. **I. G. Gass** (Ed.) (1972) *Understanding the Earth* , 2nd ed, Artemis Press, Sussex, p. 106.
12. **D. Dewer** (1957) *The Transformist Illusion*, Dehoff Publications,
    Murfreesboro, Tennessee, p. 61.

Further Reading

J. K. Anderson & H. G. Coffin (1977) *Fossils in Focus*, Zondervan, Publishing House,
Grand Rapids, Michigan.
R. Milton (1993) *The Facts of Life*, A Corgi Book, ISBN 0 552 14121.

Evolution—on the rocks?

Key Text:
Colossians 1: 16 "For by Him [Christ] all things were created that are in heaven and that are on earth, visible and invisible ... "

Endnote: 1

Typical pattern of ammonoid evolution

As ammonites grew, they added on another shell dividing wall and then inhabited the largest primary dwelling chamber; in this latter chamber was the squid-like body of the ammonite. Where the shell chamber wall cuts the inner surface of the outer shell, a suture (*"growth line"*) is formed. This is often seen on fossil ammonoids if they are internal casts. The goniatites have a simple suture with lobes and saddles: the ceratites have a simple saddle but subdivided lobe; and the ammonitic sutures have both saddles and lobes subdivided, often referred to as *"frilled"* or highly *"convoluted"* sutures. With the major extinctions of the ammonoids over geological time, some *"surviving stock"* supposedly fathered a fresh stock of rapidly and widely evolving forms. Middlemiss warns against thinking *"simple sutures are earlier, more complex sutures are later"*. He says, *"This is matter of complicated evolution within each family group, and in practice many individual Triassic genera have more complex sutures than many in the Jurassic, and likewise with the Jurassic and Cretaceous."* (Middlemiss (1971) Ibid. p. 92).

Endnote: 2

Trilobites and their Geological History

Trilobites were marine arthropods, which crawled about on the ancient sea muds. In appearance they resembled the modern wood louse; and several had the propensity to roll themselves up for protection. Periodically, trilobites would shed their skin, i.e. moult, a process aided by the presence of a facial suture. The trilobites were an amazing group, varying in size from a few millimetres to 75 centimetres in length. Although some species were blind, others (e.g. Phacops) had eyes made of calcite. K. M. Towe points out that these calcareous lenses were capable of forming inverted images over a larger depth of field, and most have been present in the living trilobite (rather than being mineralogical replacements). They appear to have provided a *"better optical system"* than that of the few living arthropods known to have corneal lenses. Geologists admit that the classification of trilobites is *"surrounded with difficulties"* mainly because no single characteristic has been found which exhibits a gradual evolutionary change within a group without being adaptational in one way or another. The original classification was based on the character of the facial suture, but this no longer tenable, and the class has been divided into 6 orders grouping together and in general of similar morphology. Over 3900 species have been described from fossil specimens.

Endnote: 3
Micraster—The Heart Urchin's evolution

The 18 differences noted by Dr. Rowe in the micraster species have been claimed as a progressive adaptation of the echinoid burrowing more deeply into the Chalk Sediment. These main changes included:

1   The test becoming broader and higher.
2   The carina (or crest) appeared and became more pronounced and the apical disc shifted backwards.
3   The anterior sulcus (groove) became deeper.
4   The ambulacral "petals" became longer and shallower, and the smooth surface between the pores became more granular.
5   The mouth shifted forward and the labrum (or lip below the mouth) made its appearance.
6   The most easily observed change was that the interporiferous areas (i.e. the middle strip of the petals between the pore pairs) passed through a series of stages: (a) smooth; (b) sutured, that is, the sutures of the plates are clearly marked; (c) inflated— they rose in a double convexity;
    (d) subdivided—that is, the middle line between these convexities became a distinct groove; and (e) divided as this groove became deep and narrow. Rhona Black (1973) in *"The Elements of Palaeontology"* says, *"There is, of course, some variation in the development of these (and other) characters in a collection of micrasters from any particular level in the Chalk, and one specimen may show a combination of characters some of which are more, and others less, advanced."* (Cambridge University Press, p. 123). Dr Dewer (1957) asks whether the micraster echinoid changed into another species. He replies, *"We do not know, because we have no means of ascertaining, whether corbovis, if crossed with coranguinum would have yielded fertile offspring, or, had the conditions that led to the formation of Coranguinum been reversed whether the latter would have gradually reverted to corbovis."* (Dewer (1957) Ibid. p. 108). He notes that

all species, when experimented with, are capable of assuming a considerable variety of form, but these are perfectly fertile when crossed with their parent form.

Questions for Further Study

1 What is claimed as one of the best evidences for evolution?
2 What is a species?
3 What are the difficulties in establishing "fossil species"?
4 Ammonites are the most complete family for which fossil records exist. What are the major differences, between them? How is this now explained?
5 What is a "septal wall"? What do you think could be its non-evolutionary significance?
6 Trilobites were very crudely like a marine version of the common wood louse. What does the phrase *"cryptogenic origin"* mean?
7 Do you think it is possible to distinguish between a *"simple"* and an *"advanced"* trilobite?
8 Dr Rowe showed that successive changes in a number of the characters of the micrasters test were regular, when the population as a whole were studied at various levels in the chalk. Do you think this variability necessarily proves evolution, or the variation possible in any given species?
9 Do you agree with zoologist Douglas Dewer who called supposed changes from phylum to phylum *"the transformist delusion"*?
10 What do you think you could illustrate using a fish tank, regarding species change?
11 What are the traditional*"proofs of evolution"*?

Food for thought:

* *"The probability of life originating by accident is comparable to the probability of the complete dictionary resulting from an explosion in a printing factory."* E. Conklin.

* *"The biggest hoax in the world for the last 150 years has been the theory of evolution."* Dr D Martyn Lloyd-Jones

On Giants' Shoulders

"Truth is always the strongest argument." Sophocles

Today, we like Newton can stand on giants' shoulders. We can see further than those who have gone before. We have the advantage of hindsight. Surprisingly, the powerful impact of Christianity was initially underestimated by early contemporary philosophers and historians. Christianity does not, however, depend solely on man seeking God—but God seeking man. The paradox of reason being used to justify reason, can only be resolved by having absolutes based on theism. Modern proponents of Darwinism (e.g. Dawkins) have as their starting point the a priori assumption of philosophical materialism; any notion of God in the equation would lose their control of the system. As Darwinian postulates cannot be verified (needing millions of years and chance mutations) it ceases to be science, and becomes scientism. Scientists have concluded that the possibility of life arising by chance on earth is imponderable, so suggest seeds from outer space. Despite this, Hoyle (not a Christian) respects the teaching of Christ. The unique claims of Christianity are highlighted by its reliance on God's grace alone and intervention in history, as the answer to man's predicament. Men and women of faith can have discernment of the times in which we live, because they can stand on giants' shoulders and apply their wisdom and knowledge to today's problems—both religious and secular. Christianity is logical and credible, given the fact that we all have either explicit or implicit "belief systems".

On that giant mass ...

The notion that knowledge and understanding progresses over time, was well stated in the twelfth century by Bernard of Chartres: *"We are like dwarfs seated on the shoulders of giants; we see more things than the ancients and things more distant, but this is due neither to the sharpness of our own sight, nor to the greatness of our own stature, but because we are raised and borne aloft on that giant mass.*" As if commenting on these very words, Isaac Newton—the great scientist—once humbly acknowledged: "*If I have seen further it is by standing on the shoulders of giants.*" [1] We can have the benefit of all the special revelation of God's Word, along with the continuous discoveries of humanity. 'Knowledge itself' as Francis Bacon admitted, 'is power'. We do have the advantage of hindsight, although sadly we are not always willing to learn from our own or others' mistakes. As the old adage puts it, "*History teaches us that history teaches us nothing.*" The First World War (1914-1918) was said to be 'The war to end wars'. Of course, we know as a sad fact, the Second World War (1939-1945) followed, and we still live in a war-torn world today.

Once it was claimed we could right the world by education ... ignorance was the great enemy. Now we have so much information, we cannot even hope to process it all—with or without the aid of technology. In addition, as the torrent of data and rapid change bombard the average person today, it is difficult for anyone to sort out the wood from the trees! There is almost unlimited knowledge available today from the internet alone; as this mass of data passes in kaleidoscopic manner before us, it is difficult to pick out the permanent or significant from the ephemeral. Historically speaking too, it seems that recognising the significant and potentially powerful forces is not a problem unique to the current age.

Brilliant galaxy of philosophers and historians

It was the rationalist historian William Lecky who pointed out that the powerful impact of Christianity was grossly underestimated by the early Roman and later philosophers: "*That the greatest religious change should have taken place under the eyes of a brilliant galaxy of philosophers and historians, who were profoundly conscious of the decomposition around them, that all of these writers should have utterly failed to predict the issue of the movement they were observing, and that, during the space of three centuries, they should have treated as simply contemptible an agency which men must now admit to have been, for good or evil, the most powerful moral lever that has ever been applied to the affairs of man, are facts worthy of meditation in every period of religious transition.*"[2] God, often works in a mysterious way His wonders to perform. The Christian church started as a small band of frightened disciples (hiding in an upper room), but succeeded in "turning the world upside down", through God's power.

God also brings about change by acting on man's heart, mind and will. The Christian believes that not only does man search for wisdom, but that wisdom also searches for him. This is well expressed in Anne Fremantle's *The Age of Belief,* where she says: *"God is not only that than which nothing greater can be imagined, but a person who, while declaring Himself to be wholly unimaginable, has yet revealed Himself and given Himself to man. There is a vast difference between arriving at a possible God at the extreme limit of man's reason, or as a First Cause in nature, and starting from a present God who gives Himself into a man's heart. .... Christian philosophy is an intellectual inquiry into the nature of being, which accepts as its premise the possible existence of a Power outside man that is both the object and the instigator of man's search; or as Christ put it, that He is Himself 'the Way, the Truth and the Life.'"*[3]

This may be an age of disbelief in the Western World, but it is clear people are looking for decisive moral and spiritual guidance, but often getting inadequate help from the established church, which in its pronouncements on current issues appears to neglect the plain teaching of Scripture and the creeds. Faith which floats around in a sea of untestable assertions is empty and deceptive. This book, *On Giants' Shoulders* has tried to highlight the ready answers and relevant principles that exist to guide the genuine intellectual enquirer. We note, however, as psychoanalyst Sigmond Freud correctly stated man is governed by his passions—not his intellect. The world news illustrates this every day!

There are many questions that we can ask to determine whether Christianity is credible. We have sought to show that there is sufficient evidence and arguments to vindicate the Christian Faith. There is always an answer. The alternative secular viewpoints, whilst initially appearing modest or objective, are found to be just as value-judgement ridden as the Christian position openly admits. They too appeal to various universals (such as there is no God) which are not provable. The issue, then, becomes whether it is true that unless the truth of Christianity is presupposed, any proof is possible. The late Professor Cornelius Van Til (Apologist) clearly stated the alternatives: *"To me the only alternatives to the Biblical teaching with respect to creation and providence is chaos or pure contingency. To speak of an order coming out of chaos is a contradiction in terms. A Christianity that comes out of chaos or that just happens by chance is not the Christianity of Scripture."*4

A question of ooze

Van Til went on to explain this line of presuppositional reasoning thus: *"I am, therefore, not begging the question when I say you must presuppose the Christian position or predication* [to assert or affirm as true or existent] *is impossible. Unless one starts by accepting on authority the words of Christ himself one has to start with man as self-sufficient and self-explanatory."* Van Til spelt out the consequences of such a position: *"In that case man has to identify himself in chaos. He has to identify facts in chaos. He has to relate these facts by logic which has itself sprung from chaos. The result of such a procedure may be seen, for instance, in the philosophy of Sartre. Sartre says that all is ooze that is chaos, but he also says that there cannot be a God. He is a bit of ooze that has sprung out of ooze, flitting about in ooze and makes universal logical negations* [for instance, there is no God] *about all future possibilities. This is, to me, the only alternative to accepting the Christian position on the authority of Christ speaking in his word."*5

Whilst such a position initially sounds fantastic, ultimately non-Christian viewpoints are only surviving by "rustling" or stealing their foundational truths. They are, in fact, sawing off the branch they are sitting on! Secular thinkers are tacitly assuming a meaningful universe (while sometimes attempting to prove the opposite!) which is open to intelligent investigation and discoverable laws. We have seen, for example, how the scientific method itself underpins a Christian view of reality and shows that most people do not live consistently with life as only chaos and old night or *"integration into the void"*. To look at life as a pure mechanical chance has a certain pointlessness about it. It results in a purposeless existence without any sense of responsibility to anyone in particular. Despite this, postmodern views hold sway and we reap the havoc of a humanism that still recognises *"man as the measure of all*

things being what they are, of things not being what they are not."
As philosopher, Martin Hollis admits: *"If all uses of evidence presuppose that things are in general orderly, then there can be no evidence for this presupposition itself. The upshot is a paradox. On the one hand we could, it seems, hardly have better evidence that we live in an orderly universe and shall continue to do so. On the other hand we seem, on reflection, to have no evidence whatever, which supports this conclusion without assuming it. Many philosophers (and others) find this an incredible result and try to show that the challenge is a bogus one. But many have accepted that Reason cannot justify Reason and have tried to live intellectually with the result. David Hume, for instance, the eighteenth-century thinker, whose A Treatise of Human Nature (1739, Volume 1, Part III) contains the most famous statement of the case, concludes that all our reasonings rest finally on custom and imagination. Similar thoughts have lately been causing upheaval in the philosophy of the sciences.*"[6]

The prevalent attitude in the academic and scientific community is that science and religion are incompatible. The two positions are characterised as follows. *"Science"* is a system of knowledge based on experimentation, observation and logic. *"Religion"* is regarded as a system based on myth, culture and ultimately self-delusion. A researcher should never let his personal faith affect his work, or he will no longer be regarded as a serious scientist. It is interesting to note, that perhaps the greatest scientist of all time, Isaac Newton, would be jettisoned on this viewpoint. He stated in his *Mathematica Principia*: *"This most beautiful system of the sun, planets, and comets, could only proceed from the counsel and dominion of an intelligent and powerful Being. This Being governs all things, not as the soul of the world, but as Lord over all, and on account of His dominion He is wont to be called Lord God, Universal Ruler.*"[7]

We have looked extensively at a materialistic model of origins. Evolution is clearly something the Creator has ordained, in so far as some limited form of micro-evolution is concerned. The case of the variability of Darwin's finches, for instance, is well known. The are fourteen different species of Darwin finches, found in the Galapagos islands. They are believed to have evolved from a single species similar to the blue-black grassquit found in South America. Some have beaks suitable for fruit eating; others have a strong grosbeak-like bill for seed eating; and insect eaters use a warbler-like insect eating bill. Another finch is a cactus eater. The size and shape of their bills reflect these specialisations, and are said to be examples of adaptive radiation. The finches still remained finches, however, despite the variations between them. They can all successfully interbreed.

Species have genetic potential or variability in their inherited characteristics. Take ourselves, (species *homo sapiens*). We have several races of mankind, with different skin colour, looks and size, but we can all marry people of different racial type and yet have children successfully. But there are clear limits to the amount of change species can undergo. If you cross a zebra with a donkey, you get a zedonk. If two zedonks try to interbreed— you find there is sterility, you are at the end of the line. The possibility of crossing the major phylum boundaries has been called the *"transformist illusion"*. There is no clear evidence of this type of evolution, a *"fishes-to-man type evolution"*, sometimes called *"macro-evolution"* or *"Evolutionism"*.

As a fully committed evolutionist, Richard Dawkins is typical of those who make their starting point the *a priori* assumption of philosophical materialism. This foundational worldview means that matter is all that exists. If materialism is the starting point of biology, Darwinism (or its modern variants) has to be true as a matter of logic. Dawkins recognises this as an evolutionist and so seeks to explain the origin of all things by purely materialistic principles. Dawkins concludes that evolution must be true, even if the evidence conflicts with it, because he already "knows" it must be true. Hence, when given examples (for instance, from Behe's analysis) of the "irreducible complexity" in living systems that appear to be inexplicable on any step-wise evolutionary processes, Dawkins retreats to a position of unfalsifiability by arguing that these examples are merely due to temporary ignorance. These problems will eventually be explained, and confirm their evolutionary origins. He believes Darwin is the greatest scientist of the millennium, and that his notion of natural selection was so emancipating from the ignorant creation ideas that went before.

Religion a mental virus

Dawkins has argued in favour of the Meme theory—which views ideas and beliefs as the mental equivalent of genes. They are hypothetical replicators which *'propagate themselves ... by leaping from brain to brain.'* (The Selfish Gene, p. 192); He regards religion as a *'mental virus'* that infects the human brain; and he thinks young people are susceptible to believe anything they are told. Whilst these are theories of how ideas spread or are propagated, they give no means of assessing the truth or falsity of those beliefs. These arguments can be equally applied to either Christianity or atheism! Research Fellow, Michael Poole has commented, *"Much of Dawkins' world-view depends on his central thesis that 'religion is a scientific theory', including his view of 'God as a competing explanation (to science) for facts about the universe and life.' I know of no professional philosopher who makes such an assertion, but as far as I know Dawkins has not yet attempted to justify this contentious claim"* (Science a stick to beat religion? N.B., June-July, the Origins debate, UCCF, p. 7.)

It is easy to understand why evolutionists are unhappy with creationism. Once you let God into the picture, you lose control of the equation. In truth, Darwinism is really scientism rather than science. After all, what repeatable experiment can be devised whose main demands are chance mutation and millions of years? This accounts for the current interest in life on Mars, and extra-terrestrial life. As scientists have failed to provide a convincing proof on Earth, they are now looking to other planets, in an attempt at verification by the back door. Even Dr Crick (the co-discoverer of the DNA code) suggested life began with an unmanned spacecraft carrying primitive micro-organisms from another planet which crash landed into the sea billions of years ago! [8] Scientists (like Oparin) have long realised that the age of the earth is not long enough for the chance formation of life's components to form.

Professor A.S. Romer, raised a vital question for geoscientists: *"Is evolution true? The answer depends upon what is considered by the questioner as valid evidence. ... But it can be said that all the known facts of palaeontology are consistent with the theory of evolution and impossible of rational interpretation on any other basis."*[9] Despite Romer's claims, it is exceedingly difficult to establish supposed evolutionary trends in any series of fossils distributed throughout the rock strata of the stratigraphical column. As one of the chapters in Hoyle's *Evolution from Space* succinctly states: *"The evolutionary record leaks like a sieve."*[10] In fact, Professor Romer's statement implies any alternative explanations of the data under review will not be seriously considered.

There are still scientists who agree with the editor of Omni (1981) when he claimed: *"So far not one shred of evidence has ever been found to support the Creationist point of view. Not a fingerbone, not a leaf, not a shard of evidence exists ... And if it did happen this way, the creating force went to incredible trouble to litter this planet with the evidence of evolution; from dinosaur fossils to hominoid teeth, from the speciation Darwin found during his voyage on the Beagle to the stages of development that the human foetus undergoes during its nine-month gestation."* Interestingly enough, this supposed "evidence" does not stand up! For instance: Darwin's finches with different beak types can still all successfully interbreed, meaning they are not new species. As has been remarked, Darwin's *Origin of Species* would be better called, "Origin of Races." The recapitulation theory has been scientifically discredited. Even the pro-evolutionary evidence presented from Dr Kettlewell's famous light and dark colourd peppered moths has been shown to be seriously flawed: **See Endnote 1.**

In the Introduction to the 1958 J. M. Dent (Everyman Library Series, no. 811) centennial edition reprint of Darwin's *Origin of Species* , Professor W. Thompson (a former Director of the Commonwealth Institute) made the following criticisms of Darwinism: *"Personal convictions, simple possibilities are presented as if they were proofs, or at least valid arguments in favour of the theory"* ... and *"To establish the continuity required by the theory, historical arguments are invoked, even though historical evidence is lacking. Thus are engendered those fragile towers of hypothesis based on hypotheses, where fact and fiction intermingle in an inextricable confusion."* As Eileen Barker (sociologist and Dean of LSE) perceptively remarked: *"The creationists do not dispute 'facts', only interpretations and, given a particular set of metaphysical assumptions and a particular perspective on the world, their position was both logical and comprehensible"* (Times Higher Educational Supplement, 27 July, 1977).

Theistic evolution?

Christians are clearly illogical if they try to adopt evolution as God's way of creating, when this explanation is founded on the a priori assumption of philosophical materialism. How can a science based on materialism be a means of investigating how God created? It is trying to marry evolution to creation, which will inevitably result in a strange hybrid! Christians do not base their presuppositions on materialism, and so it is futile to try to build a view on this foundation, then try to add God on top of it. The issues raised by evolutionism (as an all embracing philosophy) are ones which ultimately lead to despair: life is a chance occurrence and cannot be anything more than a short-lived meaningless existence, before the ageing process takes its toll. Life, in other words, is no more than a match struck in the dark and blown out again.

Fred Hoyle pointed out that, *"Everybody must wonder from time to time if there is any real purpose to life. Of course we all have immediate aims, to succeed in our careers, to bring up our children, and still in many parts of the world simply to earn enough to eat. But what of long term purpose? For what reason do we live our lives at all? Biology, as it is presently taught, answers that the purpose is to produce the next generation. But many of us are impelled to persist in wondering if that can be all ... There is nothing except continuity, no purpose except continued existence, now or in the future."*[11]

Scientists (like Hoyle) have spent considerable time investigating our ultimate origins. Professors Hoyle and Wickramasinghe admitted dissatisfaction with the prevailing establishment view that life arose here on earth, as there is insufficient time to overcome the statistical odds against it. The discovery that the odds against the *"spark of life"* occurring accidentally on earth were calculated by Professor Fred Hoyle and Professor Chandra Wickramasinghe to be as low as 10 to the power of 40,000. This simply means that the likelihood of life starting accidentally on earth is imponderable. Professor Wickramasinghe (Cardiff) said he was *"100% certain that life could not have started spontaneously on earth."*[12] He admitted that he was uncomfortable with this: *"From my earliest training as a scientist, I was very strongly brainwashed to believe that science cannot be consistent with any kind of creation. The notion has had to be painfully shed. I am quite uncomfortable in the situation.*"[13] It did not take long, however, for Wickramasinghe (as a Buddhist) to make a reaffirmation of his belief that the earth was seeded by comets, and rejection of the Genesis account. [14]

Extra-terrestrial life

The solution these two scientists came up with was to postulate that life came in the form of a seed from outer space, also that there is some cosmic designer behind it all. As theologian Berkhof has commented, *"Most of those who reject the theistic view of God still profess faith in God, but He is a God of their own imagination."*[15] The views of these two scientists still reflect a belief in a *"God of the gaps"*. We see nature cannot do it alone, so perhaps some intelligent force helped. Sir Fred Hoyle stated, *"I am not a Christian, nor am I likely to become one as far as I can tell. Yet my disbelief in Christianity as a religion does not prevent me from being deeply impressed by many of the sayings of Christ."*[16]

Jesus' teaching is indeed impressive. Jesus Christ's birth and death divides history (BC—AD). He is a fact of history, well attested to by secular historians. He went about doing good. He claimed to be not only the Son of God, but *"the way, the truth and the life."* He was either a liar, or a lunatic or else He was telling the truth. Can you really afford to ignore Him as God's provision for all our imperfections and wrong doing? To do so would involve a spiritually serious health warning, and what is worse—a lost eternity. It is only if we ask our Maker for help and guidance, that we will find lasting happiness and peace. The only way to paradise is explained in His manual—the Bible. Is this just the vague ideas of some antiquated obscurantist? We are on the verge of the new millennium .... can we still believe such teaching as true?

Bertrand Russell remarked once, *"The Christian principle, 'Love your enemies' is good ...... There is nothing to be said against it except that it is too difficult for most of us to practise sincerely."*[17] Compelling as Russell's comment is, it is not forceful enough. The Christian life is not only difficult for anybody to follow—it is impossible. The writer, Os Guinness, summed up this position succinctly by saying: *"... it is exactly here that humanism leaves off and Christianity begins. That is also why only this uniquely 'impossible' faith—with a God who is, with an Incarnation that is earthly and historical, with a salvation that is at cross-purposes with human nature, with a Resurrection that blasts apart the finality of death—is able to provide an alternative to the sifting, settling dust of death and through a new birth open the way to new life."*[18]

What makes Christianity different from all the other religions of the world? At a conference attended by Professor C. S. Lewis years ago, this question was discussed. Some contributors argued that Christianity is unique in teaching that God became man. However, someone objected that other religions had a similar notion. What about the resurrection? No, it was argued, other faiths believe the dead rise again. C. S. Lewis entering the conference late, asked, *"What's the rumpus about?"* When he learned the discussion was about the uniqueness of Christianity, he replied: *"Oh, that's easy. It's grace."* Grace is God's unmerited pardon given to rebellious sinners, through the atoning death of His Son. Lewis believed, in fact, that whatever is true in all religions is consummated in Christ.

Preacher C. H. Spurgeon said of the Biblical message, *"Many books in my library are now behind and beneath me. They were good in their way once, and so were the clothes I wore when I was ten years old; but I have outgrown them. Nobody ever outgrows Scripture; the book widens and deepens over the years."* The Bible is the most up-to-date book in the world: Its author, God, knows the end from the beginning! We, too, can humbly stand on Giants' Shoulders and see further than our forebears. We have the wisdom of the Biblical prophets and apostles, the testimonies of the martyrs, Reformers, and record of scientific, social and technological advance. We have available to us the greatest systematic minds the Christian church has ever had, and can see a lot farther humbly standing on their shoulders. This enables us to gain discernment of the times, realising that *"The fear of the Lord is the beginning of wisdom"* (Proverbs 9:10). Are we applying this knowledge and biblical principles to the defence of the faith in our current situation? ... our daily lives? If so, we will be those who need not be ashamed, earnestly contending for the truth of the Bible and its Creator God. Is the Bible believable? We can only conclude with St. Augustine of Hippo's words: *"Truth wherever it is found must be avidly accepted."*

References:

1   **Isaac Newton** (1675) *Letter to Robert Hooke*, 5th Feb. 1675.
2   **W. Lecky** (1869) *History of European Morals..*
3   **A. Fremantle** (1954) *The Age of Belief*, the Medieval Philosophers, Mentor Books, New English Library, London E. C. 1, p. 16.
4   **C. Van Til** (1967) Personal communication, October 17th, 1967.
5   **Ibid.**
6   **M. Hollis** (1985) *Invitation to Philosophy*, Blackwell, Oxford, ISBN 0 631 142266, p. 54.
7   **Isaac Newton** (1686) *Mathematical Principles of Natural Philosophy*. Motte's translation from the Latin in 1729, University of California Press, Berkeley, California, 1934.
8   **E. K. Victor Pearce** (1998) *Evidence for Truth: Science*, Eagle, Guildford, Surrey, ISBN0-86347-263-X, p. 113.
9   **A. S. Romer,** (1971) "Palaeontology" *Encyclopaedia Britannica*, 200th edition, William Benton Publisher, London, p. 150.
10 **F. Hoyle & C. Wickramasinghe** (1981) *Evolution from Space*, chapter 6, J. M. Dent, London, ISBN 0 460 04535 0, p. 77.
11 **F. Hoyle (1983)** *The Intelligent Universe*, Michael Joseph, London, ISBN 0 7181 2298 4, p. 6.
12 **P. King** (1981) *"Suddenly God's back!"*, Baptist Times, September 24, 1981.
13 **Ibid.**
14 **J. Durant** (Editor) (1985) *Darwinism and Divinity*, Basil Blackwell, Oxford, ISBN: 0 631 14188 X, p. 191.
15 **L. Berkhof** (1994) *Systematic Theology*, Banner of Truth, Edinburgh, ISBN: 0-85151-056-6, p. 25.
16 **F. Hoyle** (1983) Ibid., p. 251.
17 **B. Russell** (1945) *History of Western Philosophy*, Simon & Schuster, Bloomfield, N. J., p. 579.
18 **O. Guinness** (1973) *The Dust of Death*, Inter—Varsity Press, Leicester, p. 392.

Further Reading:

E. H. Andrews (1980) *God, Science & Evolution*, Evangelical Press, Welwyn, ISBN 0 85234 146 6.

J. Blanchard (1984) *Gathered Gold*, Evangelical Press, Welwyn, ISBN 0 85234 186 5.

B. Davidheiser (1969) *Evolution and Christian Faith*, Presbyterian & Reformed Co, Library of Congress no. 70-76782.

J. McDowell (1990) *Christianity: A Ready Defence*, Here's Life Publishers, England: Scripture Press Foundation (U.K.) Ltd, ISBN 1 872059 56 2.

J. McIntosh (1998) Genesis for Today, Day One publications, ISBN 0 902548786

A. Plantinga and N. Wolterstorff (1991) *Faith and Rationality*, University of Notre Dame Press, London, ISBN 0 268 00965 1.

F. Schaeffer (1968) *The God who is there*, Hodder & Stoughton, London, ISBN 340 04466 7.

D. Wilkinson (1997) *Alone in the Universe? The X Files, aliens and God*, Monarch Publications, ISBN: 9 781854 243737 -X.

Endnote : 1

Dr. H. B. Kettlewell (1959) called the change in ratio of dark and light moths, *"The most striking evolutionary change ever witnessed by man."* This so-called evidence has been critically reviewed by Michael Majerus (1998) in *Melanism: evolution in action*. A decade of research shows that these peppered moths do not settle on trees (except when released from traps and disorientated by daylight); neither do they choose matching backgrounds upon which to settle; furthermore, both increases and decreases in numbers of the melanic form have been seen in regions where there is no correlation with industrial pollution and environmental recovery. The causes of such variations still remains an unsolved problem. H. B. Kettlewell (1959) *"Darwin's Missing Evidence"*, Scientific American 200:3:48, March, p. 57.

Resources:

Apologetics on the internet:

Christians in science website: http:// www.csis.org.uk/fmstart.htm. has 3 papers analysing Dawkins' views by Michael W. Poole (Visiting Research Fellow in Science and Religion, School of Education, King's College, London) entitled, *Science and Christian Belief*.

http://www.leaderu.com/menus/apologetics.html (Gives apologetic material).

http://www.worldmall.com/erf/postmod.html—where a Christian doctor gives his objections to Postmodernism.

Dr D. M. Lloyd Jones Recordings: http://www.mlj.org.uk

Key Texts:

Hebrews 11: 3*"By faith we understand that the worlds were framed by the word of God, so that the things which are seen were not made of things which are visible."*

Hebrews 11: 6 *"But without faith it is impossible to please Him, for he who comes to God must believe that He is, and that He is a rewarder of those who diligently seek Him."*

Questions for Further Study

1 How does humanity advance in knowledge? Should Christians have more discernment today, than in the first century?

2 Did contemporary philosophers and historians recognise the significance of the rise of Christianity?

3 Martin Hollis admits: *"If all uses of evidence presuppose that things are in general orderly, then there can be no evidence for this presupposition itself. Many have accepted that Reason cannot justify Reason"* How do these quotes underline the importance of a need for *"absolutes"* in knowledge systems.

4 What is the popular caricature of science and religion?

5 How does Isaac Newton's comment from *Mathematica Principia* (claimed by some as one of the greatest scientific works of all time) challenge the modern conception of science.

6 Is there evidence for micro-evolution, or macro-evolution?

7 Would Dawkins be convinced by Behe's evidence against step-wise evolutionary processes?

8 *"Marrying Creation or Christianity to Evolution will result in a strange hybrid."* Do you agree?

9 What did Wickramasinghe confess he was brainwashed to believe? Contrast this with Newton's statement from *Mathematica Principia*.

10 Sir Ambrose Fleming (scientist and inventor) wrote: *"To sum up, finally, we can say that although intellectual arguments from design, beauty, or rationality in the universe are not so complete as to compel forcibly an assent to the existence of a personal Creator, they are still of such a character as to render a creational explanation of the material world vastly more probable than its production by any impersonal self-acting agency called Evolution."* A. Fleming (1938) *Evolution or Creation?*, 2nd ed., Marshall, Morgan & Scott Ltd, London, pp. 112-113.

Chapter 12

Do you agree with Sir Ambrose Fleming, or would you take a different approach?
11 What would Professor C. S. Lewis have said to Sir Fred Hoyle, when he claimed to be *"deeply impressed by many of the sayings of Christ"* but does not believe he is the Son of God?

Food for Thought

* *"Posterity will some day laugh at the foolishness of modern materialistic philosophy. The more I study nature, the more I am amazed at the Creator."* Louis Pasteur.

* *"The creation is both a monument of God's power and a looking-glass in which we may see his wisdom ..... To create requires infinite power. All the world cannot make a fly."* Thomas Watson.

* *"Consider men like Paul, Augustine, Thomas Aquinas, Luther, Calvin, Pascal and others. These are some of the giant intellects of the centuries, and they are giants because they had the wisdom to see how far reason could take them, and then to submit themselves to the revelation. They were lifted up and enlightened by the Spirit of God, and their minds and gigantic reasoning powers then began to demonstrate themselves."* D. Martyn Lloyd-Jones.

Nice one, Cyril!

"All unbelief is the belief of a lie." Horatius Bonar

A fter examining man's prejudice against God, we underline the need for Christian apologetics. Later on we analyse a case study which reflects the common objection to Christian belief. The dialogue recorded notes the evidence and necessity of the historical resurrection of Christ.

In-built prejudice

It is interesting to note that the Bible emphasises there is an in-built prejudice against believing in God (Romans 1:18). This naturally affects publication of materials in scientific journals or papers, if the establishment perceive them as a threat to the status quo. Why is it that evolution has such a stranglehold in our universities and schools today? Largely because the majority of scientists (we are told) accept it as true. Ideas filter down from centres of learning to the average man and woman. Articles on creation would be turned down by journals as unscientific. Nevertheless, because good science depends on Christian truth, it is evident that despite some speculative evolutionary theories, scientists do arrive at valid conclusions—through God's common grace—in their studies. Scientific theories come and go—as the history of scientific ideas shows. Once "continental drift" was thought impossible, for example, now it is the status quo for geologists to believe in plate tectonics.

Even in the free-thinking USA a radical secular thinker like Velikosky was initially rejected by many publishers, several decades ago. Velikosky's *Worlds in Collision* was turned down by major publishers because academics in America threatened not to use any publisher that dared to spread his catastrophic ideas of origins! Similar rejection has happened to modern secular writers, like science journalist Richard Milton. He was commissioned to write an article for *The Times Higher Education Supplement* on "*Scientific*

Censorship and Evolution" which they subsequently did not publish. Instead, Milton published the article himself on the internet.[1]

Richard Milton said the article was spiked by the THES following a campaign against it by Richard Dawkins. Milton comments, *"I believe that the great strength of science and the scientific method is its openness to debate. Science is strong because errors are exposed through the process of open argument and counter-argument. Science does not need vigilante scientists to guard the gates against heretics. If the heresy is true it will become accepted. If false, it will be shown to be false, by rational discourse. In his "The Open Society and its Enemies" Sir Karl Popper says that the great value of the scientific method is that it saves us from 'the tyranny of opinion.' If neo-Darwinists can counter the evidence I present, let them do so. If they seek to prevent my writing being published because they don't like it, then it is not just I that fall victim to the 'the tyranny of opinion', it is all of us."*[2]

Whilst many scientists are now critical of Darwin's ideas, they are sometimes prepared to accept even more incredible explanations of the origin and significance of the human race and Universe. This fact reminds us that it is a knife edge often between truth and error. At a popular level, a hydrological engineer, refutes Darwin, Genesis and evolution theories. Design is the signature of life, contends Mr El Ayouty (1998) in his book *Goodbye Darwin*, but then suggests extraterrestrial intelligence is responsible for its design, viz. scientists on Vinaka sent trilobites and crustaceans to earth in a spaceship! Aspects of the book read like someone who has taken *Star Trek* science fiction too seriously. No explanation in this scenario, however, of where these "extraterrestrial beings" got their know-how from, is given, or who 'created them'. His epilogue concludes by saying, *"I do believe that God exists one way or another; this is common sense. Otherwise , how did everything start? But I do not agree with many of man's interpretations of the main religions, as they have been manipulated in the hands of different interests and are now causing much suffering instead of relief, happiness and salvation. One day, logic and common sense will prevail."*[3] Improving ones' discernment and logic is a matter taken up by lawyer Philip Johnson.

The book *Testing Darwinism* by Philip E. Johnson (1997) reviews different methods of arguing, in a useful aid to clear thinking. These methods include: recognising the selective use of evidence, appeals to authority, ad hominem arguments (which attack the person—rather than their argument), straw-men arguments, begging the question type approaches, lack of testability, and use of vague terms—which are all reviewed by Johnson. He shows the need for spotting deceptive arguments and grasping the basic scientific issues without getting bogged down in unnecessary details.[4]

Cornelius Van Til—an apologist believed by some to be the most important Christian thinker in the twentieth century [5]—expounded an even more radical approach: *"In seeking to follow the example of Paul, Reformed apologetics needs, above all else, to make clear from the beginning that it is challenging the wisdom of the natural man on the authority of the self-attesting Christ speaking in Scripture. Doing this, the Reformed apologist must place himself in the position of his "opponent," the natural man, in order to show him that on the presupposition of human autonomy [man's supposed independence from God] human predication [setting forth of truth] cannot even get underway. The fact that it has gotten underway is because the universe is what the Christian, on the authority of Christ, knows it to be. Even to negate [or deny] Christ, those who hate Him must be held up by Him. A three year old child may slap his father in the face only because the father holds him up on his knee."*[6]

The apologist Francis Schaeffer's work was heavily indebted to Van Til's methodology, but this fact, is rarely—if ever—mentioned in reviews of Schaeffer's lifework. A balanced critique of the use of Francis Schaeffer's presuppositional approach to theistic argumentation was undertaken by Dr Thomas V. Morris. He concluded with a warning about apologetic self-exultation, emphasising our need to always be humble and make tentative presentations of our arguments:

"When we allow a human invention
to be confused with Divine intention,
Or take the current argumentation
to be equated with proclamation;

We join a friend with a stranger,
and thereby always court the danger
that weakness be found within the new
and men reject not one but two."[7]

We all have either explicit or implicit belief systems on which we live our daily lives, but many are unaware of this. Tim Keller (Pastor, New York City) said, *"Everyone has a religious faith in some source of meaning and morality. In other words, intellectually, anyone who doubts Christianity is at that moment bowing to some other "God", some other foundation for truth and life. Traditional apologetics has tended to treat the sceptic as being religiously neutral and then builds a case for Christianity made completely of evidences. Presuppositional apologetics, however, insists on showing a sceptic his or her own religious faith-assumptions and argues for Christianity by comparing the gospel with alternative world-views."*[8]

We trust there are beams beneath the floor when we walk on it, so Christians trust that God is behind all things, a sovereign protector and sustainer, unseen but for ever at hand. Man in his attempt to run away from God, is like a drowning man in the ocean attempting to make a ladder of water to escape. The attempt is doomed to failure! It was Saint Augustine who is quoted as having said—based on a passage in Isaiah— **"Understand that you might believe. Believe that you might understand."** Actually Augustine's original says: *"Accordingly here, as understanding consists in sight, and is abiding, but faith feeds us as babes, upon milk, in the cradles of temporal things (for now we walk by faith, not by sight); as, moreover, unless we walk by faith, we shall not attain to sight, which does not pass away, but abides, our understanding being purified by holding the truth;—for these reasons one says, "If you will not believe, you shall not understand;" but the other, "If you will not believe, you shall not abide."* The earlier noted popularised version is pithier! Good communication does require us to be "with it" and know modern idioms and buzz words. C. S. Lewis emphasised our need to know the common vernacular.

A conversation between an atheist (Cyril) and a Christian (Nick) provides an example of interaction between two acquaintances, based on actual incidents! This is a real popular case of apologetics in action however *"artificial"* it may seem, with limited time to respond to the objections raised. It is not possible—in such circumstances—to think of every implication of the objector's queries or comments. Nor would it be profitable always to do so. The questioner can go off at a tangent. The

Christian, however, should always be ready to give a reason for the hope that is in them (I Peter 3: 15-16).

The scenario: Nick meets Cyril

Nick: *"Hi Cyril, what do you think about the Christian message?"*
Cyril: *"I think you Christians are all so arrogant!"*
Nick: *" Why, Cyril?"*
Cyril: *"I heard a Christian preacher say once, 'To understand the Bible properly, you need the help of the Holy Spirit. He had the cheek to say: 'Without the help of God, we were like chimpanzees trying to read Shakespeare'."*
Nick: *"Well, I don't suppose he was trying to be offensive. I guess he was saying that by nature we don't want God, and so we need his Spirit to help us understand."*
Cyril: *"But, that's rubbish! Are you telling me you Christians are so gullible as to believe all the myths and fairy stories found in the Bible?"*
Nick: *"I don't think Christians are any more gullible than anyone else, and anyway some of the greatest thinkers of all time have been Christians. Think of St. Augustine of Hippo, a giant intellect; then again the apostle Paul—who has written some of the profoundest books in the Bible ......"*
Cyril: *"Yes, but you've got no Einsteins who were Christians. What about great scientists? They don't figure in your list."*
Nick: *"No, I cannot mention everything at once! Have you heard of the Magnetic Resonancing Scanner? Would you say you needed a good mind to invent something like that?"*
Cyril: *"Yes, I've heard of it."*
Nick: *"Well, the inventor of that is a Christian. He is a practising scientist and Christian in America. He trusts in the Bible. I could give you many more examples like Faraday, Ambrose Fleming, Kelvin, Maxwell and so on. Anyway even Einstein admitted that God existed. He also said he could not think of a genuine scientist without a profound faith."*
Cyril: *"Yes, but how can you believe in God, 'an old man, with a long white beard.' I think you know scientists tell us we have evolved, or haven't you heard of Darwin? We are creatures that are no different from*

insects if you like, we are products of evolution. Yes, we can think, but it's arrogant to talk about 'living forever'. I think when we die that's it...."

Nick: "Hold on a bit, Cyril. You are raising quite a few points here. We haven't got long but the points you raise all have an answer. Firstly God isn't like you portray Him. God is Spirit, and He has qualities you can find out about in the Bible. God is not like you and me, limited to time and space; He is eternal. To put it in a nutshell, as the Shorter Catechism does: 'God is a Spirit, infinite, eternal, and unchangeable in His being, wisdom, power, holiness, justice, goodness, and truth.' So there's no idea that God is like an old grandfather in the sky! He has created the whole Universe ...."

Cyril: "No, I cannot believe that! Don't you know how big the Universe is! The Sun is one star in a collection of 100 thousand million stars which make up the Milky Way galaxy. This galaxy is only one of 100 thousand million galaxies in the Universe. You think you matter when we are so small and insignificant, mere 'dots'. It's just pie in the sky when you die!"

Nick: "I think you are expressing—in part—what we find in the Bible! David says in Psalm 8 when he considers the wonder and size of the Universe, how can God be interested in us, ' grasshoppers' as it calls us elsewhere in the Bible."

Cyril: "Well, if it gives you comfort to believe that, you can. I wish I could have faith like that! But Stephen Hawking doesn't believe in God. Haven't you heard about his scientific view that the Universe has no beginning or end?"

Nick: "Yes, Stephen Hawking has done some interesting work in this area. But you know he says in his book on Black Holes and Baby Universes: 'Although science may solve the problem of how the Universe began, it cannot answer the question why does the Universe bother to exist? I don't know the answer to that.'[9] Also the problem still remains for him as to 'Why there is something rather than nothing?' You see Cyril, on the basis of the Big Bang theory of the origin of the Universe, this teacup has as much meaning as me!"

Cyril: "Yes, I agree."

Nick: "So what's the purpose of living in your scheme of things?"

Cyril: "I enjoy lots of things—sex, art, sketching, football, and playing my different musical instruments!"

Nick: *"Are you really happy to die believing that? Are you prepared to die? Christians believe the chief end of man (people) is to glorify God, and enjoy him for ever."*

Cyril: *"For me death is just the cessation of existence. We are just higher—if you like—on the scale of being than the animals—because we can think. How can you believe, if there is a God, that it makes any difference to Him—to say I believe in Him?".*

Nick: *"It was Jesus Christ who said that what we believe affects our eternal destiny, not me. I expect that you've heard it before, but Jesus said He was 'the way, the truth and the life.' And John 3:16 tells us that 'God so loved the world, that He gave His only begotten Son, that whoever believes on Him, should not perish but have everlasting life....'"*

Cyril: *"Look, I've heard all this stuff before. I cannot see how you can be so gullible as to believe all that! Anyway, if there is a God He must be bitter and twisted to allow all this suffering in the world."*

Nick: *"You have raised an important issue. I think we can learn from Biblical examples, some of the answers to pain and suffering. You may have heard of Job and the trials he went through. In Job 38 God eventually answers Job's questions by asking him where he was when the world was created. He reminds Job of his smallness, and that as it says in Genesis : '... shall not the judge of all the earth do right?' We cannot always expect God to be subject to our criteria of fairness. Nevertheless, God does restrain evil and does not always instantly judge sin or sinners. Supremely we see God's answer to suffering and pain in the death of His Son on Calvary's Hill. Not only did Jesus take away all the sin of those who would come to God, but He even purchased the time for us to repent (re-think) and turn away from our sin."*

Cyril: *"What happens to babies in Heaven, then?"*

Nick: *"The Bible does not tell us a lot about babies in Heaven. David, the Psalmist, said he hoped to see one of his sons in the next life (2 Samuel 12: 23). But Bible teaching cannot be based on a single verse alone. Overall, Scripture teaches us that we should repent and believe. Theologians have said that to do so we must clearly reach an 'age of discernment', so we can respond to God's truth. Those who are not in this normal situation, are cast on God's mercy and the saving work of Christ. This we do know:*

those who are in Heaven will be full personalities with all defects restored in a 'glorified body'."

Cyril: *"That's interesting, nobody has explained that to me before. Now, take the ten commandments—I don't believe that story. God pointing his finger at tables of stone and writing down the rules! Then Moses taking it down the Mount. It's just a system thought up by the leaders to maintain control over the people. Anyway, why doesn't God show himself to anybody? ..."*

Nick: *"Hold on a bit, Cyril! You are just firing points without any chance to answer! You see God is so powerful and holy He couldn't show himself to us in full; in our states we'd be burned up. He did in fact show Moses His 'rear parts'. God reveals Himself to humans in the 'book of nature', and the 'book of Scripture'—which needed His oversight to ensure its truthfulness. Finally, He showed Himself best to us in the person of Jesus Christ. Jesus said, 'He who has seen me, has seen the Father who sent me.' Anyway, if you remember the Bible account, Moses had a stutter, and at first did not want to be the leader—having to face Pharaoh and lead the Israelites out of Egypt. The ten commandments put God first, when people make up rules they put man's interests first!"*

Cyril: *"I like the people I know who are Christians, but I feel sorry for them ...."*

Nick: *"Cyril, don't you think you may be being programmed by the world to live for this life only? Are you being arrogant to deny the Lord Jesus and to call Him a liar, because He said these things were true. He even proved His power by conquering the grave....."*

Cyril: *"Oh, no! You cannot believe in the resurrection. Jesus has been shown to have taken a drug, offered to him on a spear, that put him in a coma, and later He revived."*

Nick: *"That's just not true! The soldier did indeed offer some vinegar and gall (nothing like you suggest) but you note the text says, Jesus after he tasted it refused to drink it (Matthew 27:34)."*

Cyril: *"O.K. convince me!"*

Nick: *"The facts speak for themselves. An atheistic Australian journalist (Tony Morphet) set out to disprove the Bible, but ended up seeing this was true—not 'make-believe.' He said the New Testament is not fiction. Not* *myth, not legend, but fact. .. The Jesus you read about in the New Testament doesn't have flaws, is nothing like a fiction writer would have made Him. But nonetheless real! God's word itself confirms the truth of the resurrection. Paul mentions the numerous post-resurrection appearances in 1 Corinthians 15. It appears that the apostles were able to declare the Resurrection largely without fear of contradiction. The Jews made up the story that the disciples removed Jesus' body, thereby confirming the reality of the empty tomb. And in the unlikely event that the disciples had done such a thing (risking their lives in the face of the Roman guards) would many of them have died to sustain a fraud?"*

Cyril: *"Yes, but stories become embellished with time!"*

Nick: *"The Resurrection was related too soon after the event to be the result of legendary development. The women discovering the empty tomb bears remarkable evidence to the genuineness of the account. Women were not acceptable as witnesses in a Jewish court of Law—so any inventor of such a story would not have placed women in this role. Any attempts to explain the Resurrection as anything other than a supernatural event have always failed. You mention that Jesus did not actually die on the cross, but fell into a coma. It is interesting to note that when the Roman soldier struck his side with his spear both blood and water gushed out—a sure sign of death. Anyway, in such a weakened condition Jesus couldn't possibly have rolled the heavy closing-stone away."*

Cyril: *"What about the possibility that the people who saw him were having 'visions'?"*

Nick: *"Yes, another old chestnut! Hallucinations or visions do not produce the same images in many different people. But in the Scriptures all reported seeing the same thing. Look I'll give you a book that explains in detail answers to the problems you raise, called 'Will the real Jesus please stand up?'—by John Blanchard if you'll promise to read it?"*

Cyril: *"Oh! alright then, I'll read it—if it makes you happy. I apologise if I lost my temper a bit, I don't really think all Christians are arrogant."*

Nick: *"Fine Cyril, let us know how you get on with your reading. We can take our discussion from there. Remember, if Jesus is risen then his people are raised with him to newness of life. And if Jesus is risen, then He really is God."*

Appendix 1

References:

1   **R. Milton** (1995) *Scientific Censorship and Evolution*, www. lauralee.comm/milton.ht
2   **R. Milton,** in an open letter to the editor of the THES (Auriol Stevens) 16 March 1995.
3   **C. El Ayouty** (1998) *Goodbye Darwin*, Minerva Press, London, ISBN 0 75410 172 X, p. 349.
4   **P. E. Johnson** (1997) *Testing Darwinism*, IVF, Leicester, ISBN 0-85111-198-X, pp. 37-52.
5   **E. Hulse** (1997) *"An Enjoyable Mind-stretcher"*, Reformation Today, No. 159, Sept/Oct, p. 19.
6   **C. Van Til** (1972) *Towards a Reformed Apologetic*, p. 16.
7   **T. V. Morris** (1976) *Francis Schaeffer's Apologetics*, The Moody Bible Institute, Chicago, ISBN 0-8024-2873-8.
8   **T. Keller** (1997) *The Gospel and the Secular Mind*, Conference Notes, London.
9   **S. W. Hawking** (1993) *Black Holes and Baby Universes*, Bantam, p. 90.

Further Reading:
Norman Geisler (1976) *Christian Apologetics*, Baker Book House Company, Grand **Rapids, Michigan,** ISBN 0-8010-3704-2.
P. E. Johnson (1995) *Reason in the Balance: The case against naturalism in science, law and education*, IVP, Downers Grove, Illinois, ISBN 08308 1610 0.
P. M. Masters (1973) *Men of Purpose*, Wakeman Publications, London.
W. Rietkerk (1997) *If Only I could Believe*, Solway, ISBN 1 900507 36 6.
J. Rendle-Short (1991) *Reasonable Christianity*, Evangelical Press, Darlington, ISBN 0-85234-289-6.

Resources:
Cassettes: The D. M. Lloyd-Jones Recording Trust, 2 Caxton House, Wellesley Road, Ashford, Kent, TN24 8ET, Tel. 01233 662262. E-mail mlj@ukonline.co.uk
Creation On-line: http:\\www.icr.org
Internet addresses:
http://www.Gospelcom.net/net/rbc/
http://www.gty.org
http://www.domini.org
http://www.whitedove.com/GoodNews/
C. S. Lewis web sites:

http://www.C.S.LEWIS. ORG/welcome/ by his step-son, Douglas Gresham, then click on to: Into the wardrode: **http://cslewis.cache.net/** where it is possible to hear his message called, *"Sounds like Lewis"* e.g. Is creation necessary?

Biblically Speaking Website: a Reformed site which links into other valuable sites: http://www.netkonect.co.uk/k/ketsvc/index.htm

Key Texts:

Isaiah 1: 18, *"'Come, now , and let us reason together,'says the Lord. "* See also : **Jeremiah 9: 23-24.**

Questions for Further Study

1   Is it an adequate response to say *"I know Christianity is true, because Jesus lives within my heart"*? If not, what scriptural and logical answers do you think a believer should give? See for instance: I Peter 3: 15-16; Isaiah 1: 18; Luke 24: 27; Proverbs 15: 2; Matthew 10:16.

2   What is the significance of the saying, *"It is possible to win the argument, but lose the soul"*? See for instance: I Corinthians 13: 1-2.

3   What strategies did Jesus Christ use to convey the truth in his teaching? (Note: Did he appeal to the conscience? Did he vary his approach to different classes of unbeliever, e.g. use shock tactics?)

4   Did the apostles get involved in apologetics? See Acts 17: 22-32.

5   Is it valid to quote secular sources to establish one's points? See Acts 17: 28-29.

6   How would you have replied to Isaac Asimov, when he said, *"Emotionally, I am an atheist . I don't have the evidence to prove that God doesn't exist, but I so strongly suspect he doesn't that I don't want to waste my time."* Source: Isaac Asimov (1982), Interview by Paul Kurtz, *"An interview with Isaac Asimov on Science and the Bible"*, Free Inquiry (vol. 2, Spring 1982), p. 9.

7   As a last resort, should we be provocative in order to make people think about life's meaning?

Food for Thought:

  * *"Blind unbelief is sure to err, and scan His works in vain, God is His own interpreter, and He will make it plain."*
  * *"Unbelief in the face of evidence is either stupidity or sin."* Anon.

Appendix 1

* *"Don't confuse me with facts, my mind's made up!" Anon.*

* *"Doubters invert the metaphor and insist that they need faith as big as a mountain in order to move a mustard seed." Webb B. Garrison.*

* *"Satan loves to fish in muddy water."* William S. Plumer.

* *"The Devil is very subtle; He knows how to bait the hook very well."* John E. Marshall

* "No difficulty in believing the gospel is intellectual, it is always moral." Dr. D. Martyn Lloyd-Jones.

The man, the myth, the legend ...

"God cannot give us happiness and peace apart from himself, because it is not there. There is no such thing." C. S. Lewis.

The following is a cameo of an internationally famous Christian writer: Clive Staples Lewis (1898—1963), a brilliant popular apologist. His stress was upon knowing your initial philosophy, presenting the facts, and putting Christianity in the popular vernacular. Both his 'strengths and weaknesses' are reported, although some of his critics could not hold a candle up to all he has achieved for the cause of Christ through his writings in the twentieth century.

The popular representation of Christians today as *mindless enthusiasts—bent on believing the impossible* is clearly refuted by the life and writings of Professor Clive Staples Lewis. Born in Dublin (Ireland) on November 29th, 1898, Clive (known affectionately to his friends as 'Jack') was raised in a Christian home. C. S. Lewis through his books, became one of the most influential defenders of Christianity in the twentieth century. His book *Mere Christianity* has sold over 10 million copies, and shows how Christianity can be mind-stretching. Another short tome on *Miracles* is one of the cleverest rebuttals of the arguments of rationalists, materialists and anti-theists. Whilst Lewis was no systematic or formal apologist, his writings give examples of some of the most influential applications of Christian truth—in popular form—in the 20th century. He knew how to communicate and point the way to faith.

Childhood grief

His father Albert (a solicitor) and mother Flora encouraged their two sons to read books. Sadly, their childhood security did not last long; when Jack was nine years old his mother died of cancer. His father was overcome by grief, and sent Jack (and brother Warren) to school in England. As an unhappy teenager, Jack rejected Christianity—being angry with God for the death of his mother. He became an atheist. When almost 16 years old he transferred to a new school and was then tutored by an old family friend, William T. Kirkpatrick. It was this Head Teacher that taught young Jack the importance of logical and systematic thinking. This was to lay the foundation for his future success as a don at Oxford University.

Soldier, soldier

Jack's classical studies were interrupted by the First World War. In 1917 he was sent to fight in the trenches of the Western Front. Wounded in battle, he returned home to England in 1918. Naturally he gravitated back to university life, where he remained as an academic—for the rest of his life. He became a fellow at Oxford (1925-1954) and was then appointed a Professor of Medieval and Renaissance Literature at Cambridge University (1954-1963). He was an expert on courtly love and medieval literature, establishing his reputation with *Allegory of Love: A study in Medieval Tradition* (1936).

On the run

Like the Old Testament prophet Jonah of old, Jack was on the run from God. This Oxford Professor of English was originally an atheist because of all the injustice in the world. Lewis concluded that injustice in the world pointed to the One who set the standard of justice. Lewis' atheism was first challenged by G. K. Chesterton's *Everlasting Man* . He began to appreciate Christianity's coherence. He saw *"the whole Christian outline of history set in a form that seemed to me to make sense."*[1] He was able to trust in Christ, after a conversation with J. R. R. Tolkien—a fellow philologist at Oxford, who became famous for *The Lord of the Rings*. Jack had long been interested in myths, especially Norse myths. Tolkien helped him understand that Christianity was a so-called *"myth"* that had really happened! In his autobiography Lewis wrote: *"You must picture me alone in that room at Magdalen [college], night after night, feeling, whenever my mind lifted even for a second from my work, the steady, unrelenting approach of Him whom I so earnestly desired not to meet. That which I greatly feared had at last come upon me. In the Trinity Term of 1929 I gave in, and admitted God was God, and knelt and prayed: perhaps that night, the most dejected and reluctant convert in all England."*[2]

Enthusiastic writer

Despite his reluctant conversion C. S. Lewis became one of the most enthusiastic and prolific Christian writers of this century. Jack was gifted with an exceptionally bright and logical mind. He wrote in a lucid, lively style, unrivalled by his contemporaries. You may have heard of his fascinating *Chronicles of Narnia* (1950) or his brilliant *Screwtape Letters* (1942) or encountered the incisive logic of *Mere Christianity* (1952). Jack wrote everything with an old-fashioned ink pen and ink stand, but his insights into religious and moral problems are still as relevant today as when he wrote them. He had a determined character, and was not concerned by the reputation he may gain for himself.

His lifework: no ivory tower

Jack wanted ordinary people to understand Christianity. He never over-simplified difficult issues, but presented arguments in a form the average person could understand. It is often said any fool can make a difficult subject more complicated, but only a brilliant communicator can make a complex subject simpler. The film *Shadowlands* records the touching romance which developed with his American wife (Joy Davidman). If this film is inadequate, it is because it underplays his constant commitment to Christian service and implies he did not know how to cope with the problem of his wife's illness. Jack, however, wrote another classic, *The Problem of Pain* (1948) which foreshadowed the ordeal he had to go through. This was undergoing the pain of his wife's premature death (at 45) with cancer, in 1959. The film implies his faith fell to bits, but in reality his faith strengthened. Lewis was like the tough grass—the more it's downtrodden the tougher it becomes and springs back into life. Naturally, he was laid low emotionally for many months by her death. Jack wrote *A*

Grief Observed after this bereavement experience, in which he charted his feelings and conflicts at this difficult time.

C. S. Lewis deals with issues like *"Was Jesus just a brilliant moral teacher or truly the Son of God?"* *"Why are some Christians rough diamonds?"* and *"If God is good and loves us why does He allow terrible things to happen?"* Lewis said it was not sexual behaviour that was at the centre of Christian morality but pride. It is pride that cuts us off from God, who is more powerful and better than us. Jack wrote: *"That raises a terrible question 'How is it that people who are quite obviously eaten up with pride can say they believe in God and appear to themselves very religious?' I am afraid it means they are worshipping an imaginary God"*.

Mere Christianity

His book *Mere Christianity* began as a series of radio talks that he gave during the Second World War on the BBC radio in a series of 15 minute talks. This became a Christian classic in which he explains the why's and wherefore's of the Christian faith. He was always a clear stylist who took great pains to make these talks both vivid and understandable. He started by explaining what good and bad mean. For instance, two quarrelling children—or grown ups—appeal to what is fair: they have a standard of justice. There is a law of Human Nature, just like the laws of nature which determine your fate if you step off a cliff. The radio audience generally had no idea he was combating relativism and positivism; it all seemed like common sense.

Lewis with his great knowledge of Classical Literature produced several works of fiction. *The Chronicles of Narnia* have remained popular with generations of children. Best known are the *Screwtape Letters* (1942). Screwtape is a senior devil who sardonically instructs his apprentice nephew (Wormwood) in methods of mortal temptation. Screwtape's imaginary correspondence is very humorous, but gets vital truths across. Not only were his writings interesting but they contain many pithy sayings. It would be possible to create a book of C. S. Lewis quotations, like Martin Luther's Tabletalk. Take for instance: *"A man can no more diminish God's glory by refusing to worship Him than a lunatic can put out the sun by scribbling the word 'darkness' on the walls of his cell."*

Lewis wrote other apologetic works: *The Pilgrims Regress* (1993); *The Abolition of Man* (1943); *The Great Divorce* (1944)—a fantasy; *Reflections on the Psalms* (1958) and *The Four Loves* (1960).

Jack Lewis did have defects in his appreciation of Christian doctrine. He was never exposed to any clear and systematic exposition of the Reformed Faith. He believed in a form of purgatory which we have shown elsewhere is not taught in Scripture (e.g. *"It is appointed for men to die once, but after this the judgement"* Hebrews 9:27). He tended to underline the beliefs that united Christians, but to draw a curtain over the vital fact that Christianity can only be adequately practised within a true and living Church. He had inadequate views too on aspects of the inerrancy of Scripture, but of course Lewis never claimed to be infallible, nor is he. Nevertheless, he was a Christian supernaturalist. He talked openly of his conversion from atheism, and his wish for others to make the same journey. Note: see the further reading section reference to Dr T. Baxter (1988).

Lewis as a biblical scholar of ancient texts said of prominent Bible critics: *"They seem to me to lack literary judgement, to be imperceptive about the very quality of the texts they are reading."* [3] Lewis criticises Rudolf Bultman's claim that the personality of Jesus was unimportant to the apostle Paul, or John. Lewis says, *"Through what strange process has this learned German gone in order to make himself blind to what all men except him see? ... These men ask me to believe they can read between the lines of the old texts; the evidence is their obvious inability to read (in any sense worth discussing) the lines themselves. They claim to see fern-seed and can't see an elephant ten yards away in broad daylight."* [4]

The legend

C. S. Lewis is still a household name. He is even available on the internet! Jack was the subject of a recent symposium entitled, *"A Christian for all Christians"*. In short, we have noted that he was a literary giant who published works on theology and apologetics, but also science fiction, scholarly reviews and seven books for children. The critic C. E. M. Joad, in reviewing one of his books said of Jack, that he *"possesses the rare gift of being able to make righteousness readable"*. Lewis firmly believed in the need to *"translate every bit of your theology into the vernacular."* He saw his apologetic task as getting people to face the facts. Lewis realised that no interpretation of reality can supersede its original assumptions. He said: *"What we learn from experience depends on the kind of philosophy we bring to experience. It is therefore useless to appeal to experience before we have settled, as well as we can, the philosophical question."*[5] Despite the limitation that Jack Lewis was not an unequivocal advocate of Reformation theology, he has probably done far more to advance Evangelical Christianity—than many of his critics.

References

1   **C. S. Lewis** (1955) *Surprised by Joy*, Harcourt, Brace and World, New York, p. 223.

2   **Ibid.,** pp. 228-229.

3   **C. S. Lewis** (1967) *Christian Reflections*, ed Walter Hooper, Eerdmans, Grand Rapids, p. 154.

4   **Ibid.,** pp. 156-7.

5   **C. S. Lewis** (1948) *Miracles*, Macmillan, New York, p. 11.

Further Reading:

1   **T. Baxter** (1988) *The Enigma of CS Lewis,* CRN Journal, Colchester, pp. 30-31.

2   **W. Hooper** (1996) *C. S. Lewis A Companion and Guide*, Fount, Harper Collins, London, W6 8JB.

3   **G. R. Lewis** (1977) *Testing Christianity's Truth Claims*, Moody Press, Chicago, ISBN 0-8024-8595-2, pp. 331-339.

Visit the C. S. Lewis web site:

http://**www.C.S.LEWIS. ORG/welcome/** by his step-son, Douglas Gresham, then click on to: Into the wardrobe: **http://cslewis.cache.net/** where it is possible to hear his message called, *"Sounds like Lewis"* e.g. *"Is creation necessary?"*

Key Texts:

Acts 11: 26 *"... And the disciples were first called Christians in Antioch."*
James 5: 11 *"Indeed we count them blessed who endure. You have heard of the perseverance of Job and seen the purpose of the Lord—that the Lord is very compassionate and merciful".*

Questions for Further Study

1   How do you account for the continued popularity of C. S. Lewis' writings?
2   What continues to be his best selling title, and what is its main purpose?
3   How did Jack's upbringing affect his reaction to Christianity?
4   What book helped Lewis see through atheism, and to consider Christianity?
5   Where does Lewis explain his conversion to Christianity?
6   List the books by C. S. Lewis you think are most influential, and indicate what the range of topics in his works indicates about his view of the relevance of Christianity.
7   What books deal with pain and suffering?
8   "To err is human ... " What aspects of C. S. Lewis' teaching fall short of the Bible's teaching?
9   What did Lewis think was essential before we can sort out our views of life and experience?
10 What impressed C. E. M. Joad about Lewis' writings?

Food for Thought

* *"I do not know what I may appear to the world, but to myself I seem to have been only like a boy playing on the sea-shore, and diverting myself in now and then finding a smoother pebble or a prettier shell than ordinary, whilst the great ocean of truth lay all undiscovered before me."* Isaac Newton.

"The intellectual critic is soon answered. We have but to ask him to explain the meaning of life and death." Dr. D. Martyn Lloyd-Jones.

Glossary

ABSOLUTE: (1) Free from limitations, qualification, or restriction, e.g. absolute being; (2) independent and not relative e.g. absolute time or space; (3) free from variability, change, error e.g. the absolute truth; (4) certain and true without reservation; (5) not arbitrary or relative.

AESTHETICS: The philosophy of the beautiful. What is art? What is beauty? Is the beauty of music beautiful for similar reasons to that of a landscape?

AGNOSTICISM: The belief that we cannot have knowledge of God and that it is impossible to prove that God exists or does not exist.

ALTRUISM: (1) The promotion of the good of others; (2) a selfless and benevolent love for humankind and dedication to achieving the well-being of people and society.

ANALOGICAL: Meaning based on analogy. Resemblance in some particulars between things otherwise unlike; e.g. a man's mind is like God's mind (not totally different—equivocal meaning—or identical—univocal meaning). The value of an analogy is often judged by criteria such as the number of similarities that exist between the things compared; the number of further resemblances suggested which on testing are verified as correct; and the number of suggestions about resemblances implied in the analogy.

ANALOGY: An expression or comparison of like or similar aspects of known objects, events and/or ideas, concepts.

ANXIETY, BASIC: Not neurotic phobia, but a realistic concern about the inescapable experience of death, for instance.

APAGOGIC: A method of argument which reduces an opposing view to absurdity.

APODICTIC: Knowledge of what must occur, as opposed to knowledge of what might occur or is capable of occurring or is actual or occurring.

APOLOGETICS: The science and art of defending Christianity's truth-claims; in theology the endeavour to rationally justify the divine origin of a faith.

A POSTERIORI: Latin, that which follows after, latter; after or coming from sense experience; proceeding from effects to causes. Opposite of A PRIORI.

A PRIORI: Knowledge of universal principles whose validity is logically independent of particular things observed by the senses. Sometimes used in a derogatory way to mean prior to critical evaluation—uncritical. In contrast to a posteriori knowledge whose validity depends on experience of things observed by the senses. (From Latin that which precedes; a, ab, from, out of, and prior, former, before).

ARGUMENT FROM DESIGN: See Teleological Argument.

ASSUMPTION: A statement (or postulate) of a concept taken for granted and not tested during particular scientific activity. These may be basic assumptions, experimental assumption, or theoretical assumptions.

ASTROLOGY: The study of the movements and relative positions of celestial bodies interpreted as an influence on human affairs.

ATOMIC FACT: the simplest, most rudimentary, elementary, and irreducible kind of fact consisting of a quality in some particular thing or a relation between particular things.

ATOMISM: GREEK The philosophy developed by Greek philosophers like Leucippus and Epicurus which maintained that reality is composed of atoms. In general, atomism is the materialistic view that the universe consists of ultimately simple, independent, and irreducible entities that are only contingently interrelated to form objects.

ATOMISM: LOGICAL the name given to the philosophic outlook identified with Bertrand Russell and Ludwig Wittgenstein characterised by such theories as: language and thought can be analysed in terms of indivisible and discrete components called atomic propositions that correspond to atomic facts.

AXIOLOGY: The theory of values; the analysis of values to determine their meaning, characteristics, origins, types, criteria, and epistomological status. (From Greek, axios, worthy, and logos, the study of.)

AXIOM: A self-evident truth with which to begin a system of deductive thought; their proof is related to the extent they can be used to construct a coherent and inclusive system. (From Greek, axioma, that which is thought to be worthy.)

BELIEF: (1) A state of mind in which confidence, trust, faith, trust is placed in a person, idea, or thing; (2) a conviction or feeling that something is real or true; (3) intellectual assent to an idea; (4) that which is asserted or contained in an idea.

CALCULATION: Some arithmetic and/or mathematical manipulation of abstract and numerical symbols.

CATEGORY: A general form of thought employed in all reasoning. Plato laid the foundation for philosophising in terms of categories.

CAUSALITY, LAW OF: The principle that every effect must have an adequate cause, that everything that happens has an explanation sufficient to produce it, a sufficient condition to account for it.

CAUSE: Whatever produces an effect; a person or thing that makes something happen (sooner or later).

CIRCULAR REASONING: Argument involving in the premises the point to be proved, assuming the thing to be established.

CLASSIFICATION: (1) The end result of ordering of objects and/or events according to stated criteria. (2) the process of ordering objects and /or events according to stated criteria.

COGITO ERGO SUM: Latin, I think, therefore I am, or I am thinking, therefore I exist. Descartes' phrase for an immediate, necessary, and indubitable intuition, in which he recognises himself as a thinking thing.

COGNITION: (1) intellectual knowledge; (2) the act of knowing.

COGNITIVE: Meaning which asserts something and hence is either true or false. Such theoretical meaning is not merely expressive of the emotions of the speaker or writer. Assertive meaning.

COMMON GROUND: Knowledge available to all men (non-Christian as well as Christian) on the basis of which Christians may reason with non-Christians in defence of their faith. Knowledge not dependent upon faith in God, Christ, or Scripture. Van Til would argue that even this is not truly "common ground" as it involves stealing "like a rustler" from the Creator those aspects of reality that really belong to Him, and ultimately only make sense when related to Him.

CONSEQUENTIALISM: The general term for any teleological system of ethics. By far the best-known example is Utilitarianism.

CONTRADICTION: Two propositions asserting and denying the same thing at the same time and in the same respect.

COSMOGONY: A list of ideas or formulations centred on origination and generation of the universe. Such conceptual patterns or models do not qualify as scientific theories since no prior observations or testable predictions about origins are possible.

COSMOLOGICAL ARGUMENT: There is a whole family of related arguments, for instance: (1) Either something must be eternal or something comes from nothing. Something does not come from nothing. Therefore something is eternal. (2) All things need an explanation. We cannot have an infinite chain of explanation, each thing explained by another, since then there would be no explanation for the chain as a whole. So there is something whch explains itself: this is God. (From T. Aquinas, *Summa Theologica*.)

COSMOLOGY: The study of the nature of the universe; use of tools and technology to describe aspects of the observable and physical universe.

CREATION MODEL: An explanatory belief system based upon existence of an eternal Creator who established a completed, finished, and functional universe in all aspects regarding elements, galaxies, stars, planets—especially the earth with mutually exclusive groups of animals and plants. Ideas have to do with conservation of known conditions; yet, changes of decay and degeneration are evident and easily documented.

DEDUCTION: Inference from a general rule or principle to particular cases. Starts with a general principle that is accepted as true and applies it to a particular case. The conclusion is true if the principle was true; e.g., All people are sinners. Y is a person. Therefore Y is a sinner. It is a conclusion deduced. A scientific example would be: All humans have two eyes (Major Premise); Freda Bloggs is a human (Minor Premise); Therefore Freda Bloggs has two eyes. Contrast with "induction."

DEISM: The belief in the existence of a supreme being arising from reason rather than revelation.

DESCRIPTION: A statement about some object and/or event in space-time. This is the lowest or basic level of scientific explanation.

DUALISM: A world-view which asserts that there are two independent and mutually irreducible ultimate beings, usually one good and one evil. In contrast, monism maintains that there is but one ultimate Being.

EFFECT: Any finite thing or event; fact. The result or consequence of an action, etc.

EMPIRICISM: The theory of epistemology that all knowledge is derived from and based on experience. No knowledge is derived from mental processes independent of experience because without the data of the senses the mind is a blank tablet (tabula rasa).

EMPIRICISM, PURE: The mind, of itself a blank tablet, obtains no knowledge independent of experience.

EMPIRICISM, RATIONAL: The mind, structured by rational categories, obtains all its knowledge through experience.

EPISTEMOLOGY: The division of philosophy which examines the sources and test of human knowledge; (From Greek, episteme, knowledge, and logos, the study of). It deals with questions like: What is knowledge? What is the difference between knowledge, belief and opinion? Can we really know anything? How can we know that we do?

EQUIVOCAL: Meaning which is vague and ambiguous because it has two entirely different meanings; e.g. man has a mind, God has a mind; but mind is used in two entirely different ways. See "analogical" and "univocal."

ESSENCE: That in virtue of which a thing is what it is; intrinsic nature; (from Latin, essentia, from esse, be); Sometimes, essence is used synonymously with form and idea.

ETHICS: The branch of philosophy and theology that studies conduct that is right or wrong; what people ought and ought not to do; morality; (from Greek, ethikos, from ethos, usage, character, custom, disposition, manners.) How should we live? Why should we live like that? What is "good" and "bad" or evil? How shall we decide that an act is unethical? What is "happiness"?

Glossary

EVIL: MORAL Evil that is the result of deliberate human action, like murder or war.

EVIL: NATURAL Evil that is the result of usual or unusual natural occurrences, such as diseases, drought, famines, hurricanes, volcanic disasters, etc.

EVOLUTION: (1) the development of a thing into a more complex and/or different organisation; (2) the development of a thing's potential toward a further result, purpose, or end. Evolutionism is the general name given to developmental views of life or the universe.

EVOLUTION MODEL: An explanatory belief system based upon eternal existence of matter from which have come an ascending series of elements by nucleogenesis, changes by stellar evolution of "young" stars into "old" stars, galaxies, planets—especially the earth with life that appeared spontaneously through molecular evolution followed by organic evolution, including human evolution. Ideas have to do with origination of order out of disorder and integration of more complex patterns out of least complex patterns.

EXISTENTIALISM, CHRISTIAN: A view of life maintaining that Christianity is to be passionately appropriated by sheer faith even though it is an implausible offence to the human mind (as for example propounded by Soren Kierkegaard).

EXISTENTIALISM, NON-CHRISTIAN: A view of life maintaining that individual existences, not essences or forms, make up reality. Since universal patterns of meaning cannot be found, life appears to be absurd and meaningless (e.g. Jean Paul Sartre views).

EXPERIMENT: A specifically designed use of equipment, tools of measurement, and controlled variable components to gain observations and descriptions usually otherwise unobtainable.

EXPERIMENTAL ASSUMPTION: A statement about that aspect(s) of experimentation (controlled or of trial-and-error category) that is taken for granted as "noncritical" and not measured in any way.

EXPLANATION: A particular frame of reference used to provide meaning for particular facts. Something has been "explained" when the statement, "I understand," can be made in response to the explanation offered.

EXPLICIT: Clearly and fully expressed or formulated, the absence of ambiguity or the need for inferring what is meant; understandable.

FACT: An object and/or event in space at some time.

FAITH: (1) Whole soul trust in an unseen reality on the ground of sufficient (seen) evidence. (2) Assent to the truth of an unprovable presupposition. (3) A passionate leap into the dark (Kierkegaard). (4) The acceptance of regulative principles or ideals that cannot be demonstrated theoretically or empirically but nevertheless are needed and used efficiently in scientific, practical, and moral affairs.

FIDEISM: (1) the doctrine that religious truth is founded on faith and not on reason or empirical evidence; (2) faith is superior to reason or science as a source of knowledge; (3) all other sources of knowledge (a) must conform to and support knowledge obtained by faith, or (b) are based on a faith in presuppositions that cannot be justified by reason or evidence.

FINITE: Having limits or bounds; a limited nature and existence because of location in space and time. See "infinite."

GENERALIZATION: A statement of common aspects of similar objects and/or events.—or an assertion that something is true about all members of a certain class of objects and/or events.

GAIA HYPOTHESIS: This theory describes how the ecosystem of a planet can be viewed as a single system. Gaia was the Greek earth goddess whose name has been adopted for the theory that the whole planet should be regarded as a living thing. Concept developed by James Lovelock (1979).

GNOSTICISM: A pre-Christian and early Christian school of religious thought distinguished by the conviction that matter is evil and that emancipation comes through a hidden or secret knowledge (Greek gnosis). Gnostics believed they had esoteric mystical knowledge; Christian heretics of the 1st-3rd century.

GOLDEN RULE: Do as you would be done by. This rule underlies the moral systems of nearly all the main religions, as well as Kantian ethics.

GUILT, REAL: Accountability, not for trifling mistakes or necessarily to civil law, but a liability to punishment for violation of God's law (Grounds).

HUMANISM: A philosophy which recognizes the value and dignity of man and makes him the measure of all things, confident that man has the capacity to shape his life in the world. A type of naturalism.

HYPOTHESIS: A tentative answer to a problem. A hypothesis is most properly expressed as an assertive statement in form suitable for testing. A tentative explanation put forward for confirmation or disconfirmation, like if X, then Y. It may also be a proposition made as a basis for reasoning, without the assumption it is true.

IDEALISM: A philosophy teaching that knowledge of separate facts is not possible because the knower brings to the observation of any single fact a comprehensive interpretative system (Van Til).

INCOMMENSURABLE: Two different paradigms are said to be incommensurable when they cannot be compared due to radical incompatibility of such things as meaning, truth, or justification. If, for instance, two paradigms are so alien to each other that the meanings of the concepts of the one cannot clearly be translated into the concepts of the other, so the paradigms cannot be compared to see if they are contradictory or not, as they do not share the same "universe of discourse".

IMMANENCE: A state of being present or dwelling within. In modern pantheism, God or the Absolute is completely within the world and identical with it. According to Deism, God is essentially absent from the world. According to theism, He is both immanent (in presence and activity) and transcendent (in essence) with respect to the world. Mysticism in its broadest sense assumes the mutual immanence of the human and the divine.

IMPLICIT: Capable of being understood from something else, though unexpressed: implied. Involved in the nature of something, though not disclosed.

INDUCTION: Reasoning from particular facts to general principles. The process by which one collects many particular cases, finds out by experiment what is common to all of them, and forms a general rule which is probably true; e.g., Every person I have observed has been a sinner so it is highly probable that X is a sinner. See "deduction."

INFINITE: Without limits or bounds; subject to no external determination; not confined by time or space. See "finite."

INTUITION: Perception of truths without reasoning; immediate apprehension (seeing) of objects as real without inductive or deductive inferences.

LOGIC: The division of philosophy that examines the methods and principles used in distinguishing correct from incorrect reasoning; the formal laws of thought that apply in reasoning about any subject matter. The subject consists of two different topics: The first is an analysis of what is meant by "truth". The second is analysis of the truth of arguments, and nowadays employs a sort of algebra which can be used to solve logical problems.

LOGICAL STARTING POINT: The highest principle which one introduces to give unity and order to one's interpretation of reality. This is why it is the logical starting point: what one logically conceives as the over-all synthesizing element which unites the particulars. For materialists, it is matter; for idealists, it is idea or principle; for empiricists, it is experience, but, for Clark, Van Til, and Carnell, it is the triune God of the Bible.

METAPHYSICS: The division of philosophy which studies the nature of ultimate reality or the characteristics common to all reality. The investigation of the underlying nature and structure of reality as a whole. It includes questions about the nature of time, about the different categories of existence and about whether there is a God.

MODEL: A physical object designed to show analogical representation of some large object(s) and /or events(s) and supposed relationships, especially associated with concepts of origination and generation.

MONOTHEISM: The belief there is one-and-only-one God; from Greek monos, one, single, alone, one-and-only plus theos, God.

MORAL RESPONSIBILITY: A view that accountability for right and wrong is not to individual tastes or to limited cultures, but to a transcultural Administrator of moral values.

MYSTICISM, CHRISTIAN: A philosophy maintaining that God is best known, not by reason but by direct personal experience occasioned by worship and Bible reading (Barrett).

MYSTICISM, NON-CHRISTIAN: A philosophy maintaining that reality is best known by an experience (sometimes drug-induced) in which the self is absorbed into ultimate reality, time stops, and words lose their meaning.

NATURALISM: A world-view that rejects the arguments for the existence of God and holds that the universe requires no supernatural cause but is self-explanatory. Nature, then, is deterministic, not fulfilling any purpose nor centred upon man. Only incidental to nature is the production of human life. Man's ethical values need no supernatural sanction, and man faces neither life after death nor an eternal destiny.

NIHILISM: (1) The rejection of all moral and religious principles. (2) An extreme form of scepticism maintaining that nothing has a real existence: Latin nihil, means nothing.

NON-CONTRADICTION, LAW OF: A law of logic in this form emphasizing that, while consistency is not a guarantee of truth, contradiction is a sure sign of error. See "contradiction."

OBSERVATION: A written or spoken record (as communication to self or another) of an awareness (perception) of an object and/or event.

OCKHAM'S RAZOR (or OCCAM'S RAZOR): The principle of simplicity or ontological economy, usually defined as 'Entities are not to be multiplied beyond necessity'. The principle implies: Firstly, that of two or more possible explanations for phenomena choose the one that (i) explains what is to be explained with the fewest assumptions and explanatory principles; and (ii) explains all, or most, of the facts that need explaining as satisfactorily as any of the other theories. Secondly, the simplest explanation is the one most likely to be true.

ONTOLOGICAL ARGUMENT: An a priori argument for the existence of God from the idea of God. God is defined as a self-existing or necessarily existing Being. Therefore God cannot not exist. His ontological Being is argued from what we mean by God. No evidence is necessary. By investigating the nature of God it is deduced that God exists. Anslem (Archbishop of Canturbury) in 1078 AD argued that God is *'something than which nothing greater can be imagined.'*

PANTHEISM: The belief that God is identical with the universe (from Greek pan, all; and theos, god). The universe taken as a whole is God. All is God and God is all. God is more than all that there is.

PARADIGM: (1) a way of looking at something; (2) in science, a model, pattern, or ideal theory, from which perspective phenomena are explained; (3) A rather vague term, meaning roughly the same as "conceptual scheme" or "framework of ideas" as for instance in "The Kantian Paradigm" or a "Christian framework".

PARADOX: (1) An apparent contradiction to attract attention, but resolvable logically upon further thought (Carnell and others); (2) A logical contradiction for both God and man (mysticism); (3) A logical contradiction only for man (Kierkegaard). (From Greek, paradoxon; from para, contrary to, and doxa, opinion).

PARANORMAL: Beyond the scope of normal objective investigation.

PARAPSYCHOLOGY: The study of mental phenomena outside the sphere of ordinary psychology; a term now replacing "psychical research" as the name for the study of ESP, PK, and other phenomena not recognised by established scientific disciplines.

PHENOMENA: (plural of phenomenon). Objects of experience in space and time known through the senses rather than intuition or mere thought. Broadly, appearance or that which appears.

PHILOSOPHY: Love of wisdom, from Greek sophos, *wise*. The study of the principles underlying all knowledge (epistemology) and all reality (metaphysics), morality (ethics), values (axiology), science (philosophy of science), history (philosophy of history), politics (political philosophy), etc. It involves the use of reason and argument in seeking truth and knowledge of reality, especially of the causes and nature of things and principles controlling existence.

PHILOSOPHY OF MIND: What is the human mind? How does it think? How is mind related to body?

PLURALISM: A metaphysical view that there are not one (monism) or two (dualism) but many ultimate substances or beings. Also a political view that the acceptable religious beliefs in a given country are not one or two but many. A philosophical system that recognises more than one ultimate principle.

POLITICAL PHILOSOPHY: What would utopia be like? Is utopia possible? How should social life be organised? From the Greek word polis, "city-state".

PRAGMATISM: A view of knowing that tests the truth and value of ideas by their practical consequences. Pragmatists agree in accepting what works as meaningful and true, but do not agree on the definition of "works."

PREDICTION: That expected or projected state of affairs or relationship of objects and/events based upon known or understood conditions; often found in an if... then expression.

PRESUPPOSITION: A specific, unprovable assertion postulated to make experience meaningful. A thing assumed beforehand as the basis for argument. It is a statement taken for granted upon which scientific activities (and intellectual arguments) are based such as:
1. Objectivity of study is possible;
2. Objects and/or events exist independent of observers;
3. Cause and effect relationships exist that may be identified;
4. Scientific ideas are testable, i.e. falsifiable, or not;
5. There is uniformity in the natural environment.

PROBABILITY: That state of coherence in which more evidences can be marshalled for a given hypothesis than can be amassed against it.

Glossary

PROBLEM: An interrogation or stated perplexity for which an answer is sought. A problem is most properly expressed in question form.

PROPOSITION: An assertion in the form, S (subject) is P (predicate). Four kinds are primary in traditional logic: (1) universal affirmative, "All S is P"; (2) universal negative, "No S is not P." Propositional content is either affirmed or denied, true or false. That meaning is distinct from the sentences and statements conveying it. It is a statement or assertion; a scheme proposed. In logic, it is a statement made up of a subject and predicate that is subject to proof or disproof.

PROOF: (1) a demonstration; a process that establishes or gives firm evidence or justification for a fact or truth; (2) in logic, the series of arguments based on the rules of inference of that logic which are used to derive the conclusion from the premises.

Q.E.D. : an abbreviation for that which was to be demonstrated (Latin).

RATIONALISM: (1) A theory of knowing asserting that knowledge is attained through the reason independent of sense perception, in opposition to empiricism. (2) More popularly, a view that all knowledge can be obtained through reason (in its broadest senses) independent of divine revelation, in opposition to the authority of sacred writings. To be contrasted with empiricism, logical positivism, intuitionism, revelationism.

REASON: (1) The ability of the human mind to make judgments and draw conclusions from observed data or from intuited or revealed truths by means of logical principles; the intellect (as in "the role of reason"); (2) The ground—evidence or argument—upon which a given conclusion (or truth-claim) is set forth, as in "give a reason for your hope." It includes the ability to infer.

RELATIVISM: The view that all ethical systems are somehow equally valid, so that a person's actions can only be judged relative to their particular culture or ethical system.

REPRESENTATIONALIST: Someone who believes that our ideas (or at least some them) accurately represent or picture or correspond to the way the world really is. For example a representationalist may believe that the human concept "electron" is an accurate representation of real things—electrons—in nature. Anti-representationalists (e.g. Rorty), are dismissive of the notion that concepts and language essentially function as "pictures" of reality; they prefer the Wittgensteinian model of language as a kind of human "tool" for interacting with the world.

SCEPTICISM: (1) The view (theory of knowledge!) that no true knowledge is possible or that in a particular area, such as religion, knowledge of truth is impossible for man; (2) a person inclined to doubt all accepted opinions; a cynic; (3) a person who doubts the truth of Christianity and other religions.

SCIENCE: An interconnected series of concepts and conceptual schemes that have been developed as a result of experimentation and observation and suggest further productive experimentation and observation; (2) The body of knowledge obtained by methods based upon the authority of observation. Science is limited to the study of nature; that is, study of matter and energy, because of limiting principles of being empirical, quantitative, mechanical, and corrective; (3) A branch of knowledge conducted on objective principles involving the systematized observation of and experiment with phenomena, especially concerned with the material and functions of the material universe; (4) A systematic and formulated knowledge of a specified type, e.g. geological science.

SCIENTIFIC LAW: A repeatedly tested and well-supported or substantiated generalization of seemingly universal application regarding a certain set of facts (a level of scientific explanation between description and scientific theory).

SCIENTIFIC METHOD: Techniques of controlled observation employed in the search for knowledge. In other words, science is knowledge obtained primarily through observation, not speculation or imagination.

Glossary

SCIENTIFIC THEORY: A list of postulates or assumptions (theoretical) usually specifying existence, relationship, and events concerning an imaginary entity (such as an atom, gene, or molecule) whereby a meaningful "explanatory system" for a range of rather diverse facts is made available. Postulates are based upon prior observations of relevant objects or events; and, in turn, are bases of predictions testable by experience, directly or indirectly. This is the highest level of scientific explanation.

SCIENTISM: (1) a method of teaching regarded as characteristic of scientists; (2) an excessive belief in the application of the scientific method, the belief that the human sciences require no methods other than the natural; (3) The belief that the only knowledge of repute and value is that obtained by means of the scientific process. (4) The belief that there is nothing but non-intelligent matter and energy.

SENSES: Any of the bodily faculties by which sensation is roused: the powers of the body and brain to see, hear, feel, taste, smell, etc.

SENSE DATA: The immediate, un-analysed presentations of colour, smoothness, loudness, etc., to the mind.

SENSE PERCEPTION: Intellectual awareness of the given data, an interpretation of it, and an assertion made on the basis of it.

SUBJECTIVISM: The view in epistemology that all that is known is the knower's (subject's) thoughts and feelings; nothing is known about alleged "objects" in reality. It implies belonging to the individual consciousness or perception.

SYLLOGISM: (1) A form of argument consisting of two propositions called premises from which is deduced a third proposition called a conclusion; e.g. All trees have roots. An oak is a tree. Therefore, an oak has roots. To be valid, this form of argument must follow a number of rules explained in most introductions to logic. (2) Deductive reasoning as distinct from induction.

SYNOPTIC: (1) taking a comprehensive mental view; (2) Affording a general view of a whole, characterized by comprehensiveness or breadth of view. In Christian apologetics e.g. the more general starting point is the common ground among all men on the basis of which to defend the distinctively Christian logical starting point—the triune God of the Bible.

SYSTEM: A regularly interacting and interdependent group of items forming a unified whole; an organized set of doctrines, ideas, or principles intended to explain the arrangement or working of a systematic whole.

SYSTEMATIC CONSISTENCY: The test of truth requiring a proposal to be logically consistent and in accord with all relevant facts.

SYSTEM OF APOLOGETICS: An organized set of consistent ideas urged in defence of a world view, such as Christianity. Here, of consistent ideas on such matters as : logical starting point, common ground, test for truth, role of reason, and basis of faith.

TABULA RASA: A smooth tablet (Latin); the human mind (especially at birth) viewed as having no innate ideas. Used by Locke and other empiricists to describe the condition of the human mind by nature, prior to its reception of experiential data. Contrast "rationalism," according to which the mind is "programmed" by nature with certain logical categories of thought or innate ideas.

TECHNOLOGY: The totality of the means employed by peoples to provide material objects for human sustenance and comfort.

THEISM: The world-view that asserts the reality of a personal infinite Creator, who is both immanent in His creation and transcendent to it. See "immanence."

THEOREM: A statement derived from assumptions of scientific theory more or less in the form of testable predictions or expectations.

Glossary

TELEOLOGICAL ARGUMENT: (1) the explanation of phenomena by the purpose they serve rather than by postulated causes. (2) In theology the teaching that the world (inorganic as well as organic) is an ordered design. Therefore the cause of the world is an intelligent Designer. More simply put: The universe is not just disordered chaos; everwhere we look are examples of order and intricate design—as complex as any pocket watch, for instance. If the world has been designed, there must be a designer, namely God.

TEST OF TRUTH: The decisive criterion by which to determine whether a proposed view is true or false; i.e. for a Christian, in correspondence with the mind of God or not.

TRANSCENDENT: (1) Surpassing ordinary limits, excelling, superior; of God, as existing prior to, distinct from, and exalted over the space-time universe. (2) Higher than or not included in any of Aristotle's ten categories in scholastic philosophy.

TRUTH: The quality of propositions which conform to reality or the quality of beings which realize in existence what ought to be; the quality of being true or correct according to some ground or test for establishing the reality of a statement (proposition, idea, thought, belief, or opinion).

TRUTH-CLAIM: A view of reality proposed for acceptance and action.

UNIVOCAL: Meaning that is one, the same in at least one respect, as opposed to equivocal and analogical meaning; e.g., to say that man has a mind and that God has a mind is to imply at least one identical aspect in the mind of man and God.

UNIVOCAL MEANING: The view that language about God is not ambiguous or merely figurative, but also in some respects identical to its meaning for man. Example: *"I am applying the word good in a univocal sense to both God and humans."*

UNMOVED MOVER, THE (Aristotle) sometimes referred to as the prime mover. This concept included the idea the unmoved is (a) eternal; (b) self-moving; (c) self-sufficient; (d) one, a unity; (e) a substance—the primary substance that is the source of all things; (f) completely actualised; (g) immaterial; (h) good; (i)unchanging; immutable (cannot be changed); and (k) divine thought or mind.

UTILITARIANISM: "Act so as to create the greatest happiness of the greatest number of people." There are numerous variations on this simple theme, and it was advocated by thinkers like Jeremy Bentham and John Stuart Mill.

VERIFIABLE: (1) A truth-claim that can be tested and confirmed as true or disconfirmed as false by observable evidence, not definition. It is the process of determining the truth of a statement by empirical methods; (2) the scientific testing of a statement to ascertain its truth.

WORLD VIEW: A systematic philosophy or insight into the movement and plan of the entire universe.

Select Bibliography

P. A. Angeles (1992) Philosophy (2nd edition) Harper Collins, New York, ISBN 0-06-271564-X.

A. Flew (Ed)(1979) A Dictionary of Philosophy, Pan Reference Book, London, ISBN 0 330 25610 6.

Resources:

Kategori—a magazine dealing with philosophical and scientific thinking from a Christian viewpoint.

Briefing—comment on current issues, from a biblical and apologetic viewpoint.

These up-to-date materials on apologetics can be purchased from: St Matthias Press, PO Box 665, London, SW 20 8RL. Telephone: 0181 947 5686.

G.L. Bahnsen (1998) *Van Til's Apologetic Readings and analysis,* Presbyterian & Reformed Co. New Jersey, ISBN 0-87552-0987; distributed by Evangelical Press, Darlington.

Also, an apologetic pamphlet on the influences of Christianity in British culture:

B.H. Edwards and **I.J. Shaw,** *AD,* Day One publications, 3 Epsom Business Park, Kiln Lane, Epsom, Surrey, KT 17 1 JF. Tel: 01372 728 300.

General index

Scripture index

Chapter 1

Also from Day One

The shout of a King

Derek Prime

Paperback
150 pages   £6.99

Many Christians overlook the fact that the Ascension was as much an act of God's power as the Resurrection. In The shout of a King Derek Prime argues that if we neglect our Saviour's Ascension and continuing work, we risk losing sight of His unique and central place in the life of the Church.

"The shout of a King" is the experience of the people of Israel in Numbers 23:21. When they appreciated this truth and lived accordingly, they were spiritually healthy and able to serve Him; but when they took their eyes off their King, they soon failed, bringing both dishonour to God and disaster to themselves. The Christian's hope will only remain vital and alive as we fix our eyes upon The ascended Lord Jesus alone. The Holy Spirit can enlighten us in our understanding of the Scriptures so that we appreciate all that God has freely given us in His Son's Ascension and continuing work on our behalf.

If the death of Jesus determines how we as Christians should live, so should His Ascension.

Reference: SK
ISBN 0 902548 90 5

Improving your Quiet Time

Simon Robinson

Large format paperback
144 pages   £6.95

'Very early in the morning, while it was still dark, Jesus got up, left the house and went off to a solitary place, where He prayed' (Mark 1:35). If the Lord Jesus needed quiet times of fellowship and prayer, how much more do we? Although there are no rules laid down in the Bible for organising our times of quiet, we often gain from the experience and advice of others. Simon Robinson's *Improving your Quiet Time* is full of practical advice which should encourage many who are struggling to achieve a better balance in their Spiritual walk. It also contains ideas for personal study plans, together with a two year Bible reading plan.

Reference: QT
ISBN 0 902548 89-1

For further information about these and other Day One titles, call or write to us:

01372 728 300

In Europe: ++ 44 1372 728 300

In North America: 011 44 1372 728 300

Day One 3 Epsom Business Park Kiln Lane Epsom Surrey KT17 1JF England

eMail—sales@dayone.co.uk   wwwdayone.co.uk